The United States and the Americas

Lester D. Langley, General Editor

This series is dedicated to a broader under-standing of the political, economic, and especially cultural forces and issues that have shaped the Western hemispheric experience— its governments and its peoples. Individual volumes assess relations between the United States and its neighbors to the south and north: Mexico, Central America, Cuba, the Dominican Republic, Haiti, Panama, Colombia, Venezuela, the Andean Republics (Peru, Ecuador, and Bolivia), Brazil, Uruguay and Paraguay, Argentina, Chile, and Canada.

The United States and the Americas

America and the Americas

Lester D. Langley

America and the Americas: The United States in the Western Hemisphere

The University of Georgia Press
Athens and London

© 1989 by the University of Georgia Press
Athens, Georgia 30602
All rights reserved

Set in 10 on 14 Palatino
The paper in this book meets the guidelines
for permanence and durability of the Committee on
Production Guidelines for Book Longevity of
the Council on Library Resources.

Printed in the United States of America

93   92   91   90   89   5   4   3   2   1

Library of Congress Cataloging in Publication Data

Langley, Lester D.
    America and the Americas : the United States
  in the Western Hemisphere / Lester D. Langley.
        p.   cm.—(The United States and the
  Americas)
    Bibliography: p.
    Includes index.
    ISBN 0-8203-1103-0 (alk. paper).—ISBN
  0-8203-1104-9 (pbk. : alk. paper)
      1. Latin America—Relations—United
  States.   2. United States—Relations—Latin
  America.   I. Title.   II. Series.
F1418.L27   1989   89-31968
303.48'7308—dc20   CIP

British Library Cataloging in Publication Data available

For

Arthur Preston Whitaker

Fredrick Pike

Jean Friedman

Contents

ix

Acknowledgments

My thanks to the authors of forthcoming books in this series, who, more than I, are sustaining it; to Malcolm Call, Doug Armato, and especially to Karen Orchard of the University of Georgia Press, who committed the Press to an ambitious series and who with patience and expertise have tutored the author in the task of general editor of the series; to Stan Lindberg of *The Georgia Review*, who wields a deceptively skillful editorial pen, for his reading of the manuscript; to Thomas Whigham, who has tried to correct many of my silly notions about Latin America; and, finally, to Fredrick Pike, who saw what I was aiming at; and David Pletcher, who alerted me to what I was missing.

No author has been better served.

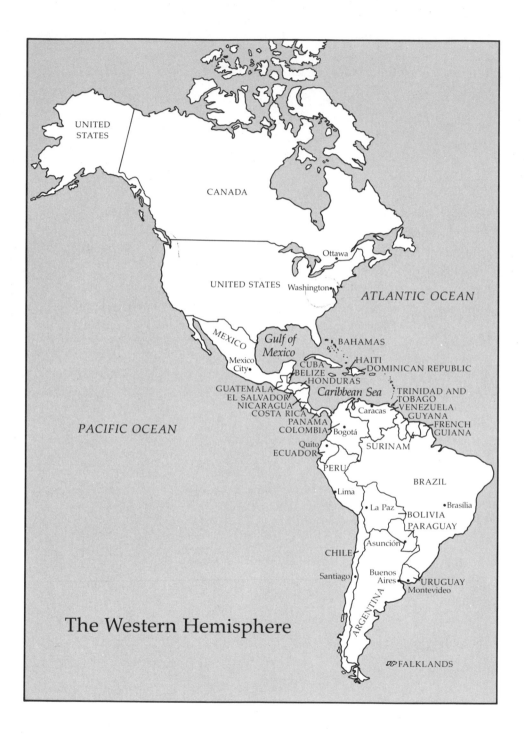

The Western Hemisphere

Introduction

America and the Americas is the general volume in a projected series on the relations between the United States and Latin America—a series intended to provide students and general readers with an accessible, up-to-date assessment of the inter-American experience. Our goal is to provide authoritative volumes that will explain the forces and issues that have shaped that experience. The authors will go beyond traditional diplomatic history and assess the internal political, economic, and especially the cultural and social considerations that inform the bilateral relationships between the United States and Canada, Mexico, Central America, Cuba, the Dominican Republic, Haiti, Panama, Colombia, Venezuela, the Andean republics (Peru, Ecuador, and Bolivia), Brazil, Argentina, Uruguay and Paraguay, and Chile. As the author of the general volume, I have tried here to provide an overview without making unnecessary intrusions into the territoriality of successive volumes; for the most part I have probed bilateral issues in detail only when they have affected U.S. policy toward the entire region.

This is not a textbook in the traditional sense. It is written for student *and* citizen. I am less interested in the formal structure of the inter-American system (that is, the Pan-American movement or the Organization of American States) than in the *idea* of the Western Hemisphere. That idea, Arthur Whitaker wrote in the mid-1950s, means simply that the peoples of the New World bear a "special relationship to one another that sets them apart from the rest of the world."[1] Their political destiny, President James Monroe declared in 1823, was republican not monarchical. Their economic obligations, the Argentine foreign minister Luis Drago said early in the twentieth century (in an era when all were debtor nations) did not justify the forcible intervention of their creditors. And their cultural bonds, the Mexican diplomat Luis Quintanilla eloquently expressed during the Korean War, were symbolized by more than geography or historical experience: "We all share in common an idea about the organization of society and of the world. In other words, to face the fact of America is to glance at any map. From pole to pole, from ocean to ocean, we are all in the same boat."[2]

The political model of republican government created by the United States found expression (at least in form if not always in substance) in all but one of the independent Latin-American states in the nineteenth century. Independent Brazil remained a monarchy until 1889.[3] Yet this adoption of similar political institutions symbolized less a community of thought about principles of government than a rejection of European colonial rule. "Home rule" became the rallying cry of Western Hemispheric political leaders as diverse as the thoroughly Anglo-Saxon Adamses of Massachusetts, the black Dessalines of Haiti, the Creole aristocrat Simón Bolívar of Venezuela, and the parish priest Manuel Hidalgo of Mexico. But for each the term carried a different meaning. For the Adamses and their generation independence meant freedom from the manipulation of European states and the creation of a *white* citizens' republic. To Dessalines, it meant rejection of *white* influence, its politics, economy, and culture. Father Hidalgo, in rallying abused Indians against their Spanish oppressors, unleashed destructive forces that menaced the social order. Bolívar, whose appeals for a defensive alliance of former Spanish colonies in the 1820s swept the hemisphere, spent his final years disillusioned with republican government and exercised authoritarian control over a people he had gloriously liberated from Spanish monarchical rule.[4]

The disciples of Latin America's founding fathers, it was generally believed in the United States, were petty tyrants, crass dictators, and/or grim military chieftains. They ruled in putatively republican societies but confronted few judicial or legislative barriers to their often arbitrary exercise of power. Curiously, despite the woeful record many in the United States perceived in the political life south of the border, there remained a belief that it could be rectified. In 1915, when the United States was alienating an entire generation of Latin Americans with its "civilizing" interventions in Mexico and the Caribbean, Secretary of State Robert Lansing proudly reaffirmed the Western Hemispheric peoples' sense of shared political identity and "common conception of human rights."[5]

Numerous other studies (some of them written a half-century ago) have described, analyzed, defended, or attacked U.S. relations with Latin America. Of the earlier studies, the most distinguished was Samuel Flagg Bemis, *The Latin American Policy of the United States*, which appeared during World War II and brilliantly assessed U.S. policy toward the region. Bemis uniformly defended the American record in the hemisphere. Among the Latin American responses to his work, few are notable, and most (such as Juan José Arévalo's *The Shark and the Sardines* or Alonso Aguilar's brief *Pan-Americanism from Monroe to the Present*) are relentlessly critical. In the past generation, political scientists and historians have produced either very structured (and often ponderous) accounts that provide a summary of the Pan-American movement and U.S. policy toward individual countries or briefer evaluations that focus on U.S.–Latin American relations since about 1960. Other works, in English and Spanish, reflect on the apparent separateness and irreconcilability of the American and the Latin American cultural traditions. Surprisingly, few have blended these themes and none, to my knowledge, has evaluated the interaction of politics, economics, and culture, of America and the United States, in the Americas.

It is that interaction that I explore in this book, and I do so in a way that demands some explanation. Earlier in my career, when I looked at Latin America more from the perspective of a U.S. diplomatic historian with an inevitable focus on policy, relations between governments, and the analytical demands they make, I was persuaded that greater understanding and sympathy with Latin America, its peoples, and their problems would do more to advance U.S. interests in the hemisphere than a Latin American policy that relied on forceful diplomacy, economic pressure, or the dispatching of troops. Now that I have shifted much more to a Latin American view, I still cling to that belief, but it is tempered by my realization that the impulses working on Latin America have largely come from within, not from the United States.

This book is also a reconsideration of U.S. policy in Latin America, but, unlike more recent studies (mostly by political scientists) it is not an advocacy tract. My purpose here is not to make the case for a hard-line policy to safeguard U.S. security interests or for a massive program to alleviate Latin America's seemingly overwhelming social and economic problems. Nevertheless, I do address such questions by asking the reader to pause and consider several issues that, in my opinion, have profoundly affected U.S. policy in the region and must be taken into account—whether the reader is radical, liberal, or conservative; believes we should apply more or less military pressure on Latin America; advocates more or less economic aid; or believes we are or are not responsible for Latin America's poverty, Castro's "conversion" to Marxism, the condition of Nicaragua, and so on.

The first of these factors complicating an assessment of U.S.–Latin American relations involves making a distinction between the "United States" and "America." Those who believe they are essentially the same and commonly use them interchangeably (as I do every day) may be irritated or even offended, but the distinction needs to be recognized because *Latin Americans* make such a distinction. Their reason lies not in resentment over our appropriation of the word *America*—in fact, they rarely refer to themselves as Latin Americans and virtually never as "Americans" but rather as Mexicans, Cubans, and so on. Instead, it is their perception that the United States and America project differing images on the hemisphere, that America "says one thing" but the United States "does another." Latin American leaders, of course, are notorious for posturing as heralds of democracy when they enter office but ruling as crass opportunists who depart it with the national treasury in tow. Political and cultural hypocrisy is a hemispheric phenomenon. My point is that the United States and America reach deep into Latin America, and the duality of their impact has, I believe, had a noticeable and occasionally determining effect on the outcome of U.S. policy. An analogy would be the bride who at first cares only that her new husband loves her, but as the marriage goes on she becomes concerned about *why* he loves her—and ultimately divorces him because he doesn't love her for the reasons most important to her.

The United States is a political entity, but "America" is a place. "America" lacks a government to articulate its foreign policies, a military to sustain them, and precise territorial jurisdiction, yet its cumulative impact on the Americas, especially in its enduring faith in human betterment and community, has been great. America and the United States have followed a parallel, sometimes reinforcing, sometimes contradictory course in the inter-American relationship. When Secretary of State John Quincy Adams and President James Knox Polk warned about European territorial expansion or political influence in the Western Hemisphere or on the North American continent, respectively, they spoke to United States interests. When President James Monroe and Secretary of State William Seward affirmed the inevitable "republican" future of the Western Hemisphere, they were invoking the credos of America. When President Ronald Reagan appealed to Americans to support U.S. policy toward Nicaragua, he was addressing U.S. national security concerns in Central America and ultimately justifing his position with reaffirmation of America's commitment to democracy. His critics (both in the United States and in Latin America) have replied with invocations of America's democratic credos. During the Mariel boatlift of 1980, when Cubans in Miami dispatched boats to ferry their friends and family members from the island to freedom, America welcomed them even as the U.S. government declared the armada in violation of its laws.

The United States is *in* the Americas, but America is *of* the Americas. The deceptively narrow but important distinction between those phrases, *evaluated historically*, is, I believe, critical for understanding U.S. policy toward Latin America and helps to explain why (as some Americans believe) it is often artfully conceived and enthusiastically supported yet ultimately fails to achieve its purpose. The United States and America have come to mean qualitatively different things to Latin Americans during the past century and a half, as the legacy of the interaction between them has bequeathed two hemispheres—the first a creature of governments and their often conflicting interests; the second a place where peoples still retain a faith that man can be liberated from the shackles of government. Latin Americans respect the United States for its power, its dynamic economy, its technical achievements, and its resolute sense of purpose in international affairs, but they can be infuriatingly condemnatory of U.S. policy, predictably when Washington enforces its strictures with troops but *even when they benefit from those policies*. At the same time it is not uncommon in Latin America to hear praise for America, its political traditions, its oft-expressed and deeply felt faith in human rights, and its nurturing of the idea of the Western Hemisphere. In this sense, an *American* (which I define as a citizen of the United States) is one who believes that the promise of America can be fulfilled in the United States.

I will also employ here a few other terms that appear precise at first glance but can be deceptive in their usage, including *Latin America* and *the Americas*. As used in this study, *Latin America* signifies not only those countries of the mainland south of the Rio Grande but also the islands of the Caribbean. Not all the English-speaking peoples of the Caribbean are Latin, and Haitians, though speaking a Latin language, are more African than French in their cultural makeup. Within the territorial outlines of Latin America live peoples from every culture of the earth—Europeans, Arabs, Africans, Asians—as well as the descendants of the great Amerindian civilizations. The colonial mix of Indian, African, and Iberian (Spanish and Portuguese) has produced in modern Latin America a symbolic cultural unity. It is more dream than reality, as the undisguised disdain with which the Argentines or Chileans regard the Bolivians or Paraguayans, for example, bears witness. But it is a hope that persists, nonetheless, as the bonds of language, devotion to ceremony and festival, or the inherited concept of an organic state whose leaders derive their "legitimacy" from "spiritual" bonds with the masses readily attest.[6]

The Americas is more problematical, for in defining it I reject the geographer's insistence on including Canada (though Canada belongs in the series). I do so for two reasons. Canada, like the former non-Hispanic colonies in the insular Caribbean, may have drawn on Europe for its political and economic institutions, but its culture and social character have not been influenced by the Hispanic and African presence. Its battle over national identity is a war between two European cultural transplants. Canadians, of course, complain as much as Latin Americans about "Americanization," but the sense of common suffering over the U.S. presence has not inspired the sense of unity that *the Americas* conveys. More important, in the inter-American experience, Canada has never been a fully committed participant. Certainly before the Dominion Act of 1867 but even after Canada had severed all but symbolic ties to the British Empire, the role of Canada in the hemisphere has been different from those of its hemispheric neighbors. Although Canada was not a signatory, it is protected under the 1947 Inter-American Treaty of Reciprocal Assistance. It does not belong to the Organization of American States but is granted permanent observer status in that body. Though in modern times Canada has had undeniable political and economic reach into Latin America—especially the Caribbean and, increasingly, Central America—its addition to the Americas, as I employ that term, merits only occasional reference.

The second key factor is that, although Americans and Latin Americans are different, the crucial differences grew out of their priorities in the political and social orders. Here I am referring especially to the American belief in a just political order and economic opportunity for the individual in opposition to the Latin American faith in the centrality of the social order and an apparent resignation to a failed political tradition and an unfair economic system. This is why I have given an inordinate amount of attention in this book to the social forces within Latin America that indirectly but consequentially affect U.S. policy. I believe that our strictures to Latin Americans over the years—even when they appear to offer political and economic benefit—have been rejected because they were ultimately threatening to the Latin American social order. The United States may be a counterrevolutionary force in Latin America, but America and especially American culture (with credos of "Be All That You Can Be" and "You

Deserve More Than Your Parents") are revolutionary notions. These credos may have little influence on the making of or justification for U.S. policy (whether forcibly or benevolently applied), but they certainly have a bearing on the success of that policy. Thus when I appear critical of U.S. policy or slight its effect, it is because I have come to the conclusion that though the United States may try to shape Latin America's future, sometimes for the region's own good, Latin America has its own agenda, which will ultimately determine the success or failure of our efforts. We don't have to like it or accept it, but we do have to live with it.

The third factor to be considered deals with our underlying assumptions. Though I still retain a liberal American's faith that our relations with Latin America will be better served by negotiation of disputes and in reaffirmation of hemispheric unity, I have belatedly acknowledged that all Americans (including policy makers) who want to improve our relations with Latin America must consider the irrational forces and changeless realities that appear not only in Latin America's history but also in our own. Political scientists remind us that Latin America has changed a great deal in the past twenty-five years. This is true, but in countless other ways neither Latin America nor the United States has fundamentally altered its early judgments about the other or been willing to discard those features of its past that frustrate the cause of hemispheric understanding. Policy makers in every government may chart diplomatic strategy on the basis of obvious, rational calculations, but all of them know that the most precisely orchestrated policy can be jeopardized by their leaders' need to "make statements" rather than carry on negotiations to resolve issues. There is some consolation in the fact that U.S. and Nicaraguan leaders are firing condemnations rather than bullets at one another, but such exchanges do not constitute dialogue or facilitate the reconciliation of disputes. The reciprocal public denunciations of the U.S. and Panamanian governments in 1988 provide yet another example of harassed leaders expressing moral outrage over the political excesses of the other when in fact both are culpable.

Latin America is neither a political nor a cultural unity, yet Latin

American governments, from right to left on the political spectrum, often seem united against U.S. policy. We Americans, accustomed to approaching hemispheric problems with "rational solutions," are often bewildered by the opposition to our policies from Latin American governments that express similar goals. Explanations for this phenomenon vary—from inherited animosities toward U.S. intervention in the hemisphere to what Carlos Rangel has called the "love-hate" duality in every Latin American when he considers the United States and everything it stands for.[7] (More frustrating for Americans are stories about Latino rabble-rousers burning the American flag one day and applying for a visa at the U.S. embassy the next.) Anti-Americanism in the hemisphere has deep historical roots, but it is not fired by religious fundamentalism, as in Iran. It is not unusual in Latin America for the same person to express both hostility to and admiration for the United States, anger at the U.S. government coupled with deep respect for American political values. Anti-Americanism runs deep in Mexico, for understandable reasons, but is also widespread in South American countries where the U.S. Marines have never marched. It is intense in Argentina but does not run as strong in Brazil, which has been far more vulnerable to U.S. interference.

Latin American democrats of every social rank who are sympathetic with U.S. goals in the hemisphere often demur from our policies and especially our practices. They do so not out of deep-seated anti-Americanism or pressures from their own people but from somber reappraisals about our priorities in Latin America. More fundamentally, they question neither our aspirations nor our objectives in Latin America but the means we often employ to achieve them. Americans should be less troubled about the occasional abusive anti-American *político* who struts across the Latin American landscape than about a far more serious problem. How are we to address the phenomenon of governments and societies that do so little for their own people yet have somehow managed to win (or exploit) their loyalty—from the social outcasts who took up arms to defend Santo Domingo in 1655 to the marginal laborer of modern Mexico? Such a conundrum perhaps has a psychological or cultural explanation (as the Spanish often say,

"It may be bad wine but at least it's ours"), but we should reflect on it as we debate U.S. policy toward the hemisphere.

Finally, I will argue that the United States and Latin American governments may have crafted a formal hemispheric organization with its attendant bureaucracy and defined purpose, but it is becoming less important for the hemisphere's future than the informal but no less vital "new" hemisphere that is emerging. The former is a political structure, but the latter is the inspiration of the peoples of the Western Hemisphere and their faith that they and not their governments retain the hemispheric vision. With their migration they are not only defying boundaries but governments' expressed notions of territoriality. With their offers of aid and friendship and their shielding of the terrified and impoverished, they reaffirm a faith in hemispheric unity that their governments seem to have abandoned. Governments may speak of extrahemispheric economic, political, and even military links, and the United States may invoke its security interests in Latin America in the service of its global needs. But the peoples of the diverse cultures of the Americas anticipate a new hemisphere in their future and in their myriad religious and humanitarian bonds are trying to achieve it. Ultimately, I believe, they will prevail on their governments to recognize the worthiness of their endeavors.

America and the Americas

Prelude:
The Western Design

The New World gave to the Old some telling phrases that portended both opportunity and uncertainty. One was "No peace beyond the line," which meant that whatever peace might prevail in Europe did not extend to the New World domains of the conquerors. The "line" was an imaginary one, symbolizing the famous demarcation in 1494 between Spanish and Portuguese claims to this still unconquered vastness, a division sanctified by the pope but defied by their rivals. Even the Catholic monarch of France, Francis I, scoffed at the notion of uncontested Iberian rule. French expeditions sailed for Newfoundland to exploit the abundant fishery of the Grand Banks, and French pirates harassed Spanish vessels in the Caribbean within a decade after Columbus's final voyage.

In the 1530s Francis openly defied a Spanish proclamation excluding all European trade from its empire but simultaneously pledged to Portugal that no French interlopers would transgress upon Portuguese outposts on the Brazilian coast. "I would like to see the clause in Adam's will," the French monarch had allegedly boasted, that denied France its destiny in the New World. The English did not require a biblical injunction to challenge the Spanish claim of exclusivity. The sixteenth century was Spain's Golden Age in the New World, but before it ended in 1600 English privateers had already transformed the Caribbean into a sea of intermittent warfare. They raided weakly defended Spanish seaports and plundered imperial treasure ships. Even after 1595, when the feared Sir Francis Drake ("Draques") succumbed to the fever off Panama, the age of privateering did not end but continued intermittently until the eighteenth century.[1]

Drake and his fellow privateer Sir John Hawkins had challenged

1

Spanish imperial domain with their predatory instincts and conviction that trade between Protestant England and Catholic overseas Spain was a "natural right." The privateers preyed on Spanish shipping with the blessing of their queen. If denied peaceful commerce with a Spanish port, trade, as Hawkins once averred, could be justifiably "forced." In this spirit of righteous entrepreneurship the most famous English privateers of the sixteenth century, with the enthusiastic support of Elizabeth I, laid waste the isolated seaports of recalcitrant Spanish officials.

For all their putatively successful raids into the Caribbean, the "Sea of the New World," Spain's rivals had little territory to show for their plunder when Elizabeth died. But the Spanish had paid a high price in the defense of their mainland empire. Their ablest imperial strategist, the fierce Pedro Menéndez de Aviles (adviser, *adelantado*, and governor of Florida), had energetically shored up the Crown's weakened defenses with fortifications at crucial sites—Havana, Santo Domingo, San Juan, and Cartagena—and instituted a convoy system to protect the treasure ships.

The Lesser Antilles and the Guianas were largely bypassed or left vulnerable to the next generation of European plunderers. By 1620 the French had already penetrated eastern Canada and established their trading posts on the St. Lawrence River. The English began their isolated colonies from Massachusetts to Virginia on territory hesitantly claimed by the Spanish monarch. And there were bolder penetrations into the heart of the Spanish Caribbean. England, France, and the Netherlands dispatched colonizing ventures into the Guianas—Sir Walter Raleigh was the most famous interloper—but eventually the Dutch prevailed. When the English under Thomas Warner abandoned the Guiana enterprise in 1624, they readily turned their attention northward to the neglected islands. Dutch intruders organized the West Indian Company, and by midcentury they were reputedly the most aggressive traders of the Spanish Main.

Unintentionally, their forays into the Spanish Empire may have prompted the English and French to look more acquisitively at the

Lesser Antilles. Ambitious English promoters, modeling their organizations on the London or Virginia companies, established diminutive outposts on Barbados, Nevis, Antigua, Montserrat, and St. Lucia. In France, Cardinal Richelieu threw his courtly energy behind a struggling French concern that had settled St. Christopher, inspiring its leaders to occupy Guadeloupe and Martinique and to import four thousand Catholics as colonizers.

But the English launched the most daring assault on Spain's Caribbean empire in the Western Design of Oliver Cromwell, Lord Protector of England, and a renegade priest, Thomas Gage. Cromwell felled the English king. Gage vowed to fell the Spanish Empire.

Like numerous later observers of Spanish colonial life who saw the Hispanic *dons* as indolent and lascivious rulers who had whipped their Indian laborers into submission, Gage believed a dramatic strike at the Spanish Empire would incite an Indian uprising. Born into an English Catholic family, Gage had entered the Dominican order and served the Spanish in Mexico. Fearing assignment to the Philippines, he joined a small band of runaway priests and headed for the kingdom of Guatemala. Their intention was to deliver themselves to a more understanding patriarch of the order. They found sanctuary in the highlands of Guatemala. Gage found more. He whetted his palate with chocolate and gathered material on the agricultural bounty of the Spanish Empire. He had the Anglo-Saxon's fascination with exotic places and distaste for their people. When he finally put to paper his stirring accounts of reprobate Spanish priests who abused their Indian charges, he drew on his own experiences in Guatemala. Over seven years of service in a local parish he acquired nine thousand pieces of eight.

In 1642 he returned to Spain and toured western Europe. Six weeks before the opening salvos of the English civil war, he publicly renounced Catholicism at St. Paul's Cathedral in a fiery sermon titled "The Tyranny of Satan." In a few months he was gleefully providing evidence against his former colleagues; on his testimony three went to the gallows. Gage's family was distraught and offered to pay for another European visit. But Gage was already writing his *Travels*,[2] which was published just as Parliament, the victor in the civil war, was readying to execute Charles I and the English were entering one of their periodic anti-Catholic, anti-Spanish outbursts. *Travels* portrays Spanish America as a tropical prize, suffering under the misrule of corrupt and cowardly bureaucrats—an empire the Protestants must conquer and redeem.

Gage's book, which radiated a tone of authenticity, galvanized the militant Protestants of Cromwellian England. And the Lord Protector himself, unsatisfied with the tiny islands that until his era constituted England's West Indian empire, reacted enthusiastically to the idea of capturing a major Spanish port. Such an invasion would be a bold stroke for Protestantism against popery and its disciples. With a modest expenditure of men and matériel, Gage assured his readers, the attack would enrich Cromwell's depleted coffers. In Mexico, for instance, the defrocked priest had watched a small band of dissidents intimidate a terrified viceroy, the Spanish Crown's most powerful official in the empire, into hiding.

In the summer of 1654, with the naval war against the Dutch in abeyance, Cromwell summoned the Spanish minister and laid down demands he knew would be unacceptable—the right of Englishmen to trade and worship as they pleased in Spain's Western Hemispheric dominion. "You have asked for my Master's two eyes," the stupefied minister responded. But Cromwell had his excuse for making war, and shortly the Lord Protector's recognized authority on Spanish imperial defense (as well as Hispanic manners and morals) found himself in the council of war plotting the Western Design.

The plan called for a strike force of three thousand crack troops against Santo Domingo, a "fat prize," weakly defended and vulnerable to English naval power. The legendary Drake with a tiny band had once held the city for a month until the Spanish king had paid a handsome ransom for its return. Cromwell's invaders were not commanded by another "Draques," however, nor did Admiral William Penn and General Robert Venables, who led this grand expedition, acquire the most professional soldiers to plunge the Protestant dagger into the Spanish heart. One chronicler described them as "cheats, thieves, lewd persons," and worse. At dockside a cavalry force had to herd them aboard ship.

Cromwell gave Venables the authority to select alternative targets (Cuba or Puerto Rico) but dispatched with the expedition a five-man commission to oversee his conduct. By the time the expedition reached West Indian waters, it had dissolved into a bickering gaggle. Still, the design had prospects for success: twenty-five hundred English rowdies and misfits may not have resembled the three thousand crack troops of the Western Design battle plan, but they should have been able to overpower a port with dilapidated fortifications and an undermanned garrison.

Ever cautious, Venables detoured to Barbados, where runaways and the seventeenth-century variety of tropical tramp flocked to the colors in such numbers that ten weeks later, when the expedition finally embarked for Hispaniola, commanders were providing the newcomers with two-thirds daily ration. The detour to Barbados was costly in another way—it gave the newly appointed local Spanish commander of Santo Domingo's weary forces (the Count of Peñalva) enough time to restore the port's fortifications and emplace several brass cannon in the shore battery. Anticipating a land assault as well, Peñalva wisely dispatched troops along the dirt road leading into town. If the English attacked overland, he reasoned, they would not be able to penetrate the thornbush-infested countryside and would have to follow that dirt road.

The expedition arrived off Santo Domingo with the commanders bickering over tactics. They finally agreed to dump the already weary foot soldiers—five regiments in all—at a site two-days' march from Santo Domingo. Poorly led, laden with rotten food, and suffering from inadequate water supplies, they trudged in the debilitating heat to do battle with a Spanish foe just as poorly provisioned. But the ambitious young Spanish commander had the advantage. He had positioned his riflemen and "cowkillers"—a motley crowd of *mestizos* and mulattoes treated as knaves and outcasts in the imperial city they were now dispatched to defend—at critical places along the road.

They fought with such ferocity that the story of Santo Domingo's defense in 1655 became enshrined in imperial military history.

The strike force reached the walls of the city but was quickly repulsed. Its reinforcements were already demoralized, their leader having departed in a huff to rejoin the waiting fleet. For a week the scattered bands of English infantrymen scurried about the countryside living off berries or hovered on the beach, in view of the supply ships that now sent them rotten provisions. In their last days ashore, the English were reduced to killing stray dogs and cats to survive. Dysentery and food poisoning soon reduced a mighty invasion force into a pitiable assemblage of the diseased and demoralized. A chronicler of the expedition captured their despair, pointing out that General Venables had his wife to comfort him, but the poor brutes ashore survived on fruit and water: "Thayer harts ware got out of thayer Dublates into thayer Breches, and wos nothing but Shiting, for thay wose in a very sad condichon, 50 or 60 stouls in a day."[3]

Miraculously, the English had lost only twenty men. Rested but led by yet another incompetent officer, they attempted a second assault on Santo Domingo. Their leader neglected to send scouts to look for the cowkillers. Once again they tromped along the dirt track toward the city, raising a dusty umbrella in their wake. The Spanish, numbering fewer than two hundred, swept down on them with a murderous ferocity, the cowkillers running down the fleeing soldiers and bayoneting them with such frenzy they were soon exhausted. When it was over, Peñalva could report almost four hundred English dead. His troops ravaged by dysentery, the reckless Venables now ordered a third attack. Peñalva's defenders had fallen back to the city walls, but the English were so frightened by the hit-and-run tactics of the cowkillers that Venables could not muster a few volunteers to drag a heavy mortar into position to shell the walls.

Thus ended Cromwell's Western Design. The abandoned weaponry of the mighty English assault force lay along a nameless dirt road in the tropics. For this debacle the high and low suffered. The incompetent adjutant-general who had masterminded the disastrous second attack was court-martialed and ordered to swab the deck of the hospital ship. A sergeant who in the thick of the fight had yelled, "We are all lost," sending the column into ignominious retreat, was hanged with a sign denoting his sin pinned to his chest. In their exaltation the Spanish commanders of Santo Domingo dispensed five hundred pesos to the poor along with virtually unworkable land grants in the wilds of Venezuela to a chosen few of the brave defenders of the city. Aboard the English ships only the enthusiasm of the irrepressible former priest Thomas Gage brightened the otherwise gloomy mood of the attackers. The hour of crisis, Gage told them, perhaps anticipating a twentieth-century homily, might also be a time of opportunity. If Santo Domingo's walls could not be breached, there lay another Spanish prize in the Golden Antilles—Jamaica, defended by a miserable and forgotten Spanish garrison. If the island of "wood and water," as the Carib Indians called this place of spectacular beauty, did not offer the English the rich mines or plantations of Hispaniola, its position in the heart of the Sea of the New World provided its conqueror with a base from which to assault the imperial mainland.[4]

When the English began to land, the Spanish, woefully undermanned, dared not resist. Far less formidable intruders had ventured here, only to abandon the island to the scattered Spanish colonists. The Spanish commander even sent out a peace delegation with a pledge to reprovision the English interlopers. But General Venables was characteristically blunt: "We came not to pillage but to plant."

The Western Design was but one of many intrusions into the Spanish Empire. Other conquerors with their threatening cultures and alien ideas would follow. Some would pillage and create havoc, then depart. Others would arrive to instruct—sometimes forcibly—in the ways of running a government or exploiting an economy. But few of the intruders with their enlightened politics or their rational economic strategies ever penetrated the culture they encountered. Like the conquering invaders of Cromwell's Western Design, they would never understand how abused peoples could defend a society that did so little for them.

1   Transatlantic Empires

Other conquests and other ventures into the Spanish Empire followed the English occupation of Jamaica. The intrusion of one culture into the domain of another became an enduring feature of Western Hemispheric history. And, too, by the end of the seventeenth century the intruders were implanting a distinct character in their imperial domains.

The eighteenth-century English assault on the Spanish Empire was principally, but not exclusively, a war of trade and commerce. Early on, the English in America joined in, but their purpose went beyond the securing of markets. Cotton Mather and Samuel Sewall, archetypal New England Puritans, identified the Spanish dominions as fertile ground for proselytizing. To them, the captive Indians of the Spanish Empire were so many abused wretches waiting the hearing of the gospel—if only New England were able to dispatch Protestant missionaries to convert them. They were alert to every effort to break the Spanish grip—from the ill-fated Scots colony in Darien to fleeting reports of unrest in Mexico and Central America. English merchants championed a vigorous expansion of the marketplace, but Sewall and Mather urged a spiritual crusade against popery in the New World. In messianic tracts they spoke of hemispheric unity, with one faith governing the spiritual and, ultimately, political and cultural life of one people. Mather wrote "An Essay to Convey Religion into the Spanish Indies," and Sewall blended religious commitment with political and commercial opportunism. In time, the religious zealots would give way to the Hispanophiles in the American Philosophical Society.[1]

But as the economic and strategic imperatives of eighteenth-century wars attained primacy in imperial politics, the sentimental but politicially naive invocations for a unity of the peoples of the Americas through faith and ideas lost their influence. They were swept

8

aside by yet another generation, who believed in strategy, interest, and advantage.

The Character of Empire

The New World economic kingdoms, in theory subordinate to the mother country, probably fit the mercantilist model until about 1700. But in the eighteenth century, even in the more closely supervised Spanish colonies, the old mercantilist controls began to weaken under the inevitable expansion of international and intraimperial commerce. What came to be known as the Atlantic economic community, with its demands for opening up more commercial opportunities, had a profound effect on Anglo-American and (after the Bourbon house assumed the Spanish throne in 1700) influenced the nominally complacent Spanish monarchs to spread the benefits of empire among a greater number of Spanish houses.[2]

If one measures the worth of the Americas by the value of production in the European colonies in the eighteenth century, the New World was a phenomenally wealthy place. Sugar, with its inordinately heavy demand for land and labor, was a plantation industry extending from New England to Brazil, but the cane thrived in the fertile soil of the West Indies. In a decade of political disturbance and slave rebellion in the 1790s, the island of Hispaniola was producing 50 million pounds of sugar annually. The British sugar islands dispatched less than one-fourth that amount during the entire eighteenth century. Rum extracted from sugar molasses became a medium of exchange used to pay for African slaves. Tobacco, indigo, and grains increased the agricultural bounty of Europe's New World domain. Added to these were the riches from extractive industries—fishing, forestry, and especially mining. The mines of Mexico and Peru, worked by Indian and black slave labor, had already begun to decline by 1700, but in the preceding two hundred years the precious metals removed from these colonies should have provided the Spanish with incalculable wealth.

Instead, their legacy was economic misfortune. Despite the obvious disparity in territory, mineral wealth, and even agricultural productivity between Spanish America and her imperial rivals, Spain was rapidly declining at the beginning of the eighteenth century. In 1715, when the transatlantic empires entered a century of conflict, Spain's population stood at 7.5 million, approximately the same as two centuries earlier. Disease and other disorders partially explained Spanish debility, but a significant number of Spaniards perished in imperial wars or died before they had children.

Another, more ominous, explanation was the economic misfortune the Spanish Empire suffered. The Spanish did not really profit from their empire, and the economic model they installed in the Western Hemisphere had a debilitating effect on imperial Spain and bequeathed the stunted economies of the modern Latin American republics. When the French Bourbons took command of the Spanish imperial treasury in 1700, they discovered it empty. The legendary treasures of Mexico and Peru had been squandered in the intermittent wars with Spain's rivals or, less noticeably, augmented the private fortunes of a string of inept monarchs, who considered the Spanish Empire theirs, not the nation's. Even more harmful was the inflationary shock the treasures of the empire imposed on the mother country. Until about 1550, when Spanish imperial power was at its height, the country was producing basic articles to meet the demands of a rapidly expanding empire, but the metallic wealth pouring into Iberia destroyed the price structure and with it nascent manufacturing. By the end of the century inexpensive clothing from Italy, France, and England was flooding the country. In agriculture there occurred a simultaneous change in emphasis away from growing foodstuffs to products for export—wool, oil, and wine—because the latter brought larger profits.

In less than a century, a proud, imperial country lost the ability to feed itself, to manage its financial affairs without interference, and to maintain the basic industrial infrastructure every modern society must have. Although the English, French, Portuguese, and Dutch empires in the Western Hemisphere were colonies, only Spanish America suffered a further debilitation: it depended on Spain, but Spain in turn depended on Europe. Spanish America was the colony of a colony.[3]

The French, English, and Dutch empires underwent dramatic changes in the two centuries after Columbus's voyage, explained variously by the economically liberating forces of the Protestant Reformation or the aggressive instincts of modernizing central governments. But the Spanish and Portuguese followed a different route. For sometimes bewildering reasons they developed no merchant or entrepreneurial class capable of sustaining the capital wealth vital to expanding capitalist economies. The Spanish merchant class scarcely existed, and all too often it reflected the hallowed Hispanic traditions of loyalty to *familia* (direct and extended) and the aristocratic values that permeated the imperial bureaucracy.

Other imperial societies questioned privilege and repudiated their medieval heritage. The Spanish did not. And in the Spanish Empire the social order, with its customs, traditions, and reassurance, assumed a primacy unequaled elsewhere in the hemisphere. The riches of Mexico and Peru made superfluous any serious limitation on the inherited *fueros* or privileges of the landed aristocracy, the military, and the church. Fearful of the latent violence in the *castas*—the layers of blacks, mestizos, and mulattoes on the bottom of society—Spanish colonial society required the stabilizing presence of these privileged institutions. In the nineteenth century, when revolutionary and republican movements sought to diminish or eliminate their continuing influence, independent Latin Americans had to create imperfect political structures to take their place.

The Americas in 1700 could most accurately be described as an ethnic and racial conglomerate: Ibero-America totaled 11 million (90 percent of them Indian) out of a total hemispheric population of 12 million. In the eighteenth century the immigration of vast numbers of white laborers to Anglo-America and African slaves to all the Americas had a dramatic racial input on hemispheric demography. By 1820, whites had risen from 11 percent of the population in 1700 to 40 percent; blacks, from 6 to 18 percent; mestizos from less than 1 to 12 percent; and mulattoes, from 1.5 to 6 percent. Indigenous peoples declined from 80 to 25 percent of the population of the Americas. But the social character remained aristocratic, with landed baron and urban merchant, yeoman and artisan, indenture and slave—a transplanted European social structure that had, sometimes imperceptibly, become distinctively New World. Everywhere, from the seigneurial estates of French Canada to the frontier of Argentina, land was the basis of wealth and social standing. And it was land and its yield that sustained the rapid expansion of cities, the growth of a merchant class, and the transatlantic commerce of the age.

In Spain, arguably, the feudal tradition of master and man, lord and manor, may not have been as vigorous as in northern Europe or England, but in Ibero-America the sway of landowner (*hacendado*) reached deep into the social structure and, ultimately, into the political and economic life of the colony. The huge estate, with its produce for export and its staples for local consumption, its human capital of slaves and landless workers, certainly existed in all the European empires. But in Ibero-American cultural life its enduring qualities were bound up with the *hacienda*, the outlying estate that served as a self-sustaining entity with its own economic, social, political, and even religious independence, or in the plantation (typified by the vast sugar *engenho* in Brazil), financed by Old World investments, which produced largely for export. Here, social status meant political influence, and even the nascent merchant classes of the cities (who in Anglo-America could aspire to social prominence) realized that everything worthwhile in life depended on the ownership of land. Realty not personalty sustained the economic, social, and ultimately the political life of Ibero-America. Families might be rich or poor, but if they held land they occupied a superior place in the social order.[4]

The Wars of Empire

In 1713, when the European powers signed the Treaty of Utrecht, the Spanish Empire remained largely intact, but it had become vulnerable to English commercial penetration. Forty years before, the English had wrested a vague Spanish recognition of their logwood camps on the eastern Central American coast, but the most ambitious Protestant outpost, William Paterson's Scots colony in the tropical wilds of Darien, had perished. In making peace the English commercial classes, who had come to prominence in public affairs, obtained something far more valuable than Spanish territory. The Peace of Utrecht had provided the coveted *asiento*, a contract for supplying Spanish America with African slaves.[5]

In the aftermath the Spanish tried to shore up their territorial guarantees in both Europe and America, but they were soon plunged into a brief war in which English warships destroyed the Spanish fleet off Sicily. The French, nominally protectors of the Spanish, seized Pensacola to strengthen the defense of a fledgling colony in Louisiana. Spain eventually recovered Pensacola, but by the 1730s its vulnerability to English commercial penetration in the Caribbean provoked a clash with its old nemesis—the militant seagoing English entrepreneur.

The immediate cause of the conflict lay in the continuing abuses of the South Sea Company, which owned a half-interest in the *asiento* and whose directors saw no reason why company ships should not engage in some profitable smuggling. English smugglers began plying the Caribbean in the tradition of Hawkins and the commercial credo of "forcing a trade." But this was the eighteenth not the sixteenth century. The Spanish had dispatched naval patrol vessels (*guardacostas*) that intercepted real and suspected violators and subjected their captains to harsh punishments. When the Spanish government refused to settle matters until its monarch received a share of South Sea Company profits, the company moguls indignantly refused. As the two governments railed at each other, an otherwise forgettable English sea captain (Robert Jenkins) appeared in Parliament with a harrowing tale about the loss of an ear to a vengeful Spanish officer. His punishment validated the Englishman's ingrained beliefs about Spanish wickedness, and his tale mobilized the anti-Hispanic elements into declaring what came to be called, fittingly, the War of Jenkins' Ear.

Already, another dispute—the settlement of Colonel James Oglethorpe in territory claimed by Spain—had exacerbated Anglo-Spanish relations. Inspired by the English merchants' fierce anti-Hispanic rhetoric and fearful of Spanish attempts to dislodge his colonists at Savannah, Oglethorpe attacked the Spanish fortification at St. Augustine in 1740. The English were repulsed, but two years later (in a counterassault) the Spanish suffered an ignominious defeat at Savannah. Afterward, Anglo-Spanish hostilities shifted to the Caribbean, where, once again, the English were determined to force a trade. By 1744 Europe was plunged into another imperial war, and along the isolated border between English and Spanish possessions, grievances festered and, years later, exploded into bitter conflict.

King George's War, as this expanded conflict was called, settled little in the Americas, but the Spanish emerged from it more determined than ever to rationalize their imperial operations in the New World. Centralization of administration and liberalization of trade policies had already become watchwords of the Spanish monarchy. In 1718, borrowing from the French colonial organization, Philip V introduced the intendancy system throughout the empire, allowing the king to govern through a limited number of loyal and presumably efficient administrators. The moribund Council of the Indies, which had become a dumping ground for family favorites under the Hapsburg dynasty, was supplanted by the Ministry of the Marine and Indies. The viceroyalty of New Granada for northern South America appeared in 1717 to join New Spain (Mexico) and Peru in the grand territorial divisions of Spain's New World empire.[6]

Even more striking were Spanish reforms under Charles III. In a symbolic gesture of royal authority, he expelled the Jesuits and ordered the destruction of their Indian missions in remote Paraguay.

Methodically, his ministers broke the commercial monopoly of Cadiz, the only Spanish port permitted to trade with the colonies, replaced the *flota* or convoy system, and expunged a host of accumulated economic obstacles inherited from the Spanish imperial past.

In appearance the reforms seemed to accommodate the administrative wisdom the Spanish perceived in the English and French models, but such reforms only whetted the Spanish colonial appetite. Even by opening up trade to Spaniards outside Cadiz, Charles was unable to supply his colonial charges, and smuggling continued. The policy of naming only *penisulares* (Spaniards born in Spain) to newly created posts further antagonized the Creoles (Spaniards born in the New World), who had already begun to call themselves "Americans." Nor could policies that seemed enlightened by Spanish standards placate the English, whose merchant ships persisted in making incursions along the Caribbean coast and abused the privilege of dispatching one ship annually to the famed Portobelo fairs in Panama, which the Spanish had granted, by anchoring the permitted vessel in the port and using it as a passage of transit to other ships that pulled alongside.

These reforms were already under way when in 1762 the Spanish court succumbed again to French pressures and brought the nation into war against the English. Spain entered the conflict at a desperate moment for its ally. At war in North America for eight years, the French had suffered one military disaster after another—ignominious defeats in Canada and naval debacles off the sugar isles in the West Indies. Facing expulsion from the New World, the French persuaded Charles III that predatory Anglo-Saxons would exploit former French possessions as bases for an attack against his empire. William Pitt the Elder, the English minister of war, who had brilliantly directed English strategy in this conflict, had professed to maintain Spanish neutrality but now refused to placate the wary Charles, who was notoriously anti-English, on outstanding issues between the two countries. Sensing opportunity, the French began to shower Charles with reassurances of support. In August 1761 the two governments allied under an encompassing principle: "Whoever attacks one crown attacks the other."

The signatories even appealed to other governments to join in the planned humiliation of England. But when the French and Spanish ministers jointly presented an ultimatum to the Portuguese king, he responded by invoking the Anglo-Portuguese alliance and declared war. A series of English victories followed. English invaders seized islands in the French West Indies and Puerto Rico. But their greatest triumph was the conquest of Havana, a military strike sustained by the determination to transform a "popish" colony into a Protestant domain while building it into a thriving English marketplace. For six months the Cubans watched as energetic merchants eager to turn a profit in the heart of the Spanish Indies descended on Havana. The experience of this occupation was to linger in Cuban history, inspiring a later generation of ambitious Creoles.

For Charles III Havana's loss was a humiliating blow. In entering the war the Spanish had sacrificed to prevent further English penetration along their frontier. In the end the French allies were the purveyors of even greater burdens. At the peace table the English demanded Florida, which they had already conquered, as compensation for restoring Havana to the Spanish. Thoroughly beaten, the French were determined to retain their hold on Martinique and Guadeloupe, the stupefyingly rich sugar isles in the West Indies, and suggested some territorial swapping. Louisiana east of the Mississippi would become English, west of the river and the Isle of Orleans, Spanish. The Spanish did not want a "white elephant" in Louisiana or the English in Florida, but they wanted even less an English presence in Havana.[7]

Spain and the American Revolution

The Spanish watched the evolving debate within the British Empire after 1763 with a hope of capitalizing on London's misfortunes tinged with apprehension about being dragged into yet another Anglo-French conflict. The Conde de Floridablanca, the unrepentantly absolutist Spanish foreign minister, regarded the American Declaration of Independence and its ringing appeal to a "candid world" as political heresy. Philosophically, the Spanish never accepted the alliance the monarchist French court fashioned with the American rebels.[8]

The Spanish, however, were not unresponsive when the first republican envoy, John Jay, descended on Madrid, soliciting recognition. Floridablanca publicly rebuffed him but arranged secret meetings with Charles's emissaries and furtive commitments of loans and subsidies. Spanish policy, geared as always to winning the fruits of victory without making an official commitment to the American cause, initially followed a prudent course. The monies flowing to the rebels, it was anticipated, would weaken the British Empire in the New World, perhaps resulting in the creation of an odious little republic, but the Spanish persuaded themselves that an independent United States would be weak and dependent on its benefactors. Thus it would fall under the sway of the only really powerful European empire in the New World. So when the French committed themselves openly in 1778 to fight until the "point of independence" was extracted from the British, the Spanish prided themselves on avoiding the republican charms of the American agents.

They were instead beguiled by their French friends. The Comte de Vergennes, the French foreign minister, was, like his predecessors, adept at playing the Spanish card in France's struggles with the British. After the Franco-American alliance of February 1778, Vergennes initiated overtures for an open Spanish commitment to the cause. The rebellion in North America, he told the Spaniards, offered Spain an opportunity to rid itself of the British presence in Central America and the Floridas. These were persuasive arguments, but Floridablanca demurred. He did not intend to be distracted from Spain's principal concern—the British foothold at Gibraltar, which had rankled a line of Spanish monarchs for half a century.[9]

At a crucial point in the negotiations Floridablanca seized on Britain's concern about fighting a larger war by offering George III what to the Spanish was a fair exchange—Spanish neutrality in return for Gibraltar and Spanish mediation of the Anglo-American civil war. Had either of George III's two predecessors received such a proposal he would doubtless have plunged his advisers into prolonged debate.

But the third Hanoverian on the British throne was an unbendingly rigid man with a finely tuned sense of rectitude about his politics and a parallel belief in the moral bankruptcy of his adversaries. His rejection took the form of a rebuke. Floridablanca was reminded of the frustrating record of Spanish diplomacy in dealing with the English. In April 1779 Spain became a belligerent.

The Treaty of Aranjuez, which brought the Spanish into open alliance with France and war with Britain, committed the French to the Spanish recovery of Gibraltar, Minorca, and the Floridas but, predictably, did not bind the Spanish to fight until American independence was achieved. That calculated omission soon became a troublesome issue for the American envoys in Europe, but the declaration of war made official two years of clandestine Spanish aid to the rebellious American colonies. Since the outbreak of the Revolution the Spanish court, following France's lead, had been channeling gunpowder, muskets, textiles, and even medicine through the dummy company the French playwright Beaumarchais had set up to aid the Americans. The supplies were shipped out of Bilbao for Havana and then on to New Orleans and the war on the Mississippi frontier. American privateers put in at Spanish ports in the Indies and from them waged a destructive campaign against British warships. Even before Aranjuez, Spanish agents had surfaced in Pensacola and Mobile and a British vessel had intercepted a ship headed up the Delaware River bearing a Spanish emissary to the Continental Congress at Philadelphia.[10]

Though both France and Spain were self-serving in this struggle, the French *had* committed themselves to American independence. Spain's intention was to exploit the American Revolution as an opportunity to protect the porous northern frontier of the poorly defended Spanish Empire. This meant retaking the Floridas and moving farther north into the vastness of interior British North America east of the Mississippi River, domain once French, now the scene of random battles less decisive in the monumental conflict east of the Alleghenies but perhaps critical in determining who would rule "inside" North America. Two thousand miles to the west, Spanish soldiers and priests, apprehensive about the meaning of Captain James Cook's

Pacific voyage, continued to push up the California coast, building presidios (forts) and missions, twin symbols of Spain's New World imperial frontier.

There would be no formal alliance with the noisome revolutionaries who had raised the flag of defiance against the British Empire. What the British and later the Americans perceived as duplicity was more accurately a trait of Spanish diplomacy that called for treating both friend and foe with considerable wariness. Unwilling to act merely as supplier for the American warriors on the Gulf coast, the Spanish planned their own assault against British Florida. Bernardo de Gálvez, the energetic and ambitious governor of New Orleans, with the timely encouragement of an American revolutionary general, James Wilkinson, struck the British on the Florida Keys and followed with blows on their weakened positions on the Mississippi. With an invading force of one thousand militiamen and Indians, Gálvez took Manchac, Baton Rouge, and Natchez, effectively destroying British power on the lower Mississippi and with it plans for an attack on New Orleans. Fired by his victories, Gálvez dispatched a naval expedition against Mobile, defended by three hundred weary soldiers, and reduced the town with an artillery barrage.

But whatever union of American and Spanish forces might have been fashioned for the planned strike against Pensacola and St. Augustine vanished with the British capture of Charleston in 1780 and the subsequent thrust inland. The Americans now directed their energies toward the more crucial battles that loomed to the north. Gálvez proved no less hesitant in their absence. He assembled a seven-thousand-man force made up of troops from Mobile, New Orleans, Havana, and even a few French volunteers and took Pensacola.[11]

Only in the interior did the Spanish lose ground. In the upper Mississippi Valley, where advancing Spanish forces had erected fortifications in anticipation of lasting American influence, the frontier revolutionary elements were more decisive. At Vincennes and Kaskaskia the victories of George Rogers Clark protected the western country against the British drive from Canada. These triumphs were not decisive in the final victory, but they signaled that the Americans would not be readily confined to the Atlantic coast.

Spain emerged from the American Revolution with a string of military triumphs but, as in the final settlement of 1763, with that inherently Spanish sense of loss and betrayal. Spanish armies had been victorious in the West Florida peninsula and the British had been repulsed in the Bay of Honduras. But in the peace Gibraltar remained British and the western country became American territory. Even in retroceding all Florida the British created yet another dispute by stipulating that west Florida's northern boundary lay, not at Vicksburg, but farther south. As in previous New World conflicts, the Spanish, in protecting territory rightfully claimed or conquering territory previously lost, were judged as duplicitous, untrustworthy, and undeserving. Trusting neither enemy nor ally, they were not trusted. As victor or loser the Spanish felt always betrayed by forces beyond their control, denied the fruits of victories nobly won, and manipulated by their allies. The Spanish effort had not been vital to victory, but Spain's contribution to American independence had not been negligible. If Gálvez and his militiamen had not shielded the Gulf coast the British might have been victorious in their southern strategy.

And for Charles III the unwritten alliance with the Americans had untoward consequences in his many kingdoms in the Indies. In the peace treaty his absolutist minister, the Conde de Aranda, had acknowledged the right of revolution. The lesson was unmistakable: if the sovereign's subject has a grievance that cannot be resolved, he can repudiate his allegiance. Britain's predicament—and Spain's exploitation of British misfortune—was widely publicized in Charles's dominion. There were revolts—the most destructive being the Inca rebellion of Tupac Amaru in Peru—of Indian against white and, more ominously, of the *castas* against whites and then of Creoles (Spaniards born in the New World) against *peninsulares* (Spaniards transplanted from the homeland).

The Creoles were the most impressionable. To them the rising of the British colonists against George III symbolized parricide, the child in arms against the father. They read the inspirational phrases of the

Declaration of Independence—noting, especially, Jefferson's exaltation that all men are entitled to "life, liberty, and the pursuit of hap-
piness" and that governments derive their "just powers from the con-
sent of the governed"—and ascribed them to Charles's empire. With
John Locke's notions of the sanctity of private property the Creoles
incorporated the credos of their favorite philospher, Jean Jacques
Rousseau, proselytizer of the "general will." Rousseau was as much a
dreamer as Columbus. He was a Calvinist with a liberated spirit. In
merging these transatlantic visions the Creoles had unknowingly
fashioned a revolutionary cause from the philosophy of reason and
that of anarchy. Their revolutionary heritage was thus a symbiotic
union of liberating vision and endless struggle. Latin American
would pay dearly for this legacy.[12]

The International Frontier

Even before independence the rebellious colonials had begun to
appropriate *American* as their own symbol of cultural unity. They
emerged from the Revolution remembering the anti-Hispanic biases
they had inherited from the long years of intermittent strife between
isolated border peoples, the anti-Catholic animus that permeated English life after Elizabeth, and the countless tales of Spanish perfidy
and wickedness. But with their colonial merchant's instincts they believed that a great commercial market still awaited them in the Spanish Empire. They had largely forgotten the faint cultural and intellectual links fashioned in the eighteenth-century Enlightenment. The
political and economic implications of the Spanish presence were uppermost in their minds.

Unlike their English forebears, Americans came to fear even a
weakened Spanish presence to the south. For a generation, an independent United States dedicated itself to breaking down the economic barriers into the Spanish entrepôt. Until the War of 1812 the
commercial rewards North Americans enjoyed with the declining
Spanish Empire more than offset losses elsewhere. And commercial

aggressiveness was accompanied by a territorial imperative—to advance the vulnerable southern frontier to the Gulf of Mexico and New Orleans. This quest, carried out against the backdrop of a momentous struggle in Europe, revealed the most acquisitive instincts of a young United States obsessed with real fears for its own survival and brought to the early relations between the United States and Latin America the most corrosive prejudices. The American priority on hemispheric security antedated even the Monroe Doctrine.

In defeat the British lost one empire but gained another, an empire of commerce and influence more lucrative than colonies because it depended on British industry, finance, and the British navy and was not burdened with the debilitating costs of the Atlantic seaboard colonies. In isolated places Englishmen suffered from the loss. The peace settlement wrought hardship on those who had settled in the Floridas after the great victory of 1763. After the American Revolution began, more than seventeen thousand Loyalists poured into the colony. With the retrocession, a few tried to build an autonomous government, presumably loyal to Spain but in reality self-governing. When this effort failed, the British migrants began yet another migration, to the Bahamas, Nova Scotia, the Mosquito coast, Louisiana, and England.

The Spanish reclaimed their lost province with typical military fanfare, fifteen ships and five hundred men sailing gloriously into the old capital, St. Augustine. Most of the British, largely Protestant, had already abandoned the colony, but about five hundred Catholic Italians, Greeks, and Minorcans the British had imported were allowed to remain. In Spanish America religious profession served as a measure of political loyalty.

Confronting an immediate problem of supplying their Indian subjects, the Spanish resorted to practical solutions. During the Revolution British officials had permitted two Loyalist merchants, William Panton and Robert Leslie, to move their operations from South Carolina and Georgia to backwater posts in Florida. By 1783 Panton, Leslie, and Company controlled the Indian trade throughout the Southeast. The Spanish could not furnish the supplies the Indians required. Rather than relinquish the trade to American traffickers and the aggressive commercial instincts of the new republic to the north, the Spanish sustained the monopoly of Panton, Leslie. And in the upper Mississippi Valley Spanish merchants continued to deal with British traders from Canada, in violation of the peace settlement. Such informal commercial links sustained frontier beliefs of an Anglo-Spanish conspiracy.

The vast territory between the Mississippi and the Appalachian Mountains was in the years after the Revolution a British protectorate in the North and a Spanish one in the South. Even in Spanish Florida the survival of Panton, Leslie, and Company meant British economic dominion of the entire lower Mississippi Valley. Isolated from the seaboard states by distance and a perceived indifference, the scattered American towns west of the mountains, which traded their corn and hogs for shirts and wares from Liverpool and Birmingham, lived within the economic and political reach of two empires. They were citizens of the Western Hemisphere's first republic, but they were marginal to its sense of identity.[13]

The struggle on the Spanish-American frontier was not, at bottom, a contest for territory—at least from London's viewpoint. From the sixteenth century the British had transformed their economy as their Spanish rival became an Old World dependency with a New World empire. The loss of the American colonies, though humiliating, brought to power a new generation of British imperialists who staked out the second British Empire—an empire of commerce and political influence protected by British seapower.

William Pitt the Younger, who came to power in the aftermath of the American Revolution, fully understood the larger stakes on the Mississippi frontier. There lay the foundation of a commercial empire stretching from Upper Canada to New Orleans and Florida, even, perhaps, beyond into the heart of the Spanish Empire. This perception explained the warm reception meted out in London to the precursors of Spanish-American revolution—Luis Vidal, who conspired against Spanish rule in New Granada; Francisco Mendiola, the Mexican seditionist; and Francisco de Miranda, the most popular Creole revolutionary in George III's kingdom.

In the 1780s and 1790s the Spanish-American frontier was alive with half-breeds, runaways, and unreconciled Loyalists, men with no political commitment to Spain, Britain, or the United States, now the nominal sovereign east of the Mississippi and north of the still uncharted Florida boundary. They hatched grandiose schemes and plots for a frontier protectorate, populated by Indians but ruled by whites with special connections in New Orleans. They had a common hatred for American expansionism. Their plan for halting the Americans at the Appalachian divide reached into high places.[14] Ultimately, their intrigue would blossom into what Andrew Jackson (who developed fierce anti-Hispanic sentiments) and his frontier cronies would refer to as the "Spanish conspiracy." Until Jackson's victory at New Orleans a generation later destroyed the notion, the British were equally devious in their intriguing, but frontier people long remembered the Spanish conspiracy and readily forgot the lingering British fascination with "undoing" the American Revolution.

"The Revolutionary War," Arthur Preston Whitaker astutely observed, "[had] . . . flung the unfortunate Spain across the path of [American] progress."[15] But the Spanish had the advantage of centralized monarchy, presumably able to direct its will to the northern periphery of its New World empire. Its challenger was a bitterly divided United States, its first years of independence an apparent mockery of the survival of republican government. As the 1790s began, their relative difference in strength was offset by the determination of the United States to reaffirm national power under the new Constitution. To do so, the Federalists accommodated British power on the high seas and confronted a weakened Spanish Empire in the North American interior.

The Spanish rightly viewed themselves as the victims of a belligerently expansionist republic in the Mississippi Valley. Agreeing on the strategic imperative of checking American expansion, Charles III's advisers could not resolve their debate on tactics to accomplish that goal. To the ineffectual Articles of Confederation government in 1785 the Spanish had proffered a liberal commercial treaty in exchange for American concessions on the navigation of the Mississippi. Political interests sympathetic to westerners had killed the measure, so the Spanish governors in New Orleans intrigued among disaffected frontiersmen fearful of losing their "natural right" to ship their tobacco, pigs, and corn down the rivers and into Spanish territory.

In the Spanish view these frontier hucksters were only slightly more deserving than the filibusters who had preyed on their vessels along the Spanish Main two centuries before. Despising the American interlopers as the advance agents of a Protestant horde, New Orleans governors were aware of the Americans' economic vulnerability and determined to exploit it. The Baron de Carondelet was the most explicit in his arguments for subverting the frontier and transforming it into a Spanish protectorate. Tolerate a few, he said, suborn their leaders, and give them minimal protection. They will be a buffer against threats to the king's prized domains farther south. Carondelet even made secret arrangements with the Kentuckians, responding to their appeals for protection against Indian attacks from Spanish Florida. James Wilkinson, the American general who dreamed of a western republic under Spanish protection, went on Carondelet's payroll.

But the line drawn against American encroachment followed a different course on maps in Madrid. In 1796, a year after the Americans committed themselves in Jay's Treaty to Anglo-American rapprochement, Carondelet threw his energies into a grand project calling for the economic subordination of the western country. The plan was reinforced by Spanish war galleys on the Mississippi. The intent was to defend Louisiana, but Carondelet had ambitious prospects for offensive action as well.

Once more, European circumstances benefited the Americans. French military triumphs against the first coalition against the Revolution had demoralized Spain and brought humiliating concessions, among them the cession of all Hispaniola. The Americans had made their concessions to Britain; now the Spanish feared that Pitt the Younger, infuriated over the concessions by his erstwhile ally against France, would retaliate, perhaps in the Gulf. Ten days after the signing of the treaty with the French, the Spanish king's minister called in an until then studiously neglected American emissary, Thomas

Pinckney, and to his consternation conceded every major issue among the list of frontier grievances—acknowledging U.S. claims to the swath of territory from the Mississippi (north of 31°) to the Chattahoochee River, navigation of the Mississippi to New Orleans, and the right to transfer goods shipped down the river on flatboats to oceangoing vessels.

These concessions considerably brightened the economic prospects for the isolated western country. Whether in north or south on the U.S. frontier, Americans who clustered in Ohio Valley settlements or in the valleys of the rivers that fed into the Ohio had a common stake in what happened in the lower Mississippi Valley. Nowhere did the impending collapse of Spain's imperial frontier advance as rapidly.

But what Spain had given up, both Americans and Spaniards knew, could just as readily be withdrawn. The more restricted right of deposit at New Orleans, which had accompanied the vital concession of free navigation for American vessels on the lower Mississippi, became in these years a symbolic test of Spanish intentions. For eight years after Pinckney's diplomatic victory in Europe, the "western question" was unresolved. Two successive Presidents—John Adams and Thomas Jefferson—correctly perceived that national unity depended on placating the continuous western demands for access to New Orleans yet were alert to the potential dangers of provoking a frontier conflict with Spain that could very well escalate into a confrontation with the French.

Sensing the American dilemma—how to push Spain out of the lower Mississippi without giving their French ally a convenient excuse to intrude—the Spanish followed their traditional diplomatic strategy of pretending to pursue one course when their goal was another. Though recognizing Louisiana's inevitable loss—as the Conde de Godoy had observed, "We can't lock up an open field," a sardonic reference to the impossibility of defending the lower Mississippi Valley—Spanish governors in New Orleans continued their generous immigration policies. They tried to lure European settlers into Louisiana and the Floridas. That failing, they revived their intrigues with the Americans they had occasionally befriended or suborned. Wilkinson, who became U.S. army commander in the West after the death of Anthony Wayne, continued to receive a subsidy from them, and he encouraged other Americans in madcap schemes to detach the western country and make it into a Spanish protectorate. In 1797, yet another Spanish conspiracy—this one involving Senator William Blount of Tennessee—collapsed under a torrent of anti-Spanish sentiment. A year later, when an undeclared naval war with France erupted on the high seas, Alexander Hamilton, and other Federalists schemed to unite east and west by declaring war on Spain and invading the lower Mississippi.

But the resolute Adams would not hear of it. His cautious diplomacy avoided a war with two European empires but did not immediately bring Louisiana into the American snare. When the United States and France ended their naval war in 1800, the Americans rid themselves of the revolutionary war alliance, but Spain had already secretly ceded Louisiana to France. The Spanish policy of maneuver and, to Americans, deception appeared vindicated. In five years of debilitating European conflict and frontier intrigue, the Spanish had sustained a weak but symbolically authoritative presence in the lower Mississippi Valley and the Floridas. A small invading force of Americans, they believed, could have taken New Orleans. But the United States had not taken advantage of Spanish military weakness in its Louisiana outpost. Adams had restrained the more aggressive instincts of his countrymen and, perhaps more important, the Spanish court had recognized that Louisiana would never be the bastion of imperial defense. Accepting that reality, the Spanish had followed a time-honored strategy of yielding but not breaking before the more powerful winds from the north.[16]

In the aftermath came Napoleon and Talleyrand's imperial design to revive New France in Louisiana and Saint-Domingue, an expanse rivaling in economic productivity the British Empire before the American Revolution. A slave revolt had erupted in Haiti in 1790 and, led by Toussaint L'Ouverture, had by the end of the decade established control over the western third of the island. Napoleon schemed to undermine Toussaint, who professed loyalty to France and the inherited rights of revolutionary France. But Toussaint had already taken advantage of French international distress. In 1798, when the undeclared naval war broke out with the United States, he confronted a powerful British army in Haiti, invited in by fearful white planters. Toussaint struck a deal with the British: he would not export his slave rebellion to Jamaica, and the British and the Americans could share Haitian trade. Recognition of Haitian independence was out of the question.

In the twilight of his presidency Adams ended the naval war with France and with it the revolutionary war alliance. He had not reckoned on French ambitions in the Western Hemisphere. He dutifully sent orders to American naval officers to cease dealing with Toussaint, then mounting a campaign to subdue the eastern portion of the island. Simultaneously, Napoleon compelled the Spanish to retrocede Louisiana and began planning to deal with the black revolutionaries in the Queen of the Antilles.

Thomas Jefferson's affections for French culture led Napoleon and his foreign minister, Talleyrand, to believe the new U.S. president would support the French cause in the Caribbean. They presumed, correctly, that the Americans feared a black republic as much as the British and that there would be no British naval interception of a French invasion force dispatched to subdue Toussaint. American officials made ambiguous statements about the ambitious French design, coupled inextricably with rumors of Louisiana's retrocession. Secretary of State James Madison told the new French chargé of American concerns. The French diplomat, alert to the nuances of American politics, asked for U.S. cooperation in keeping Toussaint from shifting into the British embrace by keeping open a small part of the American trade with the black leader. Madison then strongly hinted that if France made peace with Britain the French navy could starve the Haitians into submission. When these words reached Talleyrand, they were interpreted as a pledge of American cooperation in the French venture. In October 1801 Napoleon ceased hostilities against Britain.

Then he named his brother-in-law, Joseph LeClerc, commander of a powerful French invasion force dispatched to restore his authority over the defiant Haitians. In LeClerc's instructions, Napoleon wrote, "Jefferson has promised that from the moment the French army arrives, every measure shall be taken to starve Toussaint and to aid the army."[17]

Jefferson the Francophile and slaveholder was then in his first year as president. He was a montage of contradictions, but where Louisiana was concerned he was a strategist and opportunist, mindful of the primacy of the western question in the country's dealings with the European powers. Where black free Haiti was concerned, he was no friend of liberty. When he found out about the retrocession of Louisiana, his admiration for France slackened. His policy became fundamentally expedient, even to daring talk about allying with the British to keep the French out of Louisiana. Haiti, he had concluded, was unworthy of independence. Earlier, the more socially conservative Adams had evinced some concern for Toussaint's cause, if for no other reason than to serve American national interests, and had initiated a trade with the black leader. But Jefferson, then the presidential aspirant, had opposed even this limited contact. He told Madison in 1799, when Congress was debating the issue, "We may therefore expect black crews, and supercargoes and missionaries thence into the Southern states. . . . If this combustion can be introduced among us under any veil whatever, we have to fear it."[18] Jefferson was more prophetic than he knew about the fears the Haitian rebellion would provoke in the United States.

With an unappreciated guile and determination, Jefferson pressed the Louisiana issue. Unexpectedly, the French invasion of Haiti in late 1801 abetted his cause. The French commander, Joseph LeClerc, tricked Toussaint into surrendering, then dispatched him in chains to France. He died two years later in an Alpine prison. Across the ocean, the momentary order he had imposed lapsed into racial and class warfare, bringing with it forty thousand French casualties. Jefferson had already dispatched a special emissary, James Monroe, to treat with the French. By the time Monroe arrived, Napoleon had decided to abandon Louisiana—even before the French had formally taken possession—and in the process break his pledge to his Spanish ally not to transfer the province to a third power. Jefferson wanted New Orleans and the Floridas. Monroe bought the Isle of Orleans and the French added Louisiana to the purchase. By the end of 1802 American newspapers had picked up the rumor of the transfer. When the Spanish learned of it, they were furious and immediately restored the right of deposit they had earlier canceled.

The withdrawal of that right by Spain and, by implication, France, roused the westerners into a war fever. If Spain could not deal with the Americans on that and related matters, neither could France. In a few years the Spanish had unintentionally furthered the American cause in New Orleans by opening the city and the frontier to American commerce and Americans. When France eventually took possession of the city in early December 1803, its Americanization had already begun. Rumors of Spanish efforts to prevent the U.S. takeover had inspired volunteers from the West to invade the city and, if necessary, to seize it. The story was yet another variation of Spanish perfidy that Americans too often believed. When the American flag was unfurled a few weeks later, the volunteers were scattered about the city. But their menacing presence was unnecessary. The Spanish had no intention of fighting for a province and a city that they had already determined to relinquish. But they had never wanted to retire in disgrace. Few Americans understood this nuance of the Spanish diplomatic style.

2 America and the Revolutions of the Americas, 1800–1830

Within a year after the Louisiana purchase, the Haitian revolution ended. Out of its carnage emerged the second republic of the Americas. The upheaval dampened the spirits of even the most committed revolutionaries of Jefferson's generation. It was not technically the forerunner of the Latin American rebellion, yet its destructiveness, its symbolic horror of class and racial conflict, and its lasting imagery of mindless violence deeply affected those who shaped American policy toward the hemisphere and the precursors of Latin American independence. Even the effusive Francisco de Miranda—a transatlantic crusader—confessed to an English friend in 1798: "As much as I desire the liberty and independence of the New World, I fear the anarchy of a revolutionary system. God forbid that these beautiful countries become . . . a theatre of blood and of crime under the pretext of establishing liberty. Let them rather remain if necessary one century more under the barbarous and imbecilic oppression of Spain."[1] Simón Bolívar (who arrested Miranda for conspiring against the Crown, then himself raised the flag of revolution) was so inspired by Haiti's liberation of the slaves that he began gradual emancipation in independent Colombia, yet he feared the black revolution, that "tremendous monster who has devoured the island of Santo Domingo."[2]

For decades the "monster" served as a metaphor for the latent violence of the masses and the unpredictability of revolution begun from above but taken over by those from below. In their campaigns the Haitians resorted to a style of warfare that Americans and Europeans perceived as genocidal, a determination to drive out the whites and exterminate those who persisted in remaining. That ordinary, illiterate black slaves in rebellion fought a racial war is undeniable. In doing so they were unmindful of the judgment of a "civilized world." In the last assaults they cruelly massacred whites—men, women, and children—and destroyed the sugar economy that had made the island rich. The whites had begun the violence, and the blacks correctly sensed that if the destruction of the slave economy of sugar meant impoverishment it also ensured their freedom. The choice doomed Haiti to poverty.

The Spanish American Revolutions

For years the terrors that accompanied Haitian independence reinforced Americans' notions about the cataclysmic finality of any rebellion in the slave Caribbean, but it only moderately lessened their enthusiasm for the cause of independence on the mainland of Spanish America. They believed their own experience provided an example to these revolutions. They contributed money, supplies, and in a few cases their lives to causes they only vaguely understood but nonetheless championed. Americans remembered the narrowly defined "America" of Washington's Farewell Address, but they were captivated with the notion of liberation of an America that transcended national domain and encompassed the entire hemisphere. Thomas Jefferson described it as "one hemisphere . . . having a different system of interest" yet suffering from the "passions and wars" of European tyranny. Even his doubts that "priest-ridden people" could sustain "free civil government" did not diminish his faith that "America has a hemisphere to itself."[3]

The star-crossed plotter Miranda was perhaps the first Creole liberator Americans knew. For a generation he conspired with British ministers and American political leaders in madcap schemes for the liberation of Spanish America. The Creole malcontents had no confidence in the reformist impulses within the Spanish Empire. For them Britain and then America were symbols of a new age. Miranda had the greatness and the flaws of a generation of Hispanics born in the New World. They might have labored to change imperial Spain from within; instead they sought refuge from the Spanish tyranny in London.[4] Miranda first served the American cause during the Revolution, when he took part in Gálvez's assault on Pensacola. He obtained vital funds from a Spanish official in Havana and gave the money to the French naval commander who blockaded Yorktown. Sometime later he was secretly negotiating with the British while on a mission to Jamaica in the final years of the American Revolution. Charles III's agents were already alert to his perfidy. He fled to the newly independent United States. The American revolutionary triumph inspired him, and he found kindred spirits and, he believed, support for his own liberating cause among American leaders. He toured Europe, became a favorite of Catherine the Great, then went to London, where, during the Anglo-Spanish confrontation over Nootka Sound in 1790, he suggested to William Pitt the Younger a daring plan to liberate Spanish America. Rebuffed when the two governments settled the matter, Miranda joined the French revolutionary cause. By the end of the decade he was back in London with still more plans for revolution.

When he finally returned to the United States, he found not the revolutionary America he had first encountered but Jefferson's United States and its generation of aged rebels in power. Their cause was now the survival of the commercial republic before the onslaught of menacing and warring European empires, the national interest rather than the liberation of the hemisphere. Ultimately, as the European belligerents imperiled U.S. neutrality with such severe measures as the subjugation of U.S. merchant ships to the British rule of law on the North Atlantic and to Napoleon's continental system, which punished the United States when its government yielded to Britain's demands, the myth of New World revolutionary kindred spirits subsided before national priorities and transatlantic realities.

But the idea of an American system that reached beyond narrowly defined U.S. commercial and strategic interests had taken hold among Americans. The U.S. government may have expressed doubts about Miranda's doings, but America tolerated his presence and his plotting. Preparing for an assault on Venezuela, he obtained vital provisions and converts in the United States. Jefferson and Madison, then warily charting American policy toward Spanish America, did not commit themselves directly, but they were assured that others would support the charismatic Creole who admired British and American political culture. When he launched the ill-fated assault on Venezuela in 1807, American money, men, and matériel abetted his cause. This liberating expedition failed, but Miranda never lost that instinctively Hispanic determination to press on. He went back to London and was rewarded with a comfortable country house, a library, and a coterie of friends. Still he plotted. He wrote incendiary columns for the press, cultivated powerful British officials, and kept up a secret correspondence with rebellious Creoles in Spanish America. When in 1810 some malcontents in Venezuela raised the flag of revolution, they dispatched emissaries to London. Bolívar was among them. Despite British pledges to support his costly social life, Miranda returned with them to Venezuela and became a general in the revolutionary command. His appeal for British and American support in 1812 for a cause that few Europeans and Americans really understood went unheeded. He was captured, shipped to Spain, and died in a Cadiz prison cell four years later.

Over the preceding decade American interest in Spanish America had sharpened considerably. The first missions to the Spanish colonies after the liberalization of trade policies in 1797 were largely commercial. A U.S. consulate opened in Santiago de Cuba a year later and another in 1800 at La Guaira, Venezuela. Neither was officially recognized, but, according to local custom, they were tolerated. A few prominent Americans were later implicated in Miranda's ill-fated scheme to liberate Venezuela, and no less a vocal patriot than Andrew Jackson was mesmerized by former Vice-President Aaron Burr's bizarre plot to liberate Florida, Texas, and Mexico. A few Americans had become desultory students of Hispanic culture and were sufficiently aware of the empire's cultural achievements to offer a demurral to the more popular view of "barbarous, Popish" Spanish America.[5] Most harbored strong resentments against Spanish tardiness in recognizing American independence, conveniently forgetting about the timely Spanish aid during the Revolution. And on the south-western frontier anti-Hispanic sentiment, fueled by sporadic troubles with Florida Indians, was widespread.

The Spanish Empire had begun to crumble, and the American government was alert to the opportunity—and the consequences—of the rebellion. The revolutions in Spanish America began, as had the revolt in the English colonies to the north, as protests. In 1807 Napoleon removed Ferdinand VII from the Spanish throne and replaced him with his brother. For the Creoles who gained a political foothold in local Spanish government throughout the empire, Napoleon's act confirmed Spanish debility and in 1808 provoked the *cabildos* (the town councils) to denounce the French and reaffirm their loyalty to Ferdinand, *el deseado*, the "desired one." Two years later, revolution swept the empire. Everywhere the rallying cry was liberty, but those who raised the flag of liberation pursued a different agenda. In Mexico, the revolution portended social upheaval, pitting Indian against Spanish oppressor; in South America, it was the defiance of an alienated and opportunistic Creole elite who hearkened to the constitutional monarchism of Britain and the chorus of commercial freedom sung by Americans. Few in the revolutionary pantheon anticipated that a decade of pillage and mindless destruction lay ahead, that independence would leave in its wake a half-century of militarism, disunity, and vulnerability to the outside world.

The outbreak of revolution in 1808 brought hints of more daring policies from Washington. For a year Jefferson had watched his political reputation wither before a storm of criticism over his economic policies, especially the hated embargo, which had shut down American shipping and plunged New England into a depression. The impending collapse of Spanish authority in the New World offered yet another opportunity to take advantage of Old World distresses. Spain confronted not only rebellion in the empire but civil war at home between the *afrancesados* (those who went along with the French takeover) and the patriots loyal to the deposed Ferdinand. The latter had new-found friends among the British. For Jefferson the tumult in Spain and its fractious colonies offered the prospect for extending

American commercial interests without parallel political commitments. Anti-Jeffersonian historians have described his Latin American policies as either vacillating or self-serving. His defenders have exalted his strategic vision and even credited him with laying the groundwork for the Monroe Doctrine. He told American agents hastily dispatched to South America to make no political obligations to the rebels but to express American friendship and warn them against British or French manipulation. Sometime later, he expressed the view that American and Hispanic American revolutionaries agreed that "European influence" must be excluded from the Western Hemisphere.

Why, then, was there no enthusiastic outpouring of support for the Spanish American rebellion? The United States had been a colony and broken with its British master; now the Spanish American rebels appeared to be following a similar pattern. In truth, both were still economic colonies of the Old World. Despite Jefferson's rhetorical flourishes about the grand revolutionary community of the Western Hemisphere, his policies were determined by transatlantic realities. The controversial embargo of 1807, for example, designed to punish the British, severely damaged American commercial ties with Spanish America. The agent of the patriot party in the United States, don Federico de Onís, alertly perceived American priorities when he complained that American ships were serving as conduits between Bonapartist Spain and Spanish America. Later, he accused the Americans of abetting French efforts. To a cynical European the reasons were transparent: the United States risked much by identifying with the patriot cause and stood to gain only if its success were assured. By comparison, cooperation with France in 1810–11, when Anglo-American relations deteriorated, held out the prospect that Napoleon might compel a subservient Spanish government to cede the Floridas.[6]

Despite American hesitation, the Spanish American revolutionaries did benefit from even the limited concessions they received. The first generation of American emissaries to the revolutionary juntas may have sought commercial opportunity, yet to the Creoles who received them the gospel of commercial freedom meant, ultimately, freedom from the economic restraints of the Spanish Empire.[7] As had Jefferson, Madison avoided making political commitments, but to his credit he permitted revolutionary emissaries to purchase munitions. Agents from Buenos Aires, Venezuela, Mexico, Colombia, and even Cuba descended on Baltimore and Philadelphia, the two commercial entrepôts for the arms trade. A similar privilege was accorded de Onís when Ferdinand was restored to the throne and launched his counterrevolution. But these limited commitments to revolutionary governments supposedly fighting for the same reasons Americans themselves had struggled in their own war of independence did not provide lasting reassurances. The United States favored Latin American independence but would not recognize the fledgling revolutionary governments, nor would the private American businessmen who sold to them (such as John Jacob Astor) assume unnecessary risks. Furthermore, the American emissaries sent to treat with the rebels often found themselves outmaneuvered by British agents, who were winning commercial agreements from rebel governments even while maintaining an alliance with the Spanish Crown.

Great Britain had already surpassed the United States in the quest for Latin American commerce. Exploiting the free ports system in the Caribbean and skillfully using its naval power, Britain overcame blockades and opened revolutionary ports to merchants who had lost their markets in Europe and the United States. In Portuguese Brazil the British advance was political as well as economic. Until 1808 British ships had to sail by way of Lisbon to trade with the colony. But Napoleon's invasion of Iberia had sent the Braganza royal house to safety in Brazil aboard British warships. A commercial treaty drawn up by the British minister in 1810 virtually assured British commercial domination for a generation.

Through these years of vacillation and undisguised opportunism, American leaders continued to believe that Spanish American revolutionaries would find in the United States a political model to emulate and would, as had the United States, identify Britain as the transatlantic economic menace. Compelled to choose between national self-interest and ideological commitment to revolution, the Americans alertly and understandably chose the former. In 1811, Congress resolved that Spanish Florida must not be transferred to another non–Western-Hemispheric power. In the same year it created the Committee on the Spanish American Colonies, expressing its sympathy for the revolutionary cause and hesitantly advancing a commitment to hemispheric unity.

Clearly, then, the United States in these months before the onset of the War of 1812 placed national interest before ideological commitment. But its government and some of its more prominent publicists demonstrated more than a detached interest in the Spanish American revolutions. Latin American critics of American policy in these formative years offer an undeniable charge of American preoccupation with frontier interests in Florida and the crisis on the high seas. But just as compelling are some undeniable realities of the hemispheric situation. By 1812 the wars for independence had reached a stalemate. In Venezuela the royalist counterrevolution had apparently triumphed. In Mexico the social upheaval launched by Father Hidalgo's Indian warriors had been checked, and in faraway Buenos Aires a cabal of rebellious Creoles had become noticeably hesitant in denouncing Spanish authority. If American policies reflected international political and economic realities and, at bottom, furthered the national interest, a generation of Latin American revolutionaries shrewdly chose British over American friendship for similar reasons of statecraft, not ideological affinity.[8]

Transatlantic realities and national interest had shaken American leaders from the Western Hemispheric spell but had not destroyed their lasting faith in America. The survival of republicanism and free trade—now identified with the United States—was a more pressing issue than the uncertain cause of liberty in "greater America," certainly if one believed that the survival of the United States was ultimately vital for the survival of America. In retrospect, it is clear why few Latin American revolutionaries and Europeans believed that the United States fought the War of 1812 for principles and not, given their perceptions of U.S. territorial acquisitiveness, for national self-interest.

American determination to acquire the Floridas had figured prominently in the congressional debate over hostilities. Even before the
"no-transfer" resolution prohibiting the transfer of Florida from one
European power to another, the United States had begun a piecemeal
absorption by occupying extreme west Florida (from the Mississippi
to the Pearl River) in 1810. A year later, using as pretext the collapse of
adequate Spanish jurisdiction over the province and an impending
British invasion, President James Madison secretly encouraged an
anti-Hispanic former governor of Georgia to rouse ruffians in the
border towns for an invasion of the province. The invaders took Fer-
nandina Island and prepared for an assault on St. Augustine, but the
Spanish protested and Madison backed down. The American troops
remained for the duration of the war, and to the west the United
States occupied the remainder of the peninsula from the Pearl to the
Perdido rivers. At war's end, the Spanish had a choice: they could
hold Florida with British support or they would eventually lose it to
the persistent Americans.

In London or Madrid and in some respects even in Washington,
Florida's worth was essentially strategic. Great Britain preferred a
weak Spanish colony to the north of its West Indian possessions but
after Jackson's victory at New Orleans prudently concluded that to
defend Spanish Florida would be a tactical blunder. Rejected by London in their appeal for a British protectorate, the Spanish resigned
themselves to losing what had always been a borderland colony. But
they were determined to exact a price. In 1815, throughout Spanish
America, revolutions that had begun as protests against Napoleon's
removal of Ferdinand VII from the Spanish throne waned. Victorious
European monarchs, vowing to restore "legitimacy" on the Continent, appeared ready to aid the Spanish in restoring monarchy in
their empire. If Florida's loss to the Americans was inevitable, the
Spanish reasoned, the United States would strive to acquire it peacefully. In 1815, when the United States was finally assured that its independence would not be revoked, the Latin American revolutions
appeared doomed. Their leaders were exiled, jailed, or dead. Simón
Bolívar, who would liberate the Andes, meditated in refuge; José de

San Martín had yet to cross the Andes with his conquering army. And in Mexico, where a lowly parish priest and his marauding Indians had swept the countryside in 1810, a Spanish firing squad dispatched his successor in 1815. With the defeat of Napoleon in Europe the cause of monarchy and legitimacy triumphed. Their validation in the Spanish Empire seemed certain.

The Monroe Doctrine

The notion that the Western Hemisphere had a republican destiny and thus should be exempt from Europe's future colonization began to take shape fairly rapidly after 1815. It represented the cumulative ideological force of the "doctrine of the two spheres" and Washington's Farewell Address.[9] The War of 1812 had produced no triumph over monarchy, but it had done more than validate U.S. independence. With Jackson's victory at New Orleans Americans sensed an opportunity to stop the rapid British advance in Ibero-America. Even the cynical de Onís recognized what British miscalculation of American ambition would eventually mean for the hemisphere: "Now the United States is going to become a great nation, full of pride, presumption, and the ambition to conquer."[10]

Despite the hesitance of their government to proclaim its commitment to the Spanish American revolutionary cause, Americans seemed determined to learn more about the vast land to the south and its seemingly undifferentiated peoples. And there were revolutionary agents in the country to inform Americans—admittedly from a self-serving interest—that independent Creole republics deserved their support. William Duane of the influential *Aurora* provided Manuel Torres, the Colombian agent in Philadelphia, with letters of introduction to Congress. Torres published hortatory essays on the cause of Latin American independence in English. He knew Adams and Monroe personally. His trip in late 1822 to Washington to be received as the first Colombian minister to the United States concluded a decade of effort. Captain David D. Porter of the United States Navy promoted another rebel agent, José Carrera of Chile, who came to the United

States in 1816 and had editors and publicists in Baltimore, Washington, and Richmond trumpeting the cause of Chilean independence.

But however impressive the quickening American response to Latin America was in these years, British policy adjusted just as quickly to the prospect that the revolutionary movement might triumph. Early on, when it appeared that Britain might indeed join in the restoration of Spanish rule, British opinion viewed American overtures to the rebels somewhat harshly. Just as abruptly, following its withdrawal from the European monarchical alliance, London's policy shifted. To a generation of Latin American liberators—especially Bolívar—it was clear that British statesmen who decried revolutionary excesses were more concerned with their pocketbooks than their consciences. The prospect of losing the economic foothold they had acquired in Spanish America overcame what disdain they harbored for the Creoles. The British navy was the only viable obstacle to a Spanish reconquest, Bolívar knew. And there was a stylistic distinction between the British and Americans that persisted into the twentieth century. Republican Americans professed to treat Latin American republicans as equals but regarded them as inferiors; the British generally regarded them as dogs but treated them with a modicum of respect.

Having confronted Spanish obstinance in the political realm, American leaders displayed a predictable and for them justifiable animus when considering their official posture to Spain's rebellious Creoles. President Monroe had served his government in Spain early in the century and had acquired a working knowledge of Spanish. He left detesting Spain and the Spanish. Secretary of State Adams was often outspoken in his views on Spain and its political legacy in the New World. Understandably, he exploited the nagging Florida question as an excuse for delaying recognition to several newly independent states, but his preindependence views persevered and his contempt for the capabilities of Spain's New World children did not lessen. "As to an American system," he averred, "we have it; we constitute the whole of it; there is no community of interests or of principles between North and South America."[11] Speaker of the House Henry Clay, who knew less about Latin America than either Monroe or

Adams, unabashedly championed the cause of independence and recognition.

But the countervailing view about Latin America's pessimistic republican future gained wide currency in these formative years of U.S.—Latin American relations. H. M. Brackenridge, in a widely distributed pamphlet titled *South America*, persuasively argued the case for Latin American recognition without American aid and presented a positive assessment of Latin America's future. But even the tolerant Brackenridge believed the United States was the "natural leader" of the hemisphere. He conceded that Latin America could achieve "republican virtue" eventually. Cynics like John Randolph were probably more persuasive. They believed Latin Americans were generally inferior. When Americans fought *their* revolution, Randolph said, they were struggling for their rights as Englishmen, for they had inherited the English values of liberty and justice. Latin America's rebellious Creoles, by contrast, were the miserable children of Spanish despotism. Their struggle was not for political liberty or limited government but a Creole variant of continental despotism. "You cannot make liberty out of Spanish matter," Randolph roared, "you might as well try to build a seventy-four out of pine saplings."[12] The American variation of a damning British slur was that Hispanics displayed individual heroics but were collectively imbecilic.

Despite its controversial hesitance in recognizing the new republics, the American government tended to favor the rebels. There was a noticeable difference between rhetoric and reality, of course, but in several ways the United States indirectly abetted the revolutionary cause in Latin America. It relentlessly pursued Florida's annexation, which put the Spanish court on the defensive and weakened its counterrevolutionary efforts in the hemisphere. And, more important, the declaration of American neutrality meant, in effect, a nonbelligerence, that allowed rebel agents to operate in the United States and gave their ships access to American ports.

But the Spanish rightly convinced themselves that a republican government philosophically committed to revolution would adopt an expedient policy if the ultimate reward was the Floridas—territory crucial to U.S. defense. In 1817, when he became secretary of state, Adams charted a policy that fulfilled Spanish expectations—steady diplomatic pressure on Madrid to yield the Floridas coupled with convincing statements of American neutrality in the Spanish American revolutions. But as often happens when empires are in rapid decline, the center cannot maintain its authority in the periphery. Border ruffians commenced impromptu invasions of Florida. American troops dutifully ran them out or the American government reprimanded them. One interloper, Gregor MacGregor, assembled a crew of Spanish malcontents in Savannah and captured Amelia Island. Dislodged, he took his cause to the isolated Caribbean coast of Central America. In spring 1818 the Spanish confronted a more formidable menace, a band of Americans captained by the War of 1812's authentic hero, Andrew Jackson.

As tensions between the two governments worsened over alleged Indian raids from Spanish Florida against American settlements—a violation of the treaty of 1795—Jackson received what he later swore was authority to deal with the Indians. In his invasion of the domain of the hated Spanish dons, he burned villages and, in the most controversial incident, tried and executed two British traders (Alexander Arbuthnot and Robert Ambrister) for their "crimes" of assisting his Indian enemies. To Jackson and his frontiersmen the executions represented simple justice. But in London and Madrid (and in not a few minds in Washington) they symbolized the uncivilized behavior of scofflaws. The legal implications of the incident—the trial and execution of two British subjects in Spanish territory by Americans whose commander possessed dubious authority for his actions—were the stuff of international controversy. Jackson's improbable defender was Adams, who despised him but used the raid as yet another example of the breakdown of authority in the Spanish Empire: "Spain must immediately make her selection, either to place a force in Florida adequate at once to the protection of her territory, and to the fulfillment of her engagements, or cede to the United States a province, of which she retains nothing but the nominal possession, but which is, in fact, a derelict open to the occupancy of every enemy, civilized or savage, of the United States, and serving no other earthly purpose than as a post of annoyance to them."[13] In a brief paragraph he had not only justified the use of force but validated the foremost American concern in the Western Hemisphere—the national security of the United States.

On 22 February 1819 Adams and Onís signed the Transcontinental Treaty, declaring Florida as U.S. territory and establishing a jagged boundary between Anglo- and Hispanic America from the Sabine River to the Pacific Ocean. Two irreconcilable personalities had made possible the achievement, one a brash man of action, the other a calculating statesman and opportunist. Both were consummate American nationalists who understood the path the United States must follow in the Western Hemisphere.[14]

Creole rebels had already detected a shift in U.S. policy in Spain's favor. Another mission to the south yielded less optimistic assessments of the rebel cause than had been generally anticipated. U.S. naval vessels, sailing off the Pacific coast of South America, carried out a policing role—a tradition the navy followed into the twentieth century—with so much attention to neutrality that the Creoles were offended. In 1817 and 1818 Congress passed neutrality legislation that initially seemed to restrict Latin American revolutionary activity in the United States. Henry Clay decried the unheroic character of administration policy, but Monroe and Adams recognized a domestic reality Clay naively overlooked. Clay soon discovered that enthusiasm for the rebel cause dissipated when he pressed the issue of recognizing the Buenos Aires rebellion. The president and his secretary of state also understood, more than Clay, that a more aggressive manifestation of American concern for Latin American independence would doubtless provoke trouble with Spain and Britain.

In 1818 and the following years the European powers appeared to be organizing for a *reconquista*. The victors over Napoleon had created a counterrevolutionary alliance, which suppressed popular uprisings in Austria and Italy. It was commonly presumed, especially in the Western Hemisphere, that U.S. intervention could not safeguard the

Latin American independence movement if the British threw their
support behind Spain. London wavered on the question, however.
The British government was not ready to renounce the continental
solution of quashing revolutions before they consumed an entire
country. But British merchants were not willing to relinquish the commercial benefits accruing from the destruction of Spain's empire.
Monroe perceived the precarious nature of the situation. On the eve
of signing the Florida treaty he wrote Andrew Jackson that the European coalition must be kept out of the Western Hemisphere. Spain's
defiant colonies should be independent, he believed, but if they could
not defeat royalist armies they did not deserve independence, or, presumably, protection of the Royal Navy.[15]

Monroe's revolutionary predecessors had never accepted such a
singularity of ideological purpose that they rejected the opportunity
proffered by European politics. It was the fear of European meddling
in the aftermath of independence—an experience that had frustrated
a generation of American leaders—that now prompted hesitant in-
quiries about Anglo-American cooperation. Even "Old Buck," as the
British derisively called Adams, suppressed his natural Anglophobia
and dispatched a cordial overture to Lord Castlereagh, the British
prime minister, suggesting the inevitability of Latin American independence. When Castlereagh rebuffed the offer, Adams began to move, if
ever so cautiously, toward recognition by reassuring Buenos Aires'
agent (the American businessman David Curtis DeForest, a longtime
resident) of American wishes to trade with the port.

But the British were not to stand by and watch the Americans capture their markets. In 1818, in a conference at Aix-la-Chapelle, they
assailed the proposed European economic sanctions against the in-
surgents. In their competition for rebel commerce, both Britain and
the United States thus sustained the Latin American independence
movement, but neither appeared willing to cooperate officially. Neither could be sure about the political character the independent republics would take. The British and now the Americans had always
had lingering doubts about the mix of revolution and Hispanic

culture. It was an uncertainty that remained to baffle later generations of Americans.

Even after the Transcontinental Treaty was signed and Adams wrote effusive self-praise in his diary for settling a territorial issue that had persisted since the Revolution, the Latin American Creoles doubted American commitment. The settlement with Spain reinforced their suspicion that Washington had tarried on the issue of recognition so as to gain territorial concessions from the Spanish and now intended to continue its policy of "watchful waiting." This was inaccurate. The Spanish delayed (until 1821) in ratifying the Florida treaty because the United States had refused to pledge not to recognize the rebellious juntas. There is evidence that had Adams received more positive assurances from Castlereagh he might have pushed the issue of Anglo-American cooperation. And until 1821, when Mexican Creoles signed their pact of peace with the royalists, and the following year, when the young Brazilian monarch declared his independence of Portuguese rule, the United States would have been hard-pressed to identify a Latin American rebel government that merited recognition.

As the British warmed to his earlier argument for a more cooperative policy, Adams began shifting toward the unilateral policy that President Monroe would announce in December 1823. In part, Adams reflected the New England cynicism about Latin Americans. As his kindred spirit Edward Everett, editor of the influential *North American Review*, expressed it: "We have no concern with South America. . .we can have no well-founded sympathy with them [the South Americans]," nor could the United States hope their leaders would become George Washingtons.[16] And just as Washington had wisely chosen not to commit the United States to the cause of revolutionary France in 1793, so, too, should later governments pause before identifying too strongly with the yet unknown future of Latin America. But there were other matters to consider. One was the British move to strengthen their economic and political links with the Southern Hemisphere. Another, vaguely perceived, was the Napoleonic legacy to Latin America's first generation of leaders, the men on horseback who could blend personality and cultural identity into authoritative and commanding figures. Only the United States, Adams reasoned, could provide a New World model of government symbolized by institutions and the rule of law for Latin America, but it could not effectively do so if it joined with an Old World government, even one so widely admired by Latin America's Creole revolutionaries as Great Britain.

What made the case for Anglo-American cooperation appealing to others in Monroe's cabinet were stories of French political intrigue in the La Plata region of South America. In 1820 a Spanish army poised at Cadiz for an expedition against Buenos Aires revolted. Within a few months the rebellious officers and Spanish liberals had decreed the restoration of the constitution of 1812 and a limited monarchy. News of the events heartened the American government, but just as quickly there came rumors that the Buenos Aires Creole rebels (who were disdainful of rivalrous independence leaders in the interior) were plotting with the French to create a Bourbon empire in the La Plata. The French intrigue, coupled with a rapid lessening of Spanish resolve for a *reconquista*, confused both the British and American governments. Though Mexican and Central American independence in 1821, followed by the Brazilian declaration and Bolívar's liberation of Venezuela, New Granada (Colombia), and Ecuador in 1822, reinforced the belief that a Spanish reconquest was unlikely, the nagging French threat remained. It was strengthened in April 1823 when the French dispatched an army south to restore Bourbon absolutism on the Spanish throne.

That summer, George Canning, now British foreign minister, made his famous proposal to Richard Rush, the U.S. minister, for a joint statement on the Latin American question. The offer threw the cabinet into months of wrangling and debate. There were strategic and philosphical issues at stake. The president was alert to the expansion of Russian commercial influence in the Northwest and, presumably, responsive to congressional urging for a forthright statement on the

Greek struggle for independence. Until the final weeks, those who favored joining with the British in a collective statement were, according to Adams, in the majority. But he persisted with his pleas for a unilateral course. More than his colleagues—most of them contenders with him for the 1824 presidential nomination—he grasped the political benefits of a unilateral declaration, especially in an era when the public image of political leaders was becoming a feature of American electoral campaigns.[17] There is little evidence (save Adams's own claim) that he persuaded the others with his analysis of the British proposal; they may have intuitively sensed that a statement of national purpose would diminish the political appeal of their common opponent, Andrew Jackson.

In any event, when Monroe announced U.S. policy in December, Adams's in-house campaign for a unilateral statement won out. The message had a dual purpose: to prevent the restoration of the Spanish Empire on the Latin American mainland—the Haitian revolution had diminished American enthusiasm for the insular Caribbean—and at the same time to express American conviction about the future of the Western Hemisphere. The first was Adams's contribution, but its effective guarantee was Canning's earlier reminder to the French that the British navy would intercept any French fleet convoying a Spanish army to the New World.

Neither Adams nor Monroe intended a collective, hemispheric response to the European powers. Rather, the Monroe Doctrine skillfully blended U.S. strategic interests with a nobler purpose. Successive generations of Latin American intellectuals, assessing these early years of independence, often characterized the Monroe Doctrine as fundamentally self-serving, an early expression of U.S. opportunism in Latin America. With it, the United States established its priorities in the hemisphere. True, the doctrine eschewed the dream of a united hemisphere for the more earthly reality of national self-interest, but its plea for a New World predestined to a republican future expressed a faith that not even Bolívar retained. The first represented the expectations of the United States, but the second, undeniably, voiced the aspirations of America.

The Panama Conference

One year after Monroe's promulgation of the "destiny" of the Western Hemisphere, His Excellency, Simón Bolívar, the Liberator of Colombia and supreme commander of the republic of Peru, dispatched a momentous circular to the new governments of Spain's former colonies calling for a meeting at Panama. The purpose was to form a defensive alliance, a compact to shield against the expected assault from the Old World empires. In their labors, he solemnly observed, "will be found the plant of the first alliances that will have marked the beginning of our relations with the universe."[18]

The Liberator made no mention of Monroe's message, for good reason. Though Americans had sold arms to the rebels, issued hortatory proclamations of goodwill, and even served in their cause, the United States, in Bolívar's estimation, had contributed little to their victory. True, the United States had been the first to recognize a revolutionary government (Colombia in 1822), but it could not protect the new republics with Monroe's declaration. Rather, in Bollívar's sometimes curious logic, the United States professed to deny Britain the opportunity to safeguard Latin America's independence. In these days he was preoccupied with European intentions, believing correctly that the Spanish would require a supportive French fleet to retake their colonies. Everything thus depended on British action. If the British did not intervene against the continental allies and the Spanish landed from French warships, he would abandon the coastal cities and fight his war in the mountainous interior. A defensive alliance of the Spanish-speaking republics, with a contemplated army of one hundred thousand, posed a formidable deterrent.

To invite the Americans, Bolívar argued, would only antagonize London. So he employed a convenient excuse—the official U.S. neutrality during the long wars of liberation—to exclude them. But his putative allies, the Central Americans, who had peacefully declared their independence in 1821 and three years later had bound themselves into the United Provinces, believed the United States deserved a seat at the first great conference of the Americas. It was the begin-

ning of a long tradition among the *centroamericanos* of inviting outsiders to sit at the Hispanic family table.

By now even the outspoken Clay had become a convert to Adams's
hemispheric priorities. In the election the presidential aspirants, Clay
among them, had watched as Adams infused the nationalistic rhetoric of Monroe's message into his campaign against the most popular
figure of his generation, Andrew Jackson. When the election was
thrown into the House of Representatives, Clay had turned against
Jackson, throwing his lot (and his political future) with Adams. The
reward was the secretaryship of state, pathway to the executive man-
sion. But there is some evidence that Clay, like other Americans, had
substantially altered his views about hemispheric revolution and
American identification with the new republics. He certainly required
little convincing about rebellion in the insular Caribbean, with its incendiary Haitian symbol. In 1823, when a band of Cuban conspirators
descended on Washington looking for assistance, Adams had shun-
ted them aside, observing later that Cuba better served the United
States as a weak vassal in the Spanish Empire until the day arrived
when it would fall into America's outstretched hands. Clay still professed his old commitment to the revolutionary tradition, but his
views were moderating noticeably as the framer of American foreign
policy. The president's great worry was the rumor of a wild scheme,
bandied between the Mexicans and Colombians, calling for the liberation of Cuba. Adams surmised that such folly would, at least,
provoke the British into occupying the island and, at worst, unleash
the racial horrors of "another Haiti." Canning sensed the American
unease, and in 1825 he proposed a tripartite guarantee of Spanish
Cuba between Britain, the United States, and Spain. It was a weakly
disguised maneuver to prevent American annexation. Adams rejected the plan but carefully instructed American representatives to
the Panama Conference to block the Mexican-Colombian scheme.

The official American response to Bolívar's plan was, predictably, a
demurral of the proposal for a defensive alliance and a reassertion of
U.S. commercial interests. When Adams finally named the two American representatives (Richard Anderson, then minister to Colombia,

and John Sergeant, a Kentucky congressman), the House of Representatives (which funded their mission) plunged into a four-month debate about virtually everything but the central issue of American participation—what Monroe *really* meant, what the constitutional issues *really* were, and even the delicate matter of white Americans sitting at the conference table with black Haitians.

Clay exhausted sixty-four pages of instructions ventilating these issues. As matters turned out, one of the commissioners died en route to the meeting, and the other arrived too late, after the fretful delegates had fled the pestilential lowlands of Panama for the more salubrious climate of the Mexican highlands. Several of the new governments remained indifferent. Bolívar's emissary was able to push through a strongly worded defensive alliance. Three of his colleagues joined him in signing it. But only the Colombians, under Bolívar's prodding, ratified the pact.

The conference not only revealed the differing views of the Americans and the Latin Americans but demonstrated that the new republics were less committed to alliance than Bolívar had believed. Perhaps a European combination (with British acquiescence) offering a more realistic threat might have prompted them to create the defensive league Bolívar argued was vital to their survival. Clearly, U.S. determination to remain aloof from such political commitments jeopardized but was not decisive in the failure of the Liberator's grand design. In a sense, both Bolívar and Adams had abandoned the earlier faith in an "America" of differing cultures and differing politics but a common purpose. That misfortune ultimately lay in the U.S. decision to identify the Monroe Doctrine as its own and in Latin Americans' mutual suspicions and jealousies. The Creole liberators who guided their peoples to independence became, in triumph, leaders who turned inward to consolidate their power in societies where republican government took form but could not flourish. Some, like Bolívar himself, became dictators who despaired of the continent's future. Others fell before a rising generation of men on horseback who had little concern for hemispheric solidarity or representative government.[19]

For the United States the Monroe Doctrine ultimately assumed the lofty status of first principle of the nation's foreign policy; for Latin America it became the distortion of the Bolivarian dream by an acquisitive United States. Both interpretations were, ironically, unintended by those Americans and Latin Americans who professed faith in the nobler goal of a Western Hemisphere unshackled from European distress, a faith in America and its destiny.

3   The Model Republic
and Its Image

Ironically, the democracy that flourished in the United States in this era, though characterized by a disorderliness that often disgusted European visitors, was for a generation of Latin American intellectuals a model to be emulated. The United States was the perceived republican success of the New World. Latin America had absorbed enough of the English tradition, which a generation of rebellious Creoles had admired, and had learned of the American constitutional model, but they meshed these influences with the uncertain symbolism of the French Revolution and Napoleon. They had the task of creating republican governments for people who were illiterate and of mixed blood. In several countries, notably Chile, they looked to the United States as a guide for molding the citizen, and the participation of all classes and races in the long war for independence augured well, they believed, for a republican future. Even in imperial Brazil the notion of monarchical absolutism had perished. But they achieved few of the laudatory goals. The Spanish Empire had been a unity, though it was not unified, and it had a head, which the revolutionaries lopped off but did not provide the institutions of republican governance to supplant it.

Latin Americans may have expressed admiration for the model republic and its Constitution, but in their governance they chose to preserve the social order rather than fashion citizen republics. And they recognized an economic reality—the American traders who bore down on them with commercial treaties and goods were aggressive but more poorly provisioned than their English competitors. At the end of the revolutionary wars, before the American traders had begun arriving in significant numbers, English merchants, confronted with bulging warehouses, had dispatched these unsold goods and manufactures into Latin America. They saturated the market, often selling at losses, but they established themselves as central figures in Latin America's early commercial world. The Latin American trade may not have been vital for the emerging British Empire, but it was vital for the new republics. Only Britain could supply the quantity and quality of manufactures Latin Americans demanded.

The revolutionary generation had begun a war against a debilitated Spanish Empire in its far-flung viceroyalties, and (except for the short-lived empire of Augustín de Iturbide in Mexico) had fashioned republics. But the hostility of the periphery toward the center remained so intense among the postrevolutionary generation that regionalism plagued the new countries for the remainder of the century. From the outback came men on horseback—*caudillos*—who knew little of Enlightenment political philosophy but who understood that the vast numbers of inhabitants of the republics were essentially social conservatives. They had little aspiration beyond the expectations of their culture and were content to be ruled by someone who understood their ways and did not try to mold them into citizens.

Old Hickory in the Americas

Though Andrew Jackson had little in common with the first generation of Latin American leaders, in his personal habits, political style, and simplistic notions about right and wrong he shared some traits of their *caudillo* successors. They carved out their reputations in the interior, in the backcountry, where ordinary men admired the opportunist with ambitions to become a self-made aristocrat. In Jackson's age Latin America produced several such men on horseback —Antonio López de Santa Anna in Mexico, José Antonio Páez in Venezuela, Juan Manuel de Rosas, and lesser-known backcountry opportunists. Several were (like Jackson) upstart country aristocrats who recognized the political advantage in catering to a generation of rural people demanding a larger share of the nation's cultural identity. In his crudely articulated republican nationalism, Jackson had much in common with them.

If Jackson sensed that his Latin American contemporaries were kindred spirits, he rarely treated them as such. Expanding American commercial interests, not forging hemispheric links, was central to his Latin American policy. To Central America, which had fashioned a weak federation in 1824, Old Hickory dispatched commercial agents and canal promoters, none of whom showed much interest in the fragile cause of isthmian unity. These first emissaries to Central America were a "star-crossed lot."[1] Nor was Jackson predisposed to invoke Monroe's now vaguely remembered "doctrine." When the Central Americans requested his support in their protest against the British presence in Belize by reminding him of its prohibitions against European expansionism in the New World, they were politely but firmly rebuked. Here and elsewhere in Latin America Jackson might have exploited the growing resentment over British meddling and influence in Colombia, on the west coast, and most notably in the Falklands crisis of the early 1830s. Most Latin Americans had not yet acquired the animosity toward U.S. territorial acquisitiveness that the Mexican War later provoked.

Inept and shortsighted policies undermined what remained of inter-American goodwill. When Venezuela broke off from Colombia in 1835, the American government showed its irritation over less than satisfactory commercial relations with Bogotá by cultivating the rebellious Venezuelans. Colombia, wrote the American minister, was a "bigoted Catholic country controuled [sic] by the Priests. . .[but] Venezuela on the other hand is rapidly developing her resources and marching forward with the spirit of the age."[2] This cultural vivisection had been provoked by heavy Colombian duties on American flour. Farther down the west coast, in Chile and Peru, American determination to promote "free trade" and obtain reciprocity treaties bruised Latin American sensibilities and damaged early efforts at

Peruvian-Chilean trade agreements. With Brazil (which in independence had retained its monarchical character) the Jacksonians cultivated friendly relations; with republican Argentina they followed a policy of confrontation.[3]

In the preceding decade American shippers had descended on Buenos Aires, bearing flour, liquor, butter, salt, furniture, and lumber for a country that projected to the world the dual image of cosmopolitan elites in the capital and unlettered barbarians out in the provinces. In both city and country the Americans were distant competitors to the British. For two decades British commercial agents ruled the La Plata estuary. In the late 1820s the British had been influential in establishing the new republic of Uruguay, a buffer between the Argentines and the Brazilians. But during these years John M. Forbes, scion of an old Masschusetts commercial family, assiduously promoted anti-British resentment through his business contact among the *porteños*. On the eve of Jackson's election, an Argentine editor wrote: "Of all the nations with which we have diplomatic relations, none has rendered a more unwavering interest in the cause of liberty and independence in the hemisphere than the United States."[4]

Then "Bloody" Rosas, frontier hero and visible enemy of the Buenos Aires cosmopolites, took power and within a few months even the amiable Forbes was writing about a country fallen to "countless hordes of savages . . . at the head of which may found an undiscriminating thirst of blood and rapine."[5] Rosas might have continued indiscriminately persecuting his enemies in the spirit of national consolidation and precipitated little more than American verbal indignation, but he was determined to rectify an old Argentine grievance in the Falkland Islands (the Malvinas, as Argentines called them).

When Argentina broke from the Spanish Empire, it claimed the rights of state succession over the islands and dispatched a governor to close them off to commercial shipping from other nations. When the governor seized an American vessel for violating the ban, Jackson (in 1832) ordered a punitive retaliation—an American warship, the

Lexington, arrived off Puerto Soledad, hoisted a French flag, and dispatched a raiding party ashore to retaliate for the earlier seizures of private American vessels. Afterward, the *Lexington* sailed gloriously for Montevideo with six petty Argentine officials in shackles. To Jackson the raid was a necessary policing of an "uncivilized" society by the forces of a "civilized" nation, but Rosas, who often conflicted with British and French pretensions to "civilize" Argentine behavior, was not easily cowed. Neither was Jackson. When the Argentine government demanded an apology for the indignity, the new American minister wrote, "We have attempted to soothe, and conciliate these wayward fools long enough. *They must be taught a lesson."*[6]

Within two years diplomatic relations had deteriorated into exchanges of acrimonious official notes. The noticeable bitterness even inspired the British to reassert (with obvious American encouragement) their claims of sovereignty over the Falklands. When the British returned, the Argentine government suspended diplomatic relations with the United States and appealed to other hemispheric governments for a collective protest. Jackson weighed the issue and decided that the reoccupation of the islands did not violate Monroe's prohibition of future European territorial expansion in the New World. He could have done little to prevent British actions anyway, of course, but the reluctance to protest alienated another hemispheric republic.

The Balance of Power
in North America

With a closer nation, Mexico, diplomatic wrangling brought not only acrimony and suspicion but eventually war. For the United States the conflict was viewed as the natural consequence of an expansive republican society confronting a neighbor cursed with irresponsible leaders. The war offered Americans the martial fulfillment of a confident, romantic age. For Mexicans it has always symbolized the ignominy of losing half the nation's territory to American rapacity.

Mexico, wrote David Pletcher in the *Diplomacy of Annexation*, was the "sick man of North America" in the 1830s and 1840s.[7] In 1821 it had acquired its independence by a gentlemen's agreement between Creoles and *peninsulares* and then lapsed into a two-year monarchy under the flamboyant Iturbide. Its first constitution and federal system of government appeared to emulate the republican model of the United States, but its fundamental character differed sharply from that of its rambunctious neighbor. Its political inheritance derived from the patrimonial Spanish Crown, but its social order centered on one's place in the institutional structure, in the inherited aristocratic family, in the church, and in the military. Its political and social credos did not make Mexico the Latin American model of the Anglo republic of North America, but its distinctive pride did not permit Mexican leaders to bend too much in dealing with the United States. At the same time, U.S. determination to settle issues led a succession of diplomats and negotiators to regard Mexican pride as nothing but arrogance.

Little wonder, then, that Washington's ministers who trooped into the ancient citadel of the Aztecs with political advice (as did Joel Roberts Poinsett, who became involved in the bitter factional quarrels of Mexico in the 1820s), or generous offers to settle territorial squabbles (as did Colonel Anthony Butler, Jackson's gauche emissary) alienated a generation of Mexicans. Even the Mexican men of reason (and the early republic produced its share of enlightened political liberals who admired American political traditions) recognized that accommodation with the United States meant national dishonor.

Mexican leaders had other reasons to fear U.S. pressures. In 1819 Adams and de Onís had marked the truncated frontier from the Sabine to the Pacific in the Transcontinental Treaty in which, presumably, the Americans had relinquished all claim to Texas. But even before Mexican independence two years later, the Spanish viceroy in Mexico City (emulating the tactics of Spanish governors in New Orleans) had granted permission to Anglo families to settle west of the Sabine. Believing that isolated settlements of Americans, given large land grants and permission to retain their slaves, would create a barrier to the hordes of land-hungry farmers trying to get in, Mexico continued the policy. Mexican optimists argued that these settlers would eventually convert to Catholicism and become Mexican citizens.

In the 1820s the Texans were isolated physically but not emotionally from American culture, and the populous regions of central Mexico lay a thousand miles south. Years before, Poinsett had predicted what would happen. Texas immigrants, he wrote, were settling on the most fertile soil in the province. Given time and their obstreperous nature, they would become ungovernable. His successor, Anthony Butler, carried an almost identical message from Jackson to Mexican officials with an offer to purchase the province, from the Sabine to the "Grand Prairie." The Mexicans indignantly refused and prepared, it was rumored, a fifteen-thousand-man invasion force. The Mexican government had already begun to shift regular troops closer to the frontier and to populate the province, where Anglos now outnumbered Mexicans, with more of their own people and German and Swiss nationals.

These were mild proposals compared with the measures that would follow within the decade. In the early 1830s immigration across the virtually unguarded frontier increased. Among the newcomers were Kentuckians and Tennesseans, one of whom—Sam Houston— was a confidant (and, it was later charged, an agent) of Jackson. These recent arrivals were less accustomed to dealing with a faraway and sometimes capricious Mexican government than such veterans as Stephen F. Austin, who still believed the Mexican federalist system would tolerate the idiosyncrasies of *tejano* culture. Jackson had tried to intimidate and even bribe the Mexican government into selling Texas (all the way to the "Grand Prairie") and California from Monterey Bay north to the Oregon border and had failed. His personally chosen emissary had been duped, then rebuffed. But the transplanted Tennesseans and Kentuckians who had migrated into Texas spoiled for a fight.

In 1835 all hopes for accommodation by men of goodwill, Mexican and Texan, perished with the decision of Santa Anna to assert central authority over the defiant North. In a lofty promulgation he abrogated the constitution and the federal system it sustained. Then he grandly declared a crusade to incorporate the defiant Texans (and their Mexican kindred spirits) into the nation by summarily attaching the province to Coahuila. When the Texans raised the flag of revolt, he vowed to crush them.

In the beginning the war went badly for the "Texicans," but news of the battle of the Alamo and the "massacre" of a Texan battalion that had surrendered at Goliad inspired a generation of Americans to rally to the cause. When Jackson heard of the Goliad affair he went into an uncontrollable rage. As word of it spread from New Orleans to Mississippi and Alabama towns, Texan agents hastily set up booths to lure willing and vengeful recruits to the cause. By the time most of them got to the fighting, the decisive battle of San Jacinto had been fought, and Sam Houston had extracted his famous surrender from Santa Anna. An artist later recaptured the scene in a mural depicting a cringing Mexican pledging to respect Texas independence.

The Texas rebellion was yet another symbol of the havoc that ordinary Americans were capable of creating for two governments. But Santa Anna's surrender was the opening act in a drama for domination of the Gulf coast, from the Texas-Louisiana border round the Mexican shore, a political battle in which the expansion of statehood and slavery and the European balance of power in North America led to a larger conflict with Mexico. On one side were the small but vocal antislavery spokesmen (among them Congressman John Quincy Adams, a convert to the antiexpansionist cause) who railed against Texas annexation as a conspiracy to expand the slavocracy. Their mortal enemies were championed by John C. Calhoun, no fiery expansionist but a southern spokesman who recognized that an independent Texas might very well become, under the blandishments of British abolitionism, an independent free Texas republic and thus a magnet for runaways.

A hemispheric issue was at stake. Early in the decade the British Parliament's monumental debate over slavery in its West Indian empire had ended with a victory for the emancipationists. The American government had watched this bitterly argued matter with more than detached interest. British abolitionist propaganda increased in Puerto

Rico and Cuba, and both the British and French governments displayed an inordinate concern toward the Texas republic. Its initial overtures for statehood had floundered with Jackson's reluctance to stir up another debate over slavery. In France, the Western Hemispheric strategy took form with heavy pressure on Mexico. Using as pretext the mistreatment of French bakers in the capital, the French laid siege to Veracruz, occupying San Juan de Ulúa, the historic fortress. In the engagement the irrepressible opportunist Santa Anna lost his leg, but his daring in the battle won him (and his leg) momentary glory in Mexican history. Shortly, the French pulled back. Their attention turned northward, to the Texas republic.

American newspapers followed the "Pastry War," as the Franco-Mexican crisis was derisively referred to, with interest, but neither the press nor the American government condemned the French reprisal as a violation of Monroe's famous message. Already at odds with the Mexicans over unsettled claims reaching back to the wars of independence, the United States expediently chose a polite neutrality. Only when the French began cultivating the Texans did Washington react with alarm. There was nothing sinister about French intentions in Texas. The architect of French policy was François Guizot, Louis Philippe's foreign minister, who spoke eloquently of implanting a European balance of power in North America. The Texas republic, dependent on French military advisers against the continuing threat from Mexico, would become the bastion of a revived French Empire. A coterie of Texans had actually promoted stronger ties with Europe. Their early appeals for statehood rejected, the first generation of independent Texans had journeyed abroad looking for friends and commercial partners. They signed trade treaties with Britain and France. For a few years the French were active, offering the Texans an ambitious plan to colonize French immigrants on 3 million acres in west Texas, in defiance of the Mexican government. Guizot talked enthusiastically about constructing a line of forts from the Red River to the Rio Grande.

When the Texas assembly rejected the scheme, Guizot lost heart. But British agents now took up the challenge of transforming Texas into a protectorate. Since the American rejection of Canning's proposal for a joint declaration on Latin America, British policy had consistently sought to impede American influence everywhere, especially in Spanish Cuba and Mexico. By the 1830s Mexico was a British economic client. An independent Texas, wedged between a threatening United States and a proud but politically volatile Mexico, threatened the stability of the western Gulf. Britain had far more compelling reasons than France to act. Canada, virtually defenseless against American penetration, had just weathered a rebellion abetted by conspiring New Yorkers. A more vigorous British presence in Texas would distract the American government and prompt it to crack down on violators of the neutrality laws in upstate New York. Others saw in the Texas republic yet another opportunity. If British diplomats could persuade a generation of wastrel Mexican leaders that political wisdom dictated the survival of an independent Texas, money levied for armies to retake it might more profitably be directed to satisfying Mexico's British creditors. In London, Texas agents pestered the fiery foreign minister, Lord Palmerston, for loans. When he left office, they shuffled off to Lord Aberdeen, his successor, an unostentatious man who charmed his visitors but made few commitments to them.

In the early 1840s American diplomats began making incautious statements about a British plot to "Africanize" Texas—to ply the Texans with loans and promises if they would abolish slavery in favor of a free labor system. More outspoken British proselytizers called for a crusade to eliminate slavery not only in Texas but in Cuba and Brazil. These were incendiary words to a generation of southern politicians obsessed at being surrounded by free territory. American fears bordered on paranoia. Duff Green, confidant of Calhoun and slavery's "roving ambassador," as Adams derisively called him, spent 1840 in London attending parliamentary debates about the economic consequences of abolition in the British West Indies. British sugar planters now had to compete, to their economic detriment, with sugar economies in Cuba and Brazil based on slave labor. Green discerned a conspiracy. Refusing to admit that its free labor economy was unable to compete with the slave labor sugar isles, the British had decided to wreck the more efficient slave economies of the Western Hemisphere. Their targets were Cuba and Texas. Green's assessment of British determination but not intention was reinforced in the observation of a British diplomat the following year. "By effecting the final abolition of Slavery in Texas," he wrote, "we at once extinguish that horrid traffic in a Country which, without our interference, might become one of the most extensive Slave Markets in America."[8]

Anticipating the worst, the American government in this decade accepted as provocation to its national interests British ambitions in Mexico and Texas. And by a tortuous logic a succession of political leaders, mostly southerners, tried to persuade their northern colleagues that a slave Texas in the Union would expand the nation's internal marketplace. No one spoke more vigorously than Calhoun. In 1844, upon becoming secretary of state after the sudden death of Abel Upshur, he dispatched Upshur's hastily written treaty of annexation to the Senate with a ringing defense of slavery and its benefits. The Whig opposition, voting conscience over cotton, resoundingly turned it down. This apparent defeat of U.S. expansion inspired Aberdeen. To a peripatetic Texas agent in London he proposed a "Diplomatick Act," an Anglo-French guarantee of Texas independence and pressure on the Mexicans to recognize the republic. The only stipulation was that Texas must not become a state. When news of the offer reached Washington there was renewed alarm about British intentions. The proposal set Texans to quarreling among themselves. In Mexico the news brought renewed demands for vindicating national honor by launching a *reconquista*.

The truth of the matter was that Texas was lost to Mexico but not assured of statehood. In the elections, the Democratic candidate, James K. Polk, emulating Jackson's old fire about dealing with the Spanish dons of Florida, spoke vigorously about resolving the great territorial issues that endangered American security in the hemisphere—California, Oregon, and Texas. The rhetoric about the Oregon territory, jointly occupied since 1818 by British and Americans, was more belligerent, but Polk was less disposed to compromise with the Mexicans. Jackson had wanted to purchase Texas and California and had been rebuffed. Polk resolved to succeed where his mentor had failed. His narrow victory in the fall was sufficient inspiration for the outgoing Congress. In February 1845, a few weeks before the inauguration, Congress passed the joint resolution that formally proposed annexation of Texas.

The voting in Texas was not to occur until December, so in the months after Congress acted, there was frenzied courting of the Texans in three capitals—London, Washington, and Mexico City. In late 1844 an obscure British agent had left Mexico convinced that Santa Anna would accept Texas independence if Mexican honor could somehow be preserved and the northern frontier safeguarded against the rapacious Anglos. But it was already too late, for Santa Anna suddenly fell from public favor. Blamed for the loss of Texas, he threw himself into a battle in the national assembly to raise funds for another campaign, lost, and left for his estate in Jalapa. His detractors even stole his enshrined leg and in an act of defilement threw it into the street. He promptly went into exile in Havana.

Polk was already busily plying the Texans with lofty words about their future as a state and warning them about the perils if they rejected the American offer. In the end the resolution passed handily. Sloganeers spoke of the "reoccupation of Texas" (territory, Jackson had often argued, that was rightfully American but given away by his archenemy Adams). The newspaperman John O'Sullivan had written of "manifest destiny," by which he meant the peaceful annexation of adjacent territories and the voluntary acceptance of the "blessings of republican liberty" by the peoples of the Southwest. Polk had transformed manifest destiny into a national security issue. European intriguing in the long-standing disputes between Mexico and the United States imperiled not only American interests but the future of republican government in North America. As Secretary of State James Buchanan instructed John Slidell, sent to Mexico to purchase California and New Mexico and obtain Mexican acquiescence in Texas's annexation, the United States would not "tolerate any interference on the part of European sovereigns with controversies in America, [nor] permit them to apply the worn-out dogma of the balance of power to the free States of the Continent. . . . Liberty here must be allowed to work out its natural results; and these will, ere long, astonish the world."[9]

With these words an American secretary of state validated the use of force in the cause of republican liberty. In retrospect, O'Sullivan's belief that the example of republican government in the United States would inevitably lead neighboring peoples voluntarily to join the noble American experiment appears naive. That expansionists often employed his arguments revealed the enduring appeal of America and its hemispheric mission, now apparently subsumed in the North American strategies of the president of the United States. Neither Mexico (nor any Latin American state) would voluntarily submit to American expansion, however good or noble its intentions. And O'Sullivan was blind to the political reality Polk and his generation comprehended: manifest destiny was as much the credo of the belligerent as of the pacifist. The inspiring phrase expressed national purpose and served national self-interest. As Adams had recognized in 1823 with Monroe's pronouncement about Latin America, which Polk alertly revived to serve his continental plan, it could also enhance one's political image.

The Mexican War

Polk's principal interest lay in California, not Texas. Since the beginning of the decade the penny press had written expansively about Pacific coast issues—the Oregon dispute, until then a diplomatic matter that had quickly become a volatile political issue in 1843, and California, whose ports beckoned eastern commercial interests. In Polk's presidential campaign, however, California did not figure heavily. Only later did he revive the California issue with a warning about British intrigue in the Mexican province. Polk may have been speculating that the Californios, who had begun organizing against

Mexican rule, were readying to emulate the Texans. As things turned out, when the Mexicans abruptly rejected Slidell's offer to sell California and New Mexico, the president returned to the border squabble raised by Texas's claim to the Rio Grande as its southern boundary. An incident between Zachary Taylor's dragoons and Mexican troops on the Rio Grande provided a convenient excuse to label Mexico the aggressor, and when war commenced, Polk had a strike force on the California boundary ready to intervene and forestall any California republic.

The war began with armies penetrating New Mexico, California (which was also attacked from the sea), and northern Mexico, where General Taylor encountered unexpectedly fierce Mexican resistance. In the beginning, American military interests concentrated on the Southwest, presumably validating Polk's arguments that the war was "defensive"—asserting American claims over territories in dispute—rather than aggressive, as several outspoken New Englanders were saying. But in February 1847 Polk adopted the strategy of the Spanish conquerors of Mexico—a landing at Veracruz and a plunge into the interior of populous Mexico. His reasons were complicated. Taylor was getting more press coverage than the commander in chief and running for president from horseback in Mexico. And Polk had been duped by Santa Anna, who had persuaded the president's agent in Havana that he would end the war if the U.S. government would subsidize his return to Mexico. Instead, the Crimson Jester formed an alliance with the hated Liberals and resumed the presidency, renewing the fight. Polk vowed to reduce Mexico and its government to submission. When General Winfield Scott's invading army finally took Mexico City in September, the war was for all realistic purposes over, though sporadic fighting continued until 1848.

If one discounts the invasion of Upper Canada in the War of 1812, the Mexican War was the nation's first foreign war, a crusade that rounded out the continental domain and validated the era's romantic expressions of political and cultural superiority. For its opponents the war introduced a noticeably racist element into American diplomacy and, more disturbing, reinforced their fears that the United States had jeopardized its republican character by acquiring so much new territory. Such self-doubts about the American mission did not linger, though the rising political figure Abraham Lincoln expressed a fairly common Republican sentiment in the following decade when he described the war as the abuse of a neighboring republic. With the passage of several more generations most Americans forgot they had added roughly a third of the national domain at the expense of almost 50 percent of Mexican territory. By the end of World War I, when nationalist reaffirmation reached its zenith, Justin Smith wrote confidently in his two-volume treatise that the Mexican War represented a great crusade. A quarter-century later, during World War II, Samuel Flagg Bemis was blunter when he defended the American victory by rhetorically asking if any American retained such guilt over the immorality of the war that he would restore the Mexican cession to Mexico.[10]

Most contemporaries believed that the victory destroyed forever any possibility that the European powers might create a balance of power in North America. On the eve of the conflict the British had proposed a solution to the crisis. Had Mexico accepted London's mediation, Texas's independence would have been guaranteed, and the Mexicans would have found solace for the loss of their northeastern province by preventing the acquisitive Americans from annexing it. Two years later, following a series of stunning victories on the Rio Grande, in California, and, finally, in Winfield Scott's triumphant march from Vera Cruz into the capital of the Aztecs, Americans found another reason to celebrate. In faraway Europe, monarchy had suffered a grievous blow in the revolutions of 1848. News of the calamitous events arrived in the United States only a few weeks after a band of gloating Democrats and disconsolate Whigs joined to approve a peace treaty negotiated on the Mexican plateau between a disowned American emissary and a peace delegation with no precise authority to deal with him.

Republicanism was victorious on two continents, trumpeted the expansionist penny press editors, who had written laudatory columns about the crusade against arrogant Mexico. Some illogically attributed

the success of revolutions in the Old World to vindication of republicanism in the new. As the *New York Herald* put it, the United
States in victory had won a coveted place in "the history of civilization
and the human race."[11] To have equated "civilization" with Anglo-
Saxon cultural superiority would have been superfluous.

So pervasive were the fears of European meddling in what Americans considered a New World conflict between a righteous republican
society and a corrupt one that apprehensions over European intervention persisted well into the war. When the bellicose General Juan
Paredes had seized power a few months before the war commenced,
virtually destroying any possibility of peaceful settlement, the act appeared to confirm fears of Spanish plotting to restore the monarchy in
Mexico. Santa Anna's departure into exile in Havana inspired reports
that he had offered his services to at least three European powers.
And though British intentions appeared clear after the peaceful settlement of the Oregon question in the summer of 1846, speculation in
the British press about a British protectorate in Mexico (a young Benjamin Disraeli had expressed interest in such a plan) convinced a generation of warring Americans that they had stifled a British conspiracy. Depriving a neighbor of half its national territory was, thus, a
justifiable price to pay for the survival of republican government and
the defeat of European political intrigue in North America.

One indisputable outcome of the war lay in the victory of what
Europeans described as a ragtag army of volunteers over an army
they had always presumed was more capable. The war had advanced
something more than U.S. determination to "spread the blessings of
republican liberty" to the sparsely settled northern regions of Mexico.
It had brought a conquering army into the heart of populous Mexico,
where illiterate, rambunctious Missourians and Texans and Kentuckians marched arrogantly among once-proud savants who had
written contemptuously about the coonskin republic next door. With
Scott's plunge into the Mexican highlands the movement for the acquisition of all of Mexico gained renewed vigor, its adherents arguing
that territory acquired by conquest should not be readily given up.

But just as quickly the movement dissolved when others pointed out that absorbing populated regions of Mexico would also mean taking on that country's factious politics and alien culture.

A month after the war ended, an offer went out from isolated Yucatecos (the survivors of a murderous caste war between whites and Indians earlier in the decade), offering the province to Britain, Spain, or the United States. The penny press took up the cause of Yucatán annexation and wrote enthusiastic columns about a tropical empire. Even the poet Walt Whitman joined the crusade. Yucatán soon entered another bloody phase of its lamentable history, with pro- and antiannexationist elements battling for control and, more alarmingly, resuming the caste war. Proannexationist Yucatecos even raised the specter of European violation of the Monroe Doctrine to promote their cause. Once before, citing British interference in California, Polk had invoked the doctrine. Now he raised the issue again, warning the Europeans against creating a protectorate in the Yucatán. At the same time he rejected the notion of an American tropical empire.

Mexico lost half its national domain to the United States, but the nation's defeat, paradoxically, accomplished a long-standing political goal for Mexico in Latin American international politics. The rapidity of American conquest aroused much of Latin America to the expansionist menace from the north. Yankeephobia, until the 1840s largely unknown (except, of course, in Mexico) suddenly became an ingredient of the Latin American variation of Pan-Americanism. Its impact came too late to unite the other republics on Mexico's behalf and virtually destroyed Mexican ambitions to fashion an anti-American confederation until revolutionary Mexico undermined Woodrow Wilson's plan for a Pan-American defensive alliance in World War I.

Insensitive to the browbeating of a neighboring country and unmindful of the war's political consequences for their own country, Americans experienced in this conflict an unparalleled cultural nationalism. The United States would ultimately return to the inter-American fold, but on its own terms. The Mexican War and the surge of U.S. interest in the Caribbean and Central America that followed the war validated two disturbing elements in the relations between the United States and the other Americas.

The first was the widespread acceptance of the belief of American exceptionalism expressed as territorial aggrandizement at the expense of another hemispheric republic. For ages philosophers had debated whether creation of an empire would cause a republic to lose its political virtues. On occasion the issue had befuddled the Founding Fathers, who were sufficiently familiar with the fall of Rome to speculate about a similar fate befalling the young United States. But the conquerors of Mexico underwent little philosophical torment about this problem. Even John L. O'Sullivan, came round to Polk's forceful expression of manifest destiny. Indeed, the victors over Mexico convinced themselves that republican liberty might perish if the United States did *not* wage war against its putative tyranny. Republican institutions were sustainable not only by the dissemination of the idea but by the acquisition (forcibly if necessary) of ever greater amounts of territory on which to build those institutions. In other words, republicanism, like prosperity, had a territorial imperative.[12]

The second and equally disturbing legacy of the Mexican War lay just beneath the egalitarian surface of U.S. justification for charting a belligerent course against Mexico—ethnocentrism.[13] More bellicose exponents of manifest destiny exhibited few qualms about waging war to spread the domain not only of republican institutions but of the "Anglo-Saxon race." By the 1830s the more benign view of the first generation of independent Americans about the ability of other cultures to absorb republican values had given way to a narrower view that such accomplishments were largely confined to Americans. Sam Houston, a founding father of Texas and twice its president, often spoke of the republic as a monument to Anglo-Saxon superiority. And Thomas Hart Benton, the Missouri senator and eloquent spokesman for westward expansion, expressed his consternation that England, the citadel of Anglo-Saxon political institutions, would impede the march of that "race" in North America.

Tropical America

Even before the victory over Mexico, Latin American governments had become apprehensive about U.S. intentions in the hemisphere. Their delegates convened at Lima in 1847 (and at Santiago de Chile in 1856) to reaffirm Pan-American solidarity and a parallel commitment to national sovereignty. The first was a warning to Europe, the second, a reaction to the annexationist impulses they feared in the model republic to the north. By then, American penetration of the tropics had already begun.[14]

U.S. interest in the Caribbean—from the island of Hispaniola to Central America—soon acquired an urgency unparalleled in earlier pursuits. In the aftermath of its revolution against Haitian domination, the Dominican Republic fell prey to opportunists, among them William L. Cazneau and the American West India Company. Then diplomats and promoters descended on the Central American isthmus with treaty drafts and schemes for transisthmian commerce. The rival of American commercial ambitions was Great Britain, whose powerful influence in Guatemala and Costa Rica so antagonized Nicaragua, Honduras, and El Salvador that the latter three looked to the United States venturing south as a potential buffer. But in luring Americans, especially adventurers and promoters, the disaffected Central Americans who sought to play the British against the Americans unknowingly jeopardized isthmian security. They opened the isthmian door to a generation of frustrated Americans, many of them southerners who dreamed of a revitalized slave empire in the tropics. In the decade following the great triumph over Mexico, manifest destiny was Caribbeanized. The Sea of the New World became the American Mediterranean.

For the first time, the annexation of Cuba became a powerful issue in American politics. In 1825 John Quincy Adams had prophesied the island's fall, like a ripe apple, into an outstretched American hand. At the height of the war with Mexico, John O'Sullivan, who had the president's confidence, recommended offering Spain $100 million for the island. The Spanish rebuffed the idea with a proud reaffirmation of Spain's destiny in Cuba. In the American government the rejection confirmed long-held notions about Spanish recalcitrance. Among southerners concerned about the limits of the cotton kingdom and slavery in the West, the prospect of Cuba's liberation and then rapid acquisition as natural slave territory kindled expansionist ambitions.

Alert to U.S. instincts about Spanish rule, Cuba's putative liberators raised the flag of rebellion on American soil. They found a leader in a disenchanted Spanish soldier, General Narciso López, who had served in Venezuela and had joined the retreating Spanish army on the ever faithful isle. López found his benefactors among southern opportunists. Beginning in the summer of 1849 he launched three expeditions against Spanish Cuba. The first never left American waters, but in summer of 1850 the second embarked from the Florida Keys and struck Cárdenas, east of Havana. After a short battle López and his invaders retreated to their ships and the sanctuary of friendly Savannah. There a federal attorney charged him with violation of the neutrality laws, but he was promptly acquitted by a sympathetic jury. He headed for New Orleans to organize his third invasion. This time López had fifty Americans, among them a few sons of plantation owners, in his army. The expedition landed at Bahía Honda, an isolated cove west of Havana. A Spanish officer, alerted to their arrival, dispatched a force to intercept it, and they were all captured. Unwilling to risk arousing American wrath, the Spanish promptly tried the Americans and shipped them to Spain for a year of hard labor in the mines. The Cubans were executed. Their leader was publicly garroted in Havana Square.[15]

In the sobering aftermath the Spanish dispatched their second offer for a tripartite guarantee of Spanish Cuba (the first was in 1825) to Paris, London, and Washington. The British and French were uninterested, and the American response was even more vigorously worded than Adams's 1823 pronouncement on Cuba. The island, wrote Secretary of State Edward Everett, was a geographical extension of North America. The United States had no acquisitive designs on it but would not tolerate its transfer to another European power because Cuba's importance to American security was similar to that of Ireland in the British Empire. A New Englander, Everett was no defender of southern slavery and certainly no advocate of the nation's acquisition of more slave territory. But his successor, William L. Marcy, though no slavocrat, was nonetheless responsive to powerful Democratic pressures from the south to settle the "Cuban question." In the aftermath of López's death, the South reverberated with warnings that Spain was on the verge of abolishing slavery on the island. This would mean the "Africanization" of Cuba and the presence of a free labor economy a hundred miles from the slave South.[16]

The fear inspired one of the more bizarre episodes in the influence of slavery in the United States on the nation's evolving Latin American policy. Marcy dispatched to Madrid a passionately proslave Louisianan, Pierre Soulé, bearing an offer of $125 million for the island. When the Spanish rudely declined, the infuriated Soulé retreated to the small French border town of Aix-la-Chapelle for a strategy session with two fellow diplomats, James Buchanan, minister to Great Britain, and John Y. Mason, his counterpart in France. There they drew up a secret document (the Ostend Manifesto), which advocated American seizure of Cuba if the Spanish refused to sell. On the trip back to the United States the document was purloined from the diplomatic pouch and found its way into the abolitionist press and, ultimately, validated northern suspicions of a southern conspiracy to extend the empire of slavery into the tropics.

But in the South the dream of tropical empire did not perish.[17] After the Cuban fiasco, southern attention shifted to the isthmus, where energetic American diplomats and equally vigorous American entrepreneurs had already established a Yankee foothold in what had been a British preserve.

The British presence dated from 1824, when the five Central American states had banded themselves into a federation (the United Provinces of Central America) and promptly saddled the new federal government with an onerous loan from the London firm of Barclay, Herring, Richardson, and Company. In the following decade, as American jealousy of the British foothold mounted, the federation came asunder, mostly from provincial animosities. But the *centro-americanos* blamed the intruding British. In the seventeenth century English interlopers had begun to lay claim to the isthmus' north-eastern shore (British Honduras) and they alienated Honduras, Nic-aragua, and El Salvador (which were committed to the federal union) by encouraging separatist factions in Guatemala and Costa Rica. Nic-aragua and Honduras particularly resented the British encroachment into the Mosquitia, the vast eastern lowland the Spanish had ne-glected in the conquest. When U.S. efforts to secure tranisthmian concessions began in earnest on the eve of the Mexican War, these three states looked to the United States for help.

To the southeast lay a less vulnerable nation, New Granada (Co-lombia), where the Americans encountered yet another European rival, France. In the years after Bolívar's death the Colombians en-dured one Panamanian separatist movement after another. In 1839 they fought a bitter civil conflict over the issue of Panamanian au-tonomy. When it was over in 1841, the government began looking for guarantees of its sovereignty over the factious Panamanians. Rumors circulated about a British-supported invasion by the former Ec-uadorian strongman General Juan José Flores. And a short time later two French engineers arrived to survey for a canal or railroad. Just as the Nicaraguans and Hondurans sensed an opportunity to sign trea-ties with the Americans to offset British influence, the Colombians welcomed the opportunity to gain an American protector against their European antagonists. In 1846 they negotiated with the Ameri-can minister, Benjamin Bidlack, a treaty that opened the isthmus of Panama to free transit and gave Americans the opportunity to con-struct a transisthmian passageway across Panama. In return the U.S. government guaranteed its neutrality.

In Washington there was less timidity over the British presence in the Mosquitia, virtually ignored by the Nicaraguans until 1844, when the British government announced a protectorate over the region and began dealing with a succession of intermediaries known as the Mos-quito kings. Most of the Miskito Indians lived around Bluefields and San Juan del Norte, at the mouth of the San Juan River. As Scott's troops were making their final assault on Mexico City, Lord Palmerston was sketching a boundary for the Mosquitia and the zone of British protection over the Miskitos. This bit of cartographical imperialism completed, he dispatched agents to Nicaragua and Costa Rica to reiterate Britain's friendly intentions in the region.

If the British presence was essentially defensive, the actions of the British consul in Central America, Frederick Chatfield, were unarguably provocative. On the first day of 1848, as the United States readied for a victorious settlement with Mexico, Chatfield unleashed a ragtag Anglo-Mosquito army against defenseless San Juan. Triumphant, the invaders renamed the town Greytown and immediately announced a new tariff schedule. When the infuriated Nicaraguans retook it ten days later, Chatfield sent two warships and 250 men to drive them out. Under protest, the Nicaraguans abandoned the town and by implication acquiesced in the British protectorate.

Greytown's humiliation roused the entire Caribbean coast of the isthmus with rumors of another invasion. In Panama the American consul warned of an attack on Bocas del Toro and reported that Colombian militiamen were preparing for a British landing. Back in Washington the news of Greytown's fall prompted an official denial to British claims in the Mosquitia. The opportunistic Polk dispatched a diplomat, Elijah Hise, to treat with the wounded Nicaraguan government. An infuriated Democratic editor fumed about the Pax Britannica in the tropics: "It seems no longer agitated, whether [Great Britain] shall continue to protect the squalid nationality of some few hundred illegitimate savages, born of indiscriminate concubinage, and leprous from a commixture of every unique blood, to whom she alternately administers crowns, Christianity, and Jamaica rum. . . . What becomes of Washington's, Jefferson's, Monroe's, and Polk's defiance to Europe?"[18]

Hise was indefatigable, a necessary trait, it was often said, for dealing with Central Americans, and he was determined to outmaneuver Chatfield. The Nicaraguans were happy to comply and overwhelmed him with concessions giving the United States (or American entrepreneurs) total rights in constructing a canal using the San Juan and the interior lakes. Hise reciprocated with an unauthorized pledge that his government would safeguard Nicaraguan sovereignty. When the treaty reached Washington, the Whigs (less bellicose about isthmian questions) were ensconced in the presidency, and Hise's treaty was promptly shelved. But it was not forgotten.

Hise's successor, Ephraim George Squier, proved no less ambitious in promoting American interests in Central America and no less contentious in confronting Her Majesty's consul. He also found time to begin the first of a dozen treatises on Central America dealing with everything from the isthmus' flora and fauna to its politics and economics. John Lloyd Stephens, one of the star-crossed American emissaries of previous years, had informed his countrymen about the Mayas. Squier told them about everything else in Central America. Shortly after arriving in Nicaragua, he signed another treaty, omitting any clause guaranteeing its sovereignty. Then he moved on to Honduras and negotiated a convention with the manipulable Hondurans providing for the cession of Tigre Island in the Gulf of Fonseca, at the western terminus of the proposed transisthmian route. He dispatched the treaties with a self-congratulatory appendage about outwitting that "man of small caliber" Frederick Chatfield.[19] The "man of small caliber" promptly called on a British man-of-war to seize Tigre Island.

Secretary of State John Clayton, the recipient of this Anglophobic missive, was alert to the larger role the United States was playing in Central America; he was also apprehensive about a confrontation with the British. And his often maligned approach to isthmian questions reflected the belief that any transisthmian passage must be international—a tradition that perished a generation later with President Rutherford B. Hayes's declaration that any transisthmian canal was merely a detached portion of the U.S. coast. Clayton encouraged the French to sign a treaty with New Granada similar to Bidlack's pact and invited the British to join the United States in exercising a protective dominion over transisthmian routes from the Tehuántepec in Mexico to Panama.

Recognizing that their own interests in Central America might very

well be served by accepting his offer, the British sent a special negotiator, Sir Henry Bulwer, to Washington. In April 1850 Bulwer and
Clayton signed what was to be the most far-reaching international
agreement concerning Central America until the twentieth century.
The two countries pledged equality of treatment and a guarantee of
neutrality for any transisthmian passage. They promised not to exercise dominion of any kind over the Central American states. This
treaty gave the Americans confidence that the British would withdraw from the Mosquitia, the Bay Islands, and even British Honduras. They soon discovered that the British pledge covered only future acquisitions; interests already established, London made clear,
would be retained. The Clayton-Bulwer settlement was symbolic of
Central Americans' frustrations in trying to benefit by maneuvering
one power against another only to discover that the diplomatic combatants could withdraw to their own domain and arrive at mutually
beneficial arrangements.

And there was now another foreign presence in the isthmus—con-
cessionaires, soldiers of fortune, southern dreamers of tropical empire—presumably more amenable than the American or British governments to Central American whims.[20] For a generation the Central
Americans had welcomed the foreigners in the belief, as Francisco
Morazán had proudly declared, that the Englishman or Frenchman or
Belgian or *norteamericano* who settled in the isthmus would be transformed into a *centroamericano*. With the Liberals in the ascendancy,
Central American governments vigorously promoted foreign colonization to develop rural areas. The most ambitious of such projects
was Guatemalan president Manuel Gálvez's plan to transform the
northeastern part of the country into an agricultural preserve. The
few English who began the venture turned to hacking down mahogany trees as a livelihood.

But when the controversy over foreign interlopers reached its
zenith in the mid-1850s Nicaragua was in the eye of the storm. As the
Central American federation of 1824 collapsed in the early 1840s, the
Nicaraguan Liberals, who had supported isthmian unity, looked first
to the British and then the Americans to abet their cause. Their mortal

political enemies, the Conservatives, viewed the foreign intrusion as a menace to the social culture. But the Liberals championed a more "progressive" view. They assiduously promoted the country as a more attractive route than Panama for migrants to the gold fields in California. When Americans began swarming to the isthmus after the Mexican War, promoters eager to capture the lucrative transisthmian traffic were not far behind.

The most ambitious of these promoters was Cornelius Vanderbilt, who gathered partners to form the Atlantic and Pacific Ship Canal Company to survey a canal route. Recognizing that the gold seekers were impatient to head west, Vanderbilt also created the Accessory Transit Company, which by steamer, riverboat, and stagecoach ferried gentlemen and their "missy ladies" up the San Juan, across the interior lakes, and on to the Pacific shore. Until the Panama railway was finished in 1855, Vanderbilt's company dominated the trade. The commodore got out of the Nicaraguan venture just in time to acquire a profitable interest in its Panamanian rival.

His abrupt departure offered an opportunity to another generation of Americans with grander ambitions. Their leader was a brilliant, handsome Tennessean who had become a doctor and a lawyer— William Walker. In 1853 he led an expedition of filibusters, as this generation of mercenaries was known, into Sonora, Mexico. Failing, Walker and his men returned to California. There Walker received word about the opportunities in Nicaragua from Byron Cole, another filibuster already in Nicaragua. The Nicaraguan Liberal army was confronted with a Conservative opposition, reinforced with Guatemalan aid. In their desperation the Liberals had offered Cole and other Americans in Nicaragua bountiful land grants in exchange for their services. The message was a godsend to the languishing Walker. He was a man of lofty ambitions with the mercenary's sense of opportunity, if only he had the will to act. In June 1855, accompanied by the fifty-seven "immortals," the "grey-eyed man of destiny" set foot on Central American soil.

His initial battle was an unpropitious beginning. But Walker persisted, and by fall he had risen to commanding general of Liberal forces and had taken the old Conservative citadel of Granada. Terrified Conservatives hastily agreed to a coalition government with one of their own, Patricio Rivas, as president but with Walker as military chieftain. Ensconced as commander, Walker disbanded the Conservative army and, in keeping with an isthmian political tradition, exiled his enemies. Within a year the American minister was trumpeting the accomplishments of the regime. Commodore Vanderbilt's commercial rivals began subsidizing Walker, as they had supplemented the treasuries of his Nicaraguan predecessor. Mexican War veterans arrived with expectations of receiving a landed domain. Before long, Walker had a force of twenty-five hundred. From the isthmus came ominous rumors of a new slave state and, possibly, an attack on Spanish Cuba. Cuban revolutionaries, their cause under fire in the United States, began arriving in Nicaragua in early 1856 and joined in Walker's pacification of Nicaragua.[21]

Foreign intervention in Central America, however strong its appeal to some political elements, has always bred opposition. Central Americans can never unite, it is often said, unless they confront a common foe. In Walker they had one. The initial protests came from Conservatives in Guatemala and the Costa Ricans, who had executed Morazán and now saw themselves as the protectors of isthmian civilization and the "race" against the Protestant hordes from the north. Happily, the British funded the anti-Walker coalition, as did Vanderbilt, who was indignant that his commercial rivals were using Nicaragua to undercut his Panama route. On 1 March 1856 four Central American states formally declared war on Nicaragua.

Besieged on all sides, his troops decimated by a cholera epidemic, Walker took to the offensive. Tossing out the Conservative puppet, he proclaimed himself president of Nicaragua, declared English the official language of the country, and announced the restoration of slavery. Throughout the American South the cry went out for reinforcements. In November 1856, when the Costa Ricans sent an invading force into Nicaragua, Walker retaliated by burning Granada. He left as monument to the destruction a crude sign, "Aquí fué Granada" ("Here was Granada"). But his Central American enemies showed they could persist as well. They received aid from Peru, and a timely British blockade of Nicaragua's ports cut Walker's supply lines. In spring 1857 the Costa Rican leader sent word that any American requesting passage home would be granted safe-conduct.

Walker's men began deserting by the hundreds, leaving him with a skeletal force and almost certain defeat. But once more he was spared. President James Buchanan dispatched a U.S. warship to rescue the now famous Walker and return him home. Back in New Orleans Walker recruited another invasion force. This time he managed to reach Greytown before the U.S. Navy intercepted him and returned him to stand trial for neutrality violations. The filibuster's charm still worked its persuasiveness on juries, and he was shortly freed. Migrating to New York, he began appearing at the Metropolitan, sitting grandly in his box and occasionally acknowledging the admiring glances from the audience below with a gesture. He even found time to publish a book about his exploits, *The War in Nicaragua*.

For a year or so the dream of a southern tropical empire revived. Had Walker remained in the United States he might have found a ready outlet for his considerable martial talent in the Confederacy. But in 1860 he headed back to New Orleans and there put together his third invasion force. This time he had an "invitation" from yet another disaffected element in Central America—the English-speaking residents of the Bay Islands angry with Britain's sudden decision to restore the islands to Honduras. After a glorious welcome in the islands, he believed, there would follow a swift invasion of the Honduran mainland, then a revived isthmian union with Walker as its master.

The expedition arrived off Roatán in June 1860, discovered that the British garrison had not yet departed, and prudently sailed for Trujillo, the old port on the north Honduran coast. It quickly fell before Walker's superior force. But the captain of a patrolling British warship, alert to the nuances of Central American politics, recognized his opportunity. He sent a squad of marines ashore to arrest Walker, pledging safe passage for him and his men. When Walker surrendered the British turned him over to local Honduran officials. They quickly tried, sentenced, and dispatched the grey-eyed man of destiny into immortality. A Nicaraguan he had betrayed had already written his Central American epitaph: "God will condemn his arrogance and protect our cause."[22]

4   The Destiny
of the Americas

Latin Americans look back to the second half of the nineteenth century for formative patterns that explain their modern condition. In Abraham Lincoln they saw a leader of a northern republic that had transformed itself into a nation. After his death, when the dream of a yeoman republic gave way to a corporate industrial order, they found an economic model to emulate. Throughout the hemisphere these were years of triumphant liberalism, of an energetic state in league with ambitious entrepreneurs, of capitalists exploiting untapped human and natural resources, of visionaries who rejected the constraints of tradition for the promises of a new order. In the United States their labors brought forth an industrial democracy, unchallenged by the restraining power of a landed aristocracy, an established church, or a privileged military. But to the south the promises of modernization made the architects of a modern society abusers of their own people.

In the beginning Latin American thinkers had few doubts about the model republic. The Argentine Juan Alberdi praised England and the United States as the protectors of freedom in the nineteenth century. His compatriot Domingo Sarmiento disdained those who vilified the acquisitive Yankees: "Let us not detain the United States in its march. . . . Let us emulate the United States. Let us be America, as the sea is the ocean. Let us be the United States." As the Chilean thinker Francisco Bilbao affirmed: "Spain conquered America; the English colonized the North. With Spain came Catholicism, monarchy, feudalism, the Inquisition, isolation, deprivation, the exterminative genius, intolerance, sociability of blind obedience. With the English came the liberal currents of Reform: the law of the sovereign individual, of the thinker and worker with complete freedom. What has been the result? In the North, the United States, the foremost of nations, both ancient and modern; in the South, the dis-United States, whose progress depends on deHispanicizing itself."[1]

This statement was undeniably a distortion of reality, but it does illustrate the imprint of the two English-speaking nations on nineteenth-century Latin Americans. In their despair of finding anything similar in their Hispanic heritage they had forgotten Bolivar's warnings about a United States that clung to its own liberties but was unmindful of the liberties of others.

Lincoln and Juárez

For more than a decade from the mid-1850s Latin Americans observed two republics with differing cultures, differing economies, and differing politics—Mexico and the United States—as they searched for national identity in civil war.

After its defeat in the war with the United States, Mexico turned inward. Those who had supported the peace settlement with the Americans fell into disfavor, and in 1853 Santa Anna, the Crimson Jester from an earlier time, returned triumphantly to power. It was his last performance on the Mexican political stage, but, fittingly, he profited. The American government, which had paid only $18 million for the entire Mexican cession, provided Santa Anna with $10 million for the Mesilla Valley in southern Arizona. Two years later, his administration hopelessly indebted by the grafters and sycophants who surrounded him, he tried to sell even more of the national domain to the Yankees. This time all Mexico declared against him. His elegant yellow coach was torched and he was driven from the City of the Aztecs.

With his departure, Mexico lapsed into twelve years of civil strife and foreign intervention, even as the United States fell into discord and civil war. Their parallel internal struggles produced, at least momentarily in their troubled relationship, a sense of common struggle for nationhood. And in these struggles in both countries two remarkable leaders emerged—Abraham Lincoln and Benito Juárez—each of whom appeared unsuited for the role of building a nation.

Juárez was a Zapotec Indian from Oaxaca with a Liberal determination to drive the cleric and the soldier from their positions of privilege in Mexican society. Lincoln emerged as a regional opponent to slavery's expansion. Their rise to power was curiously parallel—Juárez's in the breakdown of the old hierarchical order before the concerted attacks of the Liberals in the mid-1850s, Lincoln's by the growing fears in the North about a national government dominated by southern sympathizers and apologists. Late in the decade, when Juárez and his political allies pushed through laws divesting the church of its lands and the military of its "rights," Lincoln and other Republicans were roundly criticizing the undisguised opportunism of James Buchanan's administration in taking advantage of Mexico's plight. In 1858 the defenders of the church and the military formed an alliance with the monarchists railing against the Liberal heathen and raised the flag of rebellion. Desperate for funds to prosecute the sedition, Mexico turned to the American government, offering transit concessions across the isthmus of Tehuántepec and the northern third of the republic (with the authority to protect the routes with American troops) for $10 million. The political outcry from Republicans, uniformly suspicious of Buchanan's motives in dealing with Mexico, prompted him to withhold the treaty from Senate consideration.[2]

In the midst of these troubles, Juárez was elected president only to have his enemies drive him from the capital. He took refuge in Veracruz. From there he waged both guerrilla and political war, sending his illiterate soldiers to ambush Conservative patrols and promulgating confiscatory decrees against his clerical enemies. In January 1861 he returned to the capital, dressed in the somber black of the Liberals and riding in a simple coach. Two months later, in similarly portentous circumstances, Lincoln took the presidential oath.

In the years that followed, two hemispheric republics plunged into civil war—the *mestizo* before the retaliation of its European creditors, the Anglo before the divisive forces the sudden conquest of territory had unleashed. In the challenge to republican government, the image of the United States in both Mexico and the rest of the hemisphere changed again.

In 1861 Great Britain, France, and Spain joined in an expedition to punish Mexico for Juárez's declaration of a moratorium on the national debt. When Mexico's creditors extended an invitation to the United States to join their pact, Seward indignantly refused, but he used the offer to extract a pledge from the British disavowing any expansionist intention in Mexico. Seward did not mention Monroe's doctrine. The British promise meant that the weak alliance with Spain and France would be of short duration. When the allies finally landed their forces at Veracruz, the Mexicans took advantage of their obvious divisions to entice the British into a separate agreement. Shortly, the Spanish, disillusioned with the notion of a *reconquista*, departed and satisfied their imperial ambitions with the reoccupation of the Dominican Republic.[3]

Only the large French army remained, under the command of a vainglorious officer with no inhibitions about retracing the conquering routes of Hernán Cortéz and Winfield Scott. By spring 1862 the French had pushed into the mountainous interior as far as Puebla. On 5 May (the *Cinco de Mayo*, a holiday now celebrated as far north as Chicago), Juárez's troops defeated them, and the French retreated to the coast. But in the following year they returned with a conquering army to install Maximilian, the Austrian archduke the Mexican Conservatives had discovered in their long European quest for a Hapsburg to sit on a restored Mexican throne. Their benefactor, Napoleon III, had often dreamed of this venture. Two decades before, in prison, he had written a tiny but ambitious volume, *The Canal of Nicaragua*, which foreshadowed the French enterprise in Panama under Ferdinand de Lesseps. A coup d'etat and accession to power brought to his court the importuning Mexican clerics, who argued for a Hapsburg to restore order and God in the heathen republic of the Liberals. The imminent collapse of republican government in Mexico and the United States provided an opportunity for action.

Viewing Mexico's defeat from afar, Seward pursued a narrow

course between condemnation, which meant invoking the Monroe Doctrine, and acquiescence in the French venture, which no dedicated proponent of republicanism could tolerate.[4] His notes to the French government on the Mexican intervention are masterpieces of diplomatic wording. France had a right to punish Mexico for its financial misdeeds, he wrote, but the Mexican people preferred republican to monarchical government.

Meanwhile, the American minister to Juárez, isolated in the remote North during these years, conveyed the repeated assurances of Seward that the cause of Juárez and the cause of Lincoln were the same. When the Confederacy dispatched its own emissary bearing promises, the stoic Zapotec was disbelieving. His patience was ultimately rewarded.

Seward's protests did little to alleviate Juárez's immediate problem or the suffering of ordinary Mexicans. But his criticism of the French venture (and the skills of the Mexican minister in Washington, Matías Romero, in rousing congressional opposition to the intervention) invigorated the *juarista* cause. As the American conflict entered its final year, a powerful sentiment took hold in the Lincoln administration to confront the French over the issue. Napoleon III, alert to the Prussian threat and the disturbing reports from his own ministers about rapidly diminishing public support for the intervention, had, apparently, already decided to withdraw French troops from Mexico. Maximilian had become a liability, the Confederacy was doomed, and Juárez's reputation was rising even among Europeans.

Seward sent the French a timetable for withdrawing their troops, which Napoleon meekly accepted. Already, the victorious Union had dispatched an army perilously close to the Mexican border, but its presence proved more symbolic than decisive in Maximilian's fall. The real victors were the *juaristas* and Juárez himself, who throughout the conflict had maintained vital links with a United States he distrusted and, at bottom, feared. While Seward pressured the French, Juárez moved against the cities of central Mexico, hoping to lure Maximilian into defending them. Taken prisoner after a hundred-day siege at Querétaro, the last Mexican emperor stood trial, was found guilty, and sentenced to death. From Europe and even the United States came pleas for clemency, but the Zapotec who had waged guerrilla war was implacable. Maximilian's execution would serve as a reminder to others who conspired to restore monarchy in Mexico. Seward had condemned the restoration of European monarchy in the Americas; Juárez and his *mestizos* had defeated it.[5]

Yet it was the American and not the Mexican struggle that inspired hemispheric admiration. And Latin Americans began to realize that the United States was far richer in its cultural and political tradition than the expansionist republic they had earlier feared. Here, again, the key issues of the American struggle—slavery, emancipation, states' rights, and military rule—were to Latin Americans of less importance than the symbol of Lincoln, whom they saw as a unifier standing against all enemies. Never again would any American leader seem to embody the traditional Hispanic traits of personalism so closely as Lincoln did for Latin Americans. The explanation lay not so much in his ultimate command of the crusade against slavery, as in his symbolic role as the "just leader" who innately senses the "will of the people" and leads them. Latin America's own experience with slavery's abolition was little affected by the tumult of abolitionism and civil war in the United States. Lincoln stood as the champion of central authority against disruptive chieftains and recognized the spiritual issues at stake in the war for the Union. His often unconstitutional exercise of power meant little to Latin Americans. What mattered was the moral legitimacy of his cause.

Cursed with political disunity, Latin Americans could readily identify with this awkward, thoroughly un-Hispanic Yankee leader. For them the powerful more often than not wore a uniform and delegated authority from horseback. Lincoln the civilian won the respect of a generation of Latin American intellectuals and civilians who decried the regional strife of their own countries or suffered the arbitrariness of petty tyrants. Lincoln, they perceived, was committed to preserve his nation without surrendering to the men on horseback. He commanded them. Alberdi, the astute Argentine political theorist who had suffered under the tyrant Rosas, identified the cause of Argentine unity with the nationalizing forces he saw in the United States. His contemporary, Sarmiento, visited Washington during the war to observe American public education and before returning wrote a laudatory biography of Lincoln.[6]

The New Empire

The ideological mentors of Latin America's first generation of rulers were French and English philosophers. Creole revolutionaries secretly read the French *philosophes* and admired the English "country Whigs" and their defiance of the English Crown. After the American Civil War they turned an admiring gaze northward to the United States, which rapidly began to demonstrate what riches a modern capitalist system was capable of generating. Political stability, Latin America's liberals recognized, permitted a new economic order of progress and technology, which in the United States meant a modern social order. American leaders accommodated their cultural and political traditions to the credos of modern capitalism, but their Latin American counterparts, fearful of the social costs of these economic transformations, only reluctantly adjusted to the political demands of the new era.[7]

The foreign entrepreneur or merchant usually conducted his business recognizing the Latin American elite's fearfulness about incorporating its industrial work force into an expanded political culture. He adjusted to the political reality or did not long survive. Those who fared well—such as W. R. Grace in Peru, who built a commercial empire on the west coast of South America—learned how to operate by the political—which meant social—priorities of the host country. A succession of Germans and Americans pushed railroad projects in Costa Rica, for example, but the wily *ticos* of the central plateau resisted until Henry Meiggs (who had laid track in Chile and the Peruvian Andes) and Minor Keith convinced them that Costa Rica's economic future lay in a rail line to the Caribbean coast. In time, of course, the entrepreneurs founded companies whose resources and clout dwarfed those of local governments. When their interests conflicted, the governments sometimes bowed and occasionally resisted. In the latter instances, Latin America became an early supporter of the Calvo doctrine, by which a foreign company agreed to settle disputes in national courts. By the twentieth century, certainly, the multinationals had begun to appeal to their own governments for support, either by diplomatic pressure or, if necessary, by more forceful means.

Mexico after Maximilian offers a good example of economic transformation and its social cost. It became the frontier of an invigorated North American industrial economy. In both Mexico and the United States political leaders sought a new economic order. Mexico again turned inward but after its victory over European monarchy strived to blend its Hispanic authoritarian past with the economic promise offered by industrial Europe and America. In Europe the modern industrial order expanded its global frontiers by extending its formal empire. The United States sought markets, bases, and influence. Mexico, like most of Latin America, adjusted because the requirements of modernization seemed to dictate doing so. It promoted industrial development by importing foreign capital, technicians, and entrepreneurs. It permitted an aggressive landed class to diminish the historic social role of the *hacienda* (where the master provided for his charges) by transforming the landed estates into plantations that produced for export, devouring small farms and those who survived on them. Its government extended to foreigners the privilege of mining for the subsoil riches of the country and the opportunity to construct rail lines to unite the domain of domestic producer with the outside world. In the process, it has been argued, an economic system was imposed from without, on the backs of downtrodden people whose only value was their labor. An informal empire took form. Its creators were Mexican and American, and its beneficiaries were Mexican and American. But its victims were *los de abajo*, those on the bottom.

In Mexico, the visible impact of the industrial revolution was impressive. This country, which Americans and Europeans had long regarded as a political and economic backwater, now had a leader, Porfirio Díaz, who brought order to the countryside and positivist credos to the state. Mexico joined the gold-standard fraternity, discouraged bullfighting and the festivities of its Indian past, and acquired a respectable image among its former detractors in Europe and America. The ideal was a modern Mexico, unified by a dynamic middle class attuned to the promise of an imported economic philosophy based on material not ideological credos.[8]

Those American leaders who charted the "new empire" did not consider their quest a traditional imperial undertaking. They were more concerned with the pursuit of markets, in the challenge posed by British economic supremacy in Latin America, and, as had earlier generations, with American security in the larger Caribbean. There was no single architect of this unified strategy, though William Henry Seward, whose career as secretary of state virtually spanned the decade of the 1860s, certainly grasped the relationship between the U.S. Navy's determination to acquire West Indian naval bases and the American farmers' clamoring for markets. In 1866 Seward commenced a vigorous campaign in the Caribbean. He signed a treaty with Denmark for the acquisition of the Danish West Indies and a canal pact with Nicaragua and initiated efforts to secure a site for a naval base in the Dominican Republic. Though none of these was approved in the nineteenth century (all but the last were achieved in the twentieth), Seward's general prediction about eventual U.S. dominance in the Caribbean was a portent of the course of American policy.[9]

His successors proved no less enthusiastic about commercial expansionism, even though they were divided on the political implications of a quest for "informal" empire. In 1870 the U.S. Senate politely asked the Ulysses S. Grant administration about the state of hemispheric trade and received from Secretary of State Hamilton Fish a reaffirmation of the Monroe Doctrine. Fish threw down the gauntlet by declaring that American economic interests in Latin America would inevitably relieve the continent from its dependence on British trade. In the ensuing years American secretaries of state pursued commercial treaties in both the independent and colonized Caribbean, urging both to accept the revered American principle of reciprocity.

Despite the urging of naval strategists such as Alfred T. Mahan and Stephen Luce and private commercial promoters for a more vigorous U.S. role in Latin America, most Americans remained apprehensive about the political implications of such ventures. The United States might achieve informal empire, they acknowledged, as had Great Britain, but it should not create formal empire, which meant the burdens of colonies and outposts to defend, an unwanted obligation the British were already reluctantly undertaking. Mahan argued that the nation did not have to emulate European colonialism to enjoy the benefits of empire—markets could be achieved without the burden of governing subject peoples. But if the nation did not modernize its navy, protect the sealanes for its commerce, and acquire political influence in strategic places, it was doomed to enter the new century in an inferior relationship to its European rivals.

Three crises of the 1870s and 1880s illustrate the changing character of the country's approach to Latin America. The first came with Grant's disastrous campaign to annex the Dominican Republic. Even before the Civil War the United States had been drawn to Hispaniola. In 1850, alert to European interests in the squabbles between Haiti and the Dominican Republic (which had won its independence in 1844 after twenty years of Haitian domination) Congress had initiated a special inquiry into the island's problems. An American emissary, William L. Cazneau, had negotiated with a larcenous Dominican executive a treaty ceding Samaná Bay for a naval base site, but French and British protests killed the plan. In 1861 Spanish troops returned, spent four years fighting a sporadic counterguerrilla war, and abandoned the republic in frustration. U.S. fascination with a Dominican navel base quickly revived, and Seward sent his son Frederick to offer the Dominican leader $2 million for a lease.

The younger Seward never consummated a deal that for the navy would have been better than Alaska. In Grant's first year as president, a band of American promoters (Cazneau among them) descended on Santo Domingo. The new Dominican leader was Buenaventura Báez, who apparently believed Cazneau was prepared to deal for the sale of the entire country. Cazneau returned to Washington and plied Grant with grandiose schemes not only for obtaining a much needed base for the U.S. Navy but also for settling remote portions of the Dominican Republic with hardy Anglo pioneers. In presenting the treaty Grant argued that annexation would raise the lowly Dominicans to a more civilized level. But the Senate was in no mood for picking up the white man's burden. Senator Charles Sumner effectively demolished Grant's argument with the persuasive logic that the Dominican Republic represented an alien culture that could not be molded into a tropical Anglo-Saxon outpost. However limited its cultural achievements, the Massachusetts solon declared, the Dominican Republic belonged to the Dominican people.[10]

Grant touted Dominican annexation as both a commercial and a moral enterprise. To Europeans, such exhortations smacked of American moralization of expansionist policies, which the European governments themselves were doing in Asia and Africa. Both were pretentious, but American pronouncements appeared to indicate that the United States really *believed* it sought a higher purpose in the world and that its empire, informal or formal, would be different. Thus in 1868, when Cuban rebels raised the flag of revolt, they aroused the country's moral conscience against "heathen Spain." Congress was swept away by pro-Cuban sentiment. But the reality of the weakness of the Cuban cause and Fish's determination to prevent a confrontation with Spain blocked the congressional firebrands' demands for action. In the first year of what became a ten-year struggle, Fish tried to negotiate Cuban independence, promising the Spanish a handsome financial settlement if they would quit the island. When they indignantly refused, another generation of American adventurers, gun-runners, and opportunists plied the waters between the Florida coast and the island.

Fish still refused to budge, though in late 1873 the capture of a U.S. gun-running vessel and the shooting of fifty-three of the crew threatened his policy of restraint. Spain apologized, paid an indemnity, and official anger over the incident dissipated. In the aftermath Fish noted perceptively that Spanish rule over the island was doomed. He championed the island's liberation (and, by implication, Puerto Rico's) but never fully accepted the notion that the island could achieve independence without American sustenance or protection. Nor could he accommodate the view of an inner circle of Cuban rebels that the real war for independence went beyond the cry for political self-rule but encompassed the dismantling of the sugar economy, source of the island's wealth but also of its social inequities.[11]

Until the 1890s the United States confined its expansionism in Latin America to commerce and, occasionally, to displays of its naval power. When the French under Ferdinand de Lesseps began dredging a canal across the isthmus of Panama (the area in which the United States had pledged in 1846 to safeguard the neutrality of the passageway) President Rutherford B. Hayes solemnly declared that *any* transisthmian canal was merely an extension of the U.S. coastline. American politicians, invoking the Monroe Doctrine, routinely denounced the 1850 Clayton-Bulwer treaty, its spirit of Anglo-American cooperation, and the hallowed idea of an international, neutral canal. Even the Colombians, long resentful of European maneuvering in the western Caribbean, appeared taken aback by American rashness. In 1885, when one of the periodic Panamanian revolts against Colombian rule could not be quelled and in the opinion of the manager of the Panama Railroad threatened the neutrality of the isthmus, the U.S. government invoked its treaty right to intervene. In the largest American military expedition to foreign soil since the Mexican War, the U.S. Navy landed several companies of marines and bluejackets and crushed the revolt. The leader of the revolution, Pedro Prestán, was publicly executed in Colón. For years afterward, observers remembered the authoritative presence of American naval power.

Pan-Americanism, Yanqui-style

Four years before the impressive demonstration of American firepower on the Panamanian isthmus, the United States had displayed its own version of Pan-Americanism in South America. Fittingly, it came from one of the more bombastic of late nineteenth-century American leaders, James Gillespie Blaine, twice secretary of state and presidential aspirant. As secretary of state in the James A. Garfield administration, he enthusiastically supported U.S. interests in Peruvian nitrates. Chilean engineers were already developing the nitrate industry in Antofagastá and Tarapacá (provinces of Bolivia and Peru, respectively). Anticipating trouble, the Peruvians and Bolivians had signed a secret pact to defend their interests. In 1879, the War of the Pacific broke out. The Chileans were victorious, routing the Bolivians and dispatching an invading army to Callao. Blaine took office just as the conquering Chileans were on the verge of a stupendous triumph. With a diplomatic naiveté that convinced the Chileans he was cleverly trying to promote U.S. economic interests in Peru, Blaine tried to mediate the conflict. As U.S. ministers in Santiago and Lima embarrassed Washington by identifying with the cause of the respective warring governments, Blaine dispatched a special emissary to the region, bearing invitations to his grand design, a Pan-American conference in the United States. Among other matters, Blaine told the Chileans, the Latin American nations would perhaps wish to discuss the recurring interstate wars of South America.

His pledge not to use the proceedings for an official inquiry into the war did not placate Chile, which announced that its government would not participate. After President Garfield's untimely death in September, Blaine lingered for several months, then left office. His successor questioned his meddling in the War of the Pacific and shelved the Pan-American venture. The Chileans had their own conception of a South American balance of power, and they expected the international powers to accept it, but they recognized their limitations in dealing with Europe and the United States.[12] They prosecuted the war against the Peruvians and in 1884 imposed what the American government considered a punitive peace settlement. Peru lost Tarapacá; Bolivia, its Pacific littoral, Antofagastá. The Peruvian provinces of Tacna and Arica, which figured prominently in Chilean calculations, fell under Santiago's domain for a decade, their future ultimately to be decided by a plebiscite.

Blaine did have a higher motive. Questioned by a suspicious Congress and rebuffed by the Chileans, he nonetheless established the view that the United States had a special obligation to mediate intrahemispheric conflicts. If its intrusion deterred European powers, so much the better. In Central America, he plunged into a long-standing territorial dispute between Mexico and Guatemala, encouraging the hapless Guatemalans to look to Washington for diplomatic protection. When the meddling Blaine formally proposed arbitration, neither Mexico nor Guatemala accepted. The United States had not yet assumed the protective role it would later play, but American intentions foreshadowed gunboat diplomacy.

Blaine returned to the State Department in 1889, in time to preside over the first modern Pan-American conference. He had lost none of his earlier commitment to a hemispheric economic war against British capital.[13] He reinforced this commitment with another popular sentiment, "America for the Americans," expressed in an ambitious but impractical proposal for a hemispheric customs union that would enhance the political image of the United States throughout the hemisphere. Contemporaneous literature, especially the hortatory (and racist) social scientific tracts, portrayed a heathenish, popish, but redeemable continent. The fundamental question was whether Latin America would be redeemed by goodwill, emulation of the United States, or forceful persuasion. When the Latin American delegates finally arrived, they were already bored with Blaine's notion of a customs union and took umbrage at his notion that American companies with legal problems in a Latin American country should have diplomatic recourse to Washington before submitting their cases to national courts.

To Blaine, economic solidarity would protect against European intrusion and, perhaps, be a forerunner of hemispheric political cooperation. All save the Dominican Republic attended this conference, but the visiting Latin American delegates saw in Blaine's slogan "America for the Americans" merely the substitution of the United States for European economic intrusion into their affairs. They approved the establishment of an International Bureau, forerunner of the Pan-American Union. Then they inspected the American industrial em-

pire, dutifully impressed with the awesome machinery that symbolized man's technological triumph but perhaps fearful of the social
disruption an industrial democracy portended.[14]

The Splendid Little War

For the United States the 1890s brought political crisis wrought by
economic dislocation. The decade ended in war and in a fervent debate over imperialism and the prosperity that some associated with it.
In Latin America these years saw a fulfillment of economic promise
for the few and the impoverishment of the many. In the United States
inequities persisted, but a dynamic capitalist economy offered at least
a limited opportunity to move up the social ladder. In Latin America,
the rulers embraced an exploitive economic system that did not
threaten the political and social culture of those who mattered.

In this decade Latin America, especially the Caribbean, took on
greater strategic importance for the United States. Its place in American calculations proved a welcome distraction from the political and
social conflict that racked the country. The Navy rapidly modernized
and ideologues talked of "looking outward." Disputes transformed
into confrontations, problems into policies, and incidents into strategies. It may be wrong to argue, as some have, that the United States
sought a fight in these years, but it did not strive to avoid one.

Early in the decade, for example, the country came perilously close
to hostilities with remote Chile. Animosities still lingered from our
meddling in the War of the Pacific and, later, from the official American sympathy with the Chilean president, Jorge Balmaceda, in the
bitter civil war between Balmaceda and the Chilean Congress in 1891.
Balmaceda, a forerunner of the modern Latin American economic nationalist, had Blaine's support. Europeans with heavy investments in
Chile feared Balmaceda would nationalize the nitrate deposits, so
they championed the congressional faction. After the Congress won,
Balmaceda took refuge in the Argentine embassy and shot himself. A
party of American sailors, on leave in Valparaiso, was mobbed by a

band of Chileans, and two Americans died. In Washington, news of the incident led the Harrison administration to demand an apology from Chile, threatening retaliation if refused. After several tense months of negotiation (interspersed with press warnings of Chilean warships steaming up to attack the defenseless California coast), the Chileans capitulated.[15]

American power intruded in other incidents and confrontations in the hemisphere. In 1894 a mutiny in the Brazilian navy, begun by monarchists intent on toppling the new republic, threatened international shipping in Brazilian ports and thus prompted a forceful American naval demonstration on behalf of the government. In the following year, Venezuela's dispute with Great Britain over the Guiana boundary brought the American government to Venezuela's defense. Secretary of State Richard Olney, responding to anti-British sentiments in the country, used the incident to inform Britain that the United States was "practically sovereign" in the Western Hemisphere and that its "fiat was law." A more blunt view, expressed by a generation of jingoistic Republicans including Theodore Roosevelt and Henry Cabot Lodge, held that Europeans could expect American interference in their disputes with Latin America.

For Venezuela and the Caribbean these statements heralded a more assertive policy with profound implications. After the Venezuelan imbroglio, the United States regarded any European gesture of force in negotiating with a Caribbean state—a not uncommon way for the nineteenth-century powers to handle their problems with smaller countries—as its own strategic concern. Europeans trying to fathom American intrusion into the Caribbean naturally assumed the United States was intent on joining the imperial family. Anti-imperialist rhetoric remained strong in the United States. Its obverse side was not identification with the Caribbean republics but reaffirmation of earlier beliefs that their political future required American guidance. The United States welcomed their break with Europe; it did not welcome them as sister republics.

The century ended with a "splendid little war" against Spain that ended one empire and imposed another that had been taking shape for three decades. To the Cuban rebels whose forerunners had fought that empire for seventy-five years their American liberators established another in its place.

When the Cuban rebellion erupted again in 1895, it quickly captured the imagination of the hemisphere. In their struggle against Spanish rule, the rebels assumed mythically heroic proportions as valiant warriors for freedom hurling themselves against an archaic political and economic system that, Americans believed, had brutalized the island for four centuries. From the beginning Washington put the Spanish government on notice that its tolerance for another prolonged struggle in Cuba was limited. Even the phlegmatic Grover Cleveland, who stood forthrightly against bellicose congressmen threatening to declare war to settle the Cuban "mess," unhesitatingly insinuated the government's moral disapprobation of Spanish rule and military measures in the Cuban conflict. The decisive difference between Cleveland and his more compliant successor, William McKinley, was the latter's willingness to accept military intervention as a solution—to wage war, as McKinley put it, in the name of humanity.

For more than a year after taking office McKinley anxiously watched the human toll the revolution and Spanish counterrevolution took on the island. As Americans cheered on the journalists and filibusters who ventured south to cover the war or to offer their services, the president realized that the combatants were waging more than a grisly conflict that sickened those Americans who read daily accounts of its human toll. If the war went on—and McKinley had the unsettling reminder of the Ten Years' War of 1868–78—the Spanish would either inflict an unacceptable punishment on the civilian population, especially in the east, or, just as ominous, the rebels would lay waste the rich sugar plantations in the west. Thus the president urgently pressed for a diplomatic solution in fall 1897 after the Spanish had cut a trench midway across the island and herded civilians into special camps in the west and after a rebel army under Antonio Maceo had begun devastating raids on the sugar plantations. When the harassed Spanish government finally succumbed to American pressures for Cuban autonomy, a proposal the rebels condemned, McKinley blamed not the Cubans but the Spanish.

The Spanish offered reforms and autonomy, but there were too few takers. The rebels wanted independence, the loyalists a vigorous prosecution of the war, the property holders U.S. intervention, and the American government the determining role in Cuba's future. In mid-February 1898, when the U.S.S. *Maine*, dispatched to Havana harbor to safeguard American lives in the beleaguered city, was blown up, the event galvanized the widespread anti-Spanish sentiment in the country. Within the U.S. government, the explosion (which the public generally attributed to Spanish saboteurs) reinforced the view that only the United States could bring a "humane" settlement to Cuba. The following month, as the Spanish anticipated American intervention and desperately sought European allies, McKinley delivered a peace proposal to Madrid that called for U.S. mediation of the conflict. For the Spanish, his ultimatum meant either humiliation or war. Spain reluctantly chose the latter.

American entry into this war was no miscalculation, no aberration brought on by frustrations generated in the bitter political divisions in the country. The United States went to war against "heathen Spain" in 1898 because the public wanted it, because American business had at last concluded that the loss of Spanish-American trade would be offset by the prospects of expanding American economic interests in the fallen Spanish Empire, because the American military (especially the navy) appeared prepared to fight it, and because the president of the United States had an uncanny ability to shield his international strategic calculations with appealing homilies. Perhaps, as Louis Pérez, Jr., has suggested, the United States went to war because it had long coveted Cuba for strategic and economic reasons, for its self-ordained role in shaping the island's future, and for its unarticulated but strongly felt conviction that the Cuban rebels were so irrational in their destructive campaigns that they could not be entrusted with power and thus required tutelage.[16]

Europeans looking at the coming of this war rightly assumed that the United States was provoking Spain into a war that would advance its ambitions in the Caribbean and the western Pacific. Though the United States pledged not to annex Cuba—a move demanded by congressmen wary of assuming the enormous Cuban debt—the intervention in Cuba (and Puerto Rico) opened up American political and military influence in the Caribbean on a scale that would, it was argued, surpass the European role in the region and facilitate American economic interests there. Less apparent to both Americans and Europeans—even those who expressed moral doubts about intruding into this conflict—was the impact of U.S. intervention on Cuba's economic and, ultimately, social and political future. The coming of American troops guaranteed one revolution but destroyed another. Americans had come to accept Cuban independence and saw themselves as the island's savior, but they had no intention of accepting its economic or social restructuring. In the past Cuban rebellion had failed, Americans told themselves, because it had not been sustained by moral resolve and determination to fight until independence was achieved.

The exhausted Cuban rebels who survived the Ten Years' War learned a different lesson: real independence could be achieved only by demolishing the island's rigid social structure, which meant destroying the sugar economy. This sentiment was not universal among the bands of revolutionaries who fled to Europe and the United States in 1878, but it was dogma to the inner core of rebels who renewed the struggle in 1895. It explains why their drive into the relatively prosperous western provinces, where the most successful sugar estates were located, left in its wake burned fields and razed mills. A goodly portion of this property represented the $50 million Americans had invested in the Cuban sugar industry. But it also symbolized a social and economic system the rebels were determined to expunge from Cuba's future—whatever the cost.

If the intervention was no misadventure or miscalculation, neither was the dispatch of American troops into the tropics a signal that the United States intended to create an empire in the American Mediterranean such as the Europeans had crafted in Africa. Europeans may have had few illusions about American purposes, but among Latin

Americans sympathy for Spain and its cultural legacy in the hemisphere was offset by widespread support of Cuban liberation, which the United States presumably guaranteed.[17] The use of American military force to settle a domestic political issue was, after all, not unprecedented. Small numbers of American marines and bluejackets had been disembarking in the tropics since 1800, when a marine contingent landed on the north coast of Hispaniola. Such interventions were never very large or lasted more than a few months. Occasionally, as in Panama in 1885, they had a decisive impact. But they were not seen as imperial ventures.

The territorial benefit of victory over Spain—military occupation of Cuba and annexation of the Philippines and Puerto Rico—did, however, provoke a debate over empire within the United States. Anti-imperial sentiment could be identified among all social and economic classes and in both political parties. But the debate was about what should be done in the aftermath of the war and not about the justification for intervening in Cuba. Throughout ran warnings and rebuttals about the fitness of those Spanish colonial charges the United States had liberated for self-government and the dangers of bringing alien cultures under U.S. rule. Equally unsettling to some was the tarnishing of America's cultural image in the experience of this war. In the hullabaloo before the war, the press portrayed the Cuban rebels as bronze variations of Anglo-Saxon warriors fighting a traditional struggle for freedom. When the Americans finally got to Cuba in June 1898, they encountered an essentially guerrilla force with unsettlingly dark-skinned common soldiers and officers. Before long U.S. officers were casually ridiculing the fighting spirit of their putative allies and praising the bravery of the Spanish enemy, a noticeably different assessment than the earlier favorable expressions about Cuban warriors from American soldiers of fortune and volunteers to the rebel cause. American blacks ("smoked Yankees") served in this campaign, earning, many of them said, more respect from the Spanish than from their own officers, who made derogatory references to the Cuban "mambises," the black shock troops of rebel contingents. After the war, when the occupying American military decided to disarm the rebel army, it did so for political and racial reasons. American troops came as conquerors, they ruled as conquerors.

The political consequences of the war proved as devastating for the Cuban rebels, it soon appeared, as for the defeated Spaniards. In waging war the United States professed no annexationist designs on the island but then refused to recognize the Cuban revolutionary government on whose behalf it was intervening. It denied the Cubans a seat at the peace table, created a postwar military government as the inherent right of the conqueror, and assumed the obligation to police a ravaged country. The independent Cuba that emerged from this experience was stunted from its birth with self-doubts about its national identity. Equally as troubling was the decision to take Puerto Rico, which had won its autonomy in 1897, as reparation. In less than a year the island passed from being a Spanish colony with considerable freedom and economic sufficiency to an outpost of the United States, conquered territory over which the U.S. flag but not the Constitution prevailed. In both islands the political culture suffered such debilitation that a major legacy of the experience was to be the Caribbean defiance that still troubles modern Americans, who believe they liberated both from Spanish oppression and prepared both for a brighter future.

The empire that the U.S. victory over Spain bequeathed was unlike any carved out in Africa or Asia by the imperial powers of Europe. It was different because America had pursued nobler goals. We had gone to war against Spain to liberate the Cubans from Spanish injustice, had taken Puerto Rico as just compensation for the cost of doing it, and had annexed the Philippines, as McKinley told a group of inquisitive clergymen, to Christianize the Filipinos. Rarely did Americans question their motives in undertaking empire; they questioned only where it should be undertaken or how it should be pursued. The peace treaty debate, which focused almost exclusively on Philippine annexation, was the last stand of the old-line antiexpansionists and their once persuasive arguments that extending American rule over other cultures would ultimately debase the character of the "model republic."

The U.S. Caribbean empire was different but not for the reasons Americans believed. In 1900 the Supreme Court, in a series of cases, declared that the Constitution did not follow the flag to Puerto Rico. The only colony in the region until 1914, when the United States purchased the Virgin Islands, remained largely neglected until the United States entered World War I. Promised its independence on the eve of war, Cuba waited four years to attain it and then, to get the Americans to leave, its leaders had to accept a constitution riddled with obligations to the United States.[18] Americans who flocked there considered Cuba as much a colony within American domain as Puerto Rico. As had those Americans who had earlier ventured into Mexico and Central America, they viewed themselves not as conquerors but as exemplars of America, especially its faith in economic opportunity and its conviction that property and its protection constituted the foundation of a modern society. In Cuba and in the banana enclaves of the Central American coast, where opportunity beckoned a generation of Americans, their impact on local economies ultimately became so large that it extended to the entire country, its politics, and even its culture.

In 1900 a thoughtful Puerto Rican emissary to the United States, Eugenio María de Hostos, solemnly informed President McKinley that by intervening in Puerto Rico the United States had an obligation either to grant the island its freedom or to annex it as a state to ensure the equality of Puerto Rican culture within U.S. domain. To do neither, he warned, would unleash powerful nationalistic outcries that would inevitably center on the disparity between U.S. actions and professions. De Hostos was more prophetic than he realized.

5   New World Policeman

In the three decades after the war with Spain, the United States expanded its interests in Latin America by every political, economic, and military measure. It had displaced the Spanish Empire in Puerto Rico and Cuba. In the western Caribbean, it had already begun to chart a more direct role for American power on the isthmus. In South America the United States had assumed a protective role over Venezuela in the 1895 boundary dispute between that country and Great Britain. With the encouragement of the Brazilian foreign minister, the Baron do Rio Branco, Washington fashioned what a later generation would call an unwritten alliance. Rejecting Argentine arguments for a hemispheric collective statement on such diverse matters as the forcible collection of international debts and the obligations of aliens to settle their disputes in the courts of the country in which they did business, the United States followed a unilateral course in the region. It asserted its military power in the Caribbean, intervening in the internal affairs of smaller states and creating a string of protectorates from Hispaniola to Panama. Its justification rested on understandable strategic arguments, questionable economic policies, and, in retrospect, political and cultural pretensions bordering on the arrogant.[1]

As the British had already discovered, informal empire with its large benefits and modest overhead ultimately gave way to formal empire with its obligations and increasing imperial surcharges. By the end of the century, a disconsolate inner group of British imperialists had come to the somber conclusion that the British Empire on which the sun never set had gotten too costly, but it had to be defended from without and, increasingly, from within. The United States had no colonial service, no colonial army, and no colonial economic bureaucracy, nor did the American government feel a need to create them. Ultimately, as strategic imperatives, economic interests, and political realities dictated, they took shape in one form or another. Taking on the imperial burden for the noblest of intentions did not lessen the obligation of defending it. As German interest in the Caribbean and in Mexico heightened after the turn of the century, so did U.S. opposition to it. As American companies intruded in the tropics, especially in Cuba and Central America, the American government articulated its Caribbean strategy in political and economic terms.

When the charges of American empire became more unruly or more defiant, they were "chastised" with stern warnings or, if they persisted in the "revolutionary frame of mind," with a "spanking" by U.S. military forces. If their outburst proved threatening to long-term American interests, they suffered occupation, which meant stern-minded military proconsuls in charge of their affairs. In Theodore Roosevelt's day, Americans enthusiastically took on the imperial mission. By Franklin Roosevelt's day, they had grown weary of it.[2]

The Big Stick

Theodore Roosevelt had set the standard for official behavior in the Caribbean even before he became president. When the McKinley administration negotiated a new treaty with the British, pledging the neutrality of a future canal, Roosevelt, then governor of New York, denounced the pact for failing to permit the United States to defend the waterway. The treaty was altered to meet his specifications. As president he withdrew American troops from Cuba in 1902 only when the Cubans accepted the Platt Amendment, which made the island a protectorate, then reluctantly sent them back four years later when the country was plunged into a civil war and both sides believed U.S. intervention would advance their respective causes. He plunged into a debts controversy between Venezuela and Britain and Germany in late 1902, virtually sponsored the Panamanian revolution of 1903, announced in 1904 that the United States would exercise a policeman's role over indebted and disorderly Caribbean states to prevent their harassment by European creditors, and declared in 1905 a customs receivership in the Dominican Republic.

These actions, Roosevelt argued, were necessary and unobjectionable, representing not aggressive behavior but forceful restraint, a policy of "velvet on iron." He correctly surmised that Great Britain would tolerate (indeed, welcome) a more dominating American political and military presence in the Caribbean. And he sensed that the American public would look on the heightened German presence in the region with misgivings. He mixed bellicose rhetoric with determined action. The intent was to achieve precisely enough involvement in Latin America to ward off European interference yet avoid becoming bogged down in turbulent internal problems that continually beset the smaller republics. The *public* Roosevelt insisted on American domination of the canal, demanded protectorate status for Cuba, warned against the German peril in the Venezuelan debts crisis, and talked of a policing role among turbulent little republics whose leaders often got in the "revolutionary frame of mind" and had to be chastised. The *private* Roosevelt confided to his transatlantic pen pal, the anti-imperialist George Otto Trevelyan, that his dispatch of troops into tropical places was not an American version of European imperial behavior.[3] In summer 1906, as the Cuban political situation deteriorated, Roosevelt insisted it was the Cubans with their endless bickering who were trying to compel him to intervene. He "reluctantly" acquiesced a few months later, calling the troops an army of pacification. He employed virtually the same words to describe how the rambunctious Dominicans were urging him to annex their country, which he compared to devouring a porcupine. There, at least, he settled for controls that gave American overseers virtual dominance over the republic's external finances.

Roosevelt was an imperialist but a somewhat reluctant one. In the Venezuelan crisis, for example, he waited until the public furor over the Anglo-German blockade before criticizing the Germans for their actions, then maneuvered the American fleet in the West Indies in such a way as to demonstrate American resolve without unduly provoking the European intruders. In the Dominican case, which had larger implications for Europeans because of the republic's heavy indebtedness, he probed into the country's internal affairs only to the extent necessary to get the customs receivership. When the Senate questioned his intentions, he confirmed the arrangement as an executive agreement and waited two years for the Senate to acquiesce in a formal treaty. He was unforgivably insensitive toward the Colombians when they debated the canal treaty Secretary of State John Hay had proffered and doubtless provoked them to reject it by his callous remarks. He did not plot the Panamanian revolt of November, though he certainly provided reassurances to the plotters. He did have legal authority to safeguard the passageway under the 1846 treaty with Colombia. Contemporaries who condemned his peremptory action forgot how many times American troops had landed to enforce it. The difference in 1903 was that the treaty was invoked *against* Colombia, to whom the pledge of maintaining the neutrality of the isthmus had been granted, which not a few lawyers considered a baffling interpretation. He got a better deal with Panama (which was to nurture a bitterness until 1979 because their negotiator in Washington, Philippe Bunau Varilla, had mortgaged the republic's sovereignty to give the Americans virtually a free hand in the Canal Zone). Roosevelt naturally accepted the concessions, but he was reluctant to fashion an American colony in the Canal Zone.[4]

More significant than Roosevelt's imperial posturing was his explicit rejection of hemispheric unity in the face of European pressures. In 1902, on the eve of the Anglo-German blockade of Venezuela, the Argentine foreign minister Luis M. Drago boldly proposed that Latin America's heavy debt should not be cause for European intervention in hemispheric affairs. Though schooled in international law, Drago took his case into the court of American politics. Praising the United States for its opposition to European territorial aggrandizement—in effect, lauding the Monroe Doctrine—Drago argued that Europe's gunboat diplomacy on behalf of its creditors threatened hemispheric integrity. Financial pressures, he believed, led inevitably to intervention. A united hemispheric protest under the rubric of a multilateral doctrine was necessary.

Never, perhaps, had a Latin American managed to articulate a more persuasive argument for collective action only to reinforce a unilateral policy. What Drago had not perceived was the acceptance within the U.S. government and the public generally of an imperial posture in the Western Hemisphere. Rejecting the charge that the United States was imitating the European powers, Secretary of State Hay articulated, and Roosevelt forcefully demonstrated, the modern American role in Latin America. The external menace, Hay informed Drago, lay not so much in the political threat (save, perhaps, for the visible though exaggerated German meddling in the Caribbean) but in the more aggressive economic penetration of European capitalism sustained by the imperial state. As a heavy investor in Cuba and Mexico, the United States (though still a debtor nation) sympathized with European creditors trying to collect from Latin American mendicants. Given its strategic interests in Latin America, especially in the Caribbean, the U.S. government could not permit European powers to collect their Latin American debts by forceful means. Neither did it wish to relinquish the Monroe Doctrine to the Pan-American system.

Within a few years, Roosevelt had rallied public sentiment against European interference in the Caribbean and then declared that the United States must police the region to ward off future European meddling. Drago watched disconsolately as the debts question dragged on in the Permanent Court of Arbitration The Hague, where the blockading powers against indebted Venezuela won first priority for payment of claims, and must have been perplexed at Roosevelt's contention that "intervention to prevent intervention" was justifiable. There was a Pan-American system, which dealt with apolitical questions such as commercial accords or mundane matters. A U.S. system for the hemisphere, however, dealt with political questions, particularly those relating to American security interests. Drago had unintentionally transformed an economic question into a political issue, and neither Roosevelt nor his successors seriously considered submitting it for hemispheric approbation. Drago posed a Pan-American corollary to the Monroe Doctrine; TR responded with the Roosevelt corollary. As

Adams had recognized in 1823, Roosevelt instinctively sensed the domestic political appeal of a unilateral rather than a collective response to the European challenge. In declaring that the United States must carry out the role of policeman in the hemisphere, Roosevelt assumed obligations that his successors and the U.S. military rapidly wearied of carrying out.[5]

At the third Pan-American conference in Rio de Janeiro in 1906, the new secretary of state, Elihu Root, emasculated Drago's doctrine, but he did so with such diplomatic skill (and polite reassurances of his respect for the Argentine statesman) that Drago lost none of his admiration for the United States. Root, who genuinely liked Latin Americans, spoke grandly of strengthening the commercial ties of the Americas and the U.S. commitment to the rule of law. But in reality, the commitments the United States had assumed had already begun to impose unwanted and reluctantly taken actions in the Dominican Republic and especially in Cuba.

With Cuba the United States had the Platt Amendment of 1902, which had created the "special relationship" Cubans came to hate, so Roosevelt was able to say that he had no choice but to intervene to "safeguard" the island's independence. But just as quickly he was plunged into another familial quarrel in Central America. In 1907, with Mexican support, Roosevelt and Root gave their approval to a series of treaties aimed at bringing peace among the warring Central American states. They agreed not to recognize governments that came to power by bullets instead of ballots and to respect the neutrality of Honduras, the warring ground of Central American armies. A Central American court was launched with American blessing. But within two years American hostility to a nationalistic Nicaraguan leader, José Santos Zelaya (who hounded foreign entrepreneurs, exiled his political enemies, and meddled incessantly in his neighbor's politics) made the American government a violator of its own principles. Alienated Nicaraguan conservatives found adherents and financial support from the United Fruit Company (UFCo), which along with lumbering and mining companies dominated the economy of eastern Nicaragua. When the revolution broke out, Roosevelt had already left office. He had not hesitated to "chastise" unruly governments that ran afoul of American strictures with selective, limited use of troops. His successor, William Howard Taft, convinced of the need for financial reorganization of small economies with the support of Wall Street's investment houses, undertook to safeguard American political interests with dollars not bullets. "Dollar diplomacy" became the motto for maintaining Central American security.

The plan was apparently working in the Dominican Republic. But Central America is not an island, and from the beginning its five states resisted "Wall Street" and its foreign economic manipulations. They could not hold back the penetration of "Market Street"—American companies whose go-getter entrepreneurs were less interested in monetary reforms or honest customs collectors than in paying what was necessary for their political champion to gain power so they would not have to pay any duties on goods they imported for their business. The prototype of "Market Street" was Sam "the Banana Man" Zemurray, who in 1911 financed a revolution plotted in a New Orleans bordello that eventually gave him a stake in a Honduran banana empire. In all save Nicaragua, dollar diplomacy was a failure, though the private American economic presence, reinforced by stern diplomatic pressures and the occasional appearance of American warships, reminded the republics of Washington's policing role.

In Nicaragua dollar diplomacy succeeded only when the United States forced Zelaya to flee, then dispatched a major military expedition into the country to protect his pro-American successor with bullets. Two thousand American troups—sent by a government whose leaders believed they confronted in Nicaragua a Latin American variation of the Boxer Rebellion with its attendant disorder—swept through Nicaragua's populous west. To this day Nicaraguans date the immersion of their country into the American empire from this era, and when the last marines finally departed a generation later the memory of the American intervention remained fixed in their collective psyches.[6]

Pan-American Visions
and Latin American Realities

Among the ironies of the Latin American policy of the United States is the record of Woodrow Wilson, who condemned the interventionism of his predecessor and chastised the economic imperialists yet became the greatest interventionist of his age. The difference, explained his defenders to a largely unreceptive Latin American audience, lay in the purpose of his hemispheric policies, not in the sometimes forceful way he applied them. For Wilson and his contemporaries, imbued with a sense of American mission and the best of intentions, Latin Americans still reserve a special antipathy. Roosevelt may have treated them contemptuously, but at least he possessed the good sense to believe there was little to be gained in trying to remold their political culture. Wilson accepted their reformation as a challenge. Three-quarters of a century later, the United States has yet to shake off the cultural paternalism he grafted onto the Pan-American tissue.

Wilson, a historian, may have known little of Latin America, its social frustrations, and its felt sense of manipulation by the industrial nations, but he saw his ignorance as no hindrance to offering the hemisphere's leaders his advice. After all, he had experienced first-hand the ravaged American South and its efforts to overcome war's devastation and the onslaught of outsiders trying to extract its wealth and mold its politics to their will. The problem lay in his inability to rectify errors in the American treatment of smaller hemispheric countries and preserve the strategic commitment wrought by sixteen years of Republican foreign policy. McKinley had accepted the colonial burden, Roosevelt had refined it with limited interventions in the Caribbean, and Taft had belatedly acknowledged that brute force, not dollars, was sometimes necessary to maintain American interests. Reviewing this legacy of unparalleled American intrusion into neighboring republics, Wilson was pointedly critical of the stifling of "legitimate aspirations" of captive peoples, yet he could not bring himself to admit that they might willingly choose a distinctly un-American path to the present. He sought a united hemisphere but was never able to shape a policy that fused his rhetoric with Latin American realities.

The problem was that the unified hemisphere of which Wilson spoke depended on U.S. direction and guidance. He condemned European economic imperialism in Latin America but with the precision of a social scientist crafted an American-directed hemispheric economic strategy. As a political thinker, he championed Latin America's striving for political liberty and "decent government," but as president he unleashed his verbal wrath upon revolutionary leaders who defied his prescriptions. Despite his professions of a new era in U.S.–Latin American relations, Wilson was, at bottom, as deeply committed as Roosevelt to the maintenance of U.S. strategic interests in the hemisphere. Unlike Roosevelt he genuinely believed a more amicable and certainly more acceptable Latin American policy could be fashioned. He accepted much of the inherited anti-imperialist dogma about the evils of export capitalism and specifically condemned dollar diplomacy. But on taking office he quickly discovered that any desire to chart a new course in hemispheric affairs assumed a secondary role to dealing with immediate problems, as in Mexico, or safeguarding vital military stakes such as the Panama Canal. To his credit, he showed a reluctance to advance the cause of private economic interests in Latin America, as had Taft, yet to the dismay of Latin Americans he undertook even bolder involvement in their internal affairs— to a degree unprecedented in the historical record. His was the classic example of good intentions transmuted into benevolent imperialism. Roosevelt had elected to chastise Latin Americans if they got in the "revolutionary frame of mind." Wilson chose to instruct them forcibly "to elect good men."[7]

Everywhere in the Caribbean Wilson inflicted punishment in the service of laudatory causes—in Haiti, where a high-minded naval officer landed troops in summer 1915 (after a mob had murdered the president and political rivals had plunged the country into a rebellion); in the neighboring Dominican Republic, where Wilson imposed his plan for running the country and, when the Dominican leaders defied him, sent in troops to run them out and install a military government; and in Mexico, which sank into revolution in 1910. Like many Americans, Wilson cheered the ousting of the Mexican dictator Porfirio Díaz and believed his successor, Francisco Madero, who had plotted his rebellion in the United States, a kindred political spirit. Three weeks before Wilson's inauguration, Madero was toppled in a military coup and then taken out and shot. Wilson never recognized the man who replaced him, Victoriano Huerta, and, because other revolutionary aspirants raised the revolutionary banner against Huerta, naively believed he could "direct" Mexico's revolutionary course.

Wilson sent emissaries into every Mexican revolutionary camp and stationed the Atlantic Fleet off Mexico's Gulf shore. He twice dispatched American troops onto Mexican soil—to Veracruz in April 1914 in an occupation that lasted seven months, and into northern Mexico in 1916 in a futile chase after Pancho Villa. The justification for the first lay in Wilson's determination to bring down a government whose leader had, indisputably, ordered the murder of his freely elected predecessor, the second, as retaliation for Villa's raid against Columbus, New Mexico. In Veracruz the American military erected an undeniably honest government in an unarguably corrupt city, a record that earned for the United States not the lasting gratitude but the enduring enmity of Mexico, Mexicans, and, indeed, most Latin Americans. In the Villa chase, the punitive expedition led by John Pershing not only failed to capture Villa and his band but found itself confronting regular Mexican troops in two engagements. The cumulative animosities wrought by American policy toward Mexico in these years gravely affected their relations until World War II.

In the aftermath of the Nicaraguan intervention of 1912, which Wilson had roundly criticized, Secretary of State William Jennings Bryan concluded a canal pact with a compliant Nicaraguan diplomat and with it expanded U.S. economic and political influence in Nicaragua. He tried to impose on Nicaragua a variation of the Platt

Amendment but failed when incensed Republicans (among them former Secretary of State Elihu Root) stopped him. The Wilson administration used the recurring internal discord in Haiti and the Dominican Republic as an excuse to install de facto military governments
that persisted for nineteen years in Haiti and eight years in the Dominican Republic. In the same era the Canal Zone was Americanized
to a degree the president who had "taken" it would have disap-
proved, and Cuba, which had emerged in 1909 from its second military occupation by American troops, was thoroughly subordinated to
American economic and political domination. Even Costa Rica, which
had already demonstrated its distinction among Central American
states for political sophistication, incurred Wilson's wrath in 1917
when the Tinoco brothers seized power. The president, employing
the stipulation against recognition of revolutionary governments in
the 1907 isthmian treaties, refused to recognize the new government.

Yet, paradoxically, he advanced a Pan-American pact to bind the
hemispheric republics in a defensive alliance that, on paper, was
stronger than Bolívar's of ninety years before. In 1913 Wilson had
pledged in an oft-quoted speech at Mobile that the United States
sought no new territorial aggrandizement in the Western Hemisphere. Latin Americans were heartened by his profession of a new
era in American policy. Yet they were quickly disheartened by
Wilson's interpretation of what a reformed Latin American policy
meant. Condemning European economic imperialism in the hemisphere, he sought to advance the economic reach of the United
States. Castigating the gunboat diplomacy of his predecessor, he followed with interventionist policies of his own. As often happened,
the profession of its "civilizing mission" by America (which called for
Latin American cooperation) and the strategic interests of the United
States (which required hemispheric domination) were not easily reconciled. As Herbert Croly had noted in his stimulating book *The
Promise of American Life* (which deals mostly with the domestic polity),
the United States must carry out its "great work" in the hemisphere
as well. Ideally, hemispheric governments would cooperate in the

endeavor to shut out European imperialism. In reality, none save the United States was strong enough to contain the external threat.[8]

Thus the "civilizing mission" of America that Wilson proclaimed joined with the "protective imperialism" of the United States that Roosevelt had earlier applied. Viewed in that way, Wilson's interventionist policies appeared reasonable and logical. But Wilson might have had to do less intervening had he preached less about the mission. Latin Americans judged him mostly on what he did for the United States and its interests, not what he said he wanted to do on behalf of America and its mission. As Americans are fond of saying— and as Latin Americans know—actions speak louder than words.

The Pan-American proposal went out to the Latin American governments just as the Veracruz affair was winding down. A number of them had tried to mediate between the Americans and Mexicans, with limited success; now the Yankees were refurbishing the Bolivarian design and presenting it to them for approval. Six governments, representing mostly small countries under close American scrutiny, heartily approved. But the larger countries, even nominally sympathetic Brazil, expressed strong reservations. And Mexico, now ruled by the determined (and defiant) Venustiano Carranza, who chafed under American incursions into his country, rallied Latin America against Wilson's pact. In both Haiti and the Dominican Republic, where Wilson had proposed undeniably beneficial political advice, the diplomats ultimately turned over matters to the U.S. military, which reluctantly but forcefully carried out his strictures. Inevitably, he turned his concerns to the European war, and in the process the international community he had strived for took on a transatlantic not a hemispheric shape. Not until the eve of World War II did plans for a Pan-American alliance reappear in the U.S. hemispheric strategy.

"To make the world safe for democracy" evoked a higher purpose to American entry in World War I, but Latin Americans had good reason to distrust the credos of America. More than a decade before, at Rio de Janeiro, Elihu Root, had tried to persuade doubtful Latin American delegates that Theodore Roosevelt's bullying actually represented the policy of restraint. Since then, the United States had reoccupied Cuba, launched a major invasion of recalcitrant Nicaragua, established blatantly military governments in Haiti and the Dominican Republic, and twice invaded Mexico. In every case, American officials pointed out, the situation had warranted our course of action, but the collective impact of these incursions alienated a generation of Latin American intellectuals and disabused their political leaders from looking northward for the model political culture.

Even more befuddling were Washington's policies toward its tropical wards, which vacillated between benign neglect and intensive efforts to reorder what Americans considered backward places. Puerto Rico, largely forgotten since its annexation, achieved a measure of status in 1917 with the Jones Act, which made its inhabitants citizens but did not accord the island the rights of a state in the Union. Then the island lapsed into colonial desuetude until the mid-1930s, when the Franklin D. Roosevelt administration dramatically publicized another salvage operation. At the southern extremity of empire lay the Panama Canal Zone, technically only a leasehold from Panama. With the opening of the canal in 1914 it was transformed into a utopian socialist enclave with propertyless white American supervisors and their West Indian labor force. In Central America lay captive Nicaragua and Honduras—the first an American protectorate and the second an independent country with a political and economic system largely beholden to American fruit companies. In Haiti and the Dominican Republic, the civilians bequeathed to the American military two more protectorates, ruled by officers committed to implanting the American sense of community in cultures they considered generally unsuited for it.

Not unexpectedly, then, Latin Americans were somewhat skeptical about American rhetoric when the United States entered World War I in April 1917. Yet except for Argentina and Mexico, where Wilson's meddling had given German agents an opportunity to conduct a secret war intended to provoke a Mexican attack on the United States, Latin American countries were not hostile to American aims. They had rejected Wilson's Pan-American pact and continued to condemn

American imperialism, but they did not embrace the German cause. For the smaller republics of the Caribbean, strategic realities made traditional neutrality an impossibility. As American investment and influence diminished with the Mexican Revolution, it advanced in the Caribbean. As Europeans retreated, the long-sought South American market in oil, cables, and finance capitalism expanded. When the war ended the process accelerated, and with it came American cultural pretensions.

The weak Caribbean republics had already bowed to the American presence, but the mainland South American countries were more insulated and resisting. Argentina looked upon the "civilizing mission" of American trade, investments, and missionary diplomacy as a threat to its own considerable prospect for leading the Pan-American movement. Only the Brazilians, who already spoke of their "special relationship" with the United States, perceived little threat in Wilson's vigorous diplomacy. They had recognized economic realities when their European credit markets collapsed; from 1914 on they had had to look to the larger banking houses of New York. At the urging of J. P. Morgan the largest of these lending institutions had formed a South American Group, agreeing to pool their resources in extending loans.[9] Direct investments and greater commercial links followed as American lenders were no longer dependent on the Latin American branches of European banks to act as intermediaries. In the summer of 1915, when the administration lifted the ban on loans to belligerents, some of these funds found their way back to Europe, but the general conditions laid the foundation for a veritable American financial assault on Latin America after Versailles.

With U.S. entry into the war came the inevitable proliferation of bureaucracies and their coteries of agents, investigators, and experts dispatched to missions in Latin America. They kept watch on German spies and tried to prevent vital products from reaching the European enemy. There was a minor brouhaha over Mexican sisal from Yucatán when enterprising Mexican factors demanded what American officials considered an exorbitant price. Herbert Hoover, czar of the Food Administration, responded with threats to use corn, a staple in the

Mexican diet, as a weapon. In the conduct of policy the State Department often found its goals confounded by such intrusions. The Shipping Board and the War Trade Board were especially meddlesome.

The most crucial issue, of course, was Latin America's position on the war. Within the State Department there was apprehension that the animosity against the military governments in Haiti and the Dominican Republic would seriously damage U.S. wartime diplomacy in South America. Washington arrogantly expected the smaller countries to do their duty and declare war. Costa Rica, Nicaragua, Panama, Honduras, Guatemala, Cuba, and Haiti willingly complied. In South America only Brazil followed their lead. Argentina and Mexico were determinedly neutral; Chile, Colombia, Paraguay, Venezuela, and El Salvador joined them. The remainder—Bolivia, Ecuador, Peru, Uruguay, and the Dominican Republic—broke diplomatic relations with Germany and her allies. (The U.S. military government in the Dominican Republic refrained from declaring war to relieve Washington of obligations for economic assistance.) In declaring its neutrality, the Uruguayan government announced what eventually became a principle of inter-American public law: though itself a neutral in the conflict, Uruguay regarded other hemispheric countries that declared war as nonbelligerents.

John Barrett, the former diplomat who had become director of the Pan-American Union, zealously argued that South Americans were not pro-German. When several governments criticized him for impertinently speaking for them, he compounded his gaucherie by suggesting that official envoys be dispatched into Latin America to solicit support for the war effort. In the end he lost his job as director of the Pan-American Union and slipped into obscurity. Washington followed this embarrassment with yet another. George Creel, head of the Committee on War Information, launched a propaganda drive to persuade Latin Americans that the United States was fighting for ideals, not territory, in Europe.[10] The Mexicans were unconvinced, but the Argentines, usually condemnatory of U.S. policy, lauded American entry into the war as inspiration for a new Pan-Americanism. But the Argentine president, Hipólito Irigoyen, was not sufficiently moved to break diplomatic relations with the Central Powers.[11]

Latin America's greatest burden remained the dislocation of its economies brought on by the loss of European markets. The hemisphere was largely unprepared for the economic impact World War I had on the republics. In 1915, at the First Pan-American Financial Conference, the delegates had discussed problems in trade, transportation, and finance and made minor adjustments, but they could not realistically anticipate that more severe measures might be required. Guatemala, which had sold its high-quality coffee to Germany, was compelled to dump the crop of 1917–18 at low prices in San Francisco. Other commodities, such as iron and steel, now came from the United States, which imposed limits on exports of vital wartime materials or, when available for the hemispheric market, charged exorbitant prices for them. Most Latin American countries found themselves far down the priority list for goods now obtainable only from the United States.

As Americans replaced European lenders and suppliers, Washington expected hemispheric governments to cooperate in everything from confiscating German property to blacklisting native firms doing business with German companies. With these measures the Wilson administration interfered in such mundane transactions as the import of coal in Argentina and the sale of Chilean nitrates. In its determination to wrest control of Latin American trade from British domination the United States occasionally took reprisals against British companies. Toward the end of the war the Departments of War and Navy objected to Britain's sale of war supplies to South American governments and opposed a British coaling station in Peru. The answer to European military influence in Latin America, the admirals said, was the prompt dispatch of U.S. military missions.

Ariel and Caliban

One legacy of the war was that the United States supplanted Europe in the economic balance of power in Latin America. The erosion of Europe's position had begun before the war and escalated rapidly in its aftermath, and it represented not a simple Marxian evolution of the dollar following the flag (or the flag in supportive pursuit of the dollar) but, more precisely, the parallel endeavors of private and public economic interests.

During the war, when it was apparent that the patterns of U.S. commerce and investment in Latin America were shifting, Congress became more supportive of private economic interests in the region. The Edge and Webb-Pomerene acts permitted American banks to establish branch offices in foreign cities and freed export houses that combined efforts to gain access to foreign markets from prosecution under the antitrust law. There was immediate concern that at war's end European competitors would challenge the United States in controlling Latin American petroleum reserves and cables (then of considerable strategic value) and regain domination of the Latin American credit market. The threat of this economic challenge turned out to be greatly exaggerated, and within a few years the State Department declared that it would no longer render judgments on private loans to Latin American governments. American petroleum, cable, and international investment concerns had already grown weary of the political restraints imposed from Washington.

There were exceptions to this apparent divorce between public and private actors on the hemispheric economic stage. In Mexico, where revolutionary nationalism, expressed in the 1917 constitutional declaration that the nation's subsoil wealth belonged to the people, collided with long-standing foreign mining and petroleum leases, the department doggedly supported the American companies.[12] And in the Caribbean, where the United States was dismantling the military occupations of the previous decade, it insisted on retaining certain financial prerogatives. As part of the price for ridding themselves of American proconsuls, the Dominicans obligated themselves to pay off the bonds issued by the occupation government. In Cuba, the U.S. ambassador often imparted his financial guidance to usually compliant Cuban leaders.

Contemporary critics, particularly the vocal socialist analysts of export capital in the 1920s, saw little substantive difference between dollar diplomacy, which symbolized the official promotion (and use) of private investment, and the diplomacy of the dollar, which stood for a less conspiratorial relationship between Washington and Wall Street. The latter brought supportive technical advice to Latin American governments improperly schooled in public finance. Under the stern guidance of Secretary of Commerce Herbert Hoover and the chief of the Bureau of Foreign Trade, Julius Klein, Washington insinuated an unexpected moral tone in this effort. Klein perhaps best expressed this blending of American cultural and economic credos. Latin American countries, he wrote, "deserve the most effective collaboration from their Northern Anglo-Saxon neighbors, not simply in capital, but in technically trained personnel and in schooling for their own native experts. . . . Indeed, the whole of our westward march across the continent, our struggles with precisely similar frontier difficulties, and our prolonged experiences with the same problems in transportation, mining, forestry, and agriculture, should certainly provide abundant sources of helpful experiences in solving these problems."[13]

On a hemispheric scale, then, Hoover sought the same cooperation with the private sector that he pursued on the domestic front—the associationist state with Washington acting as friendly mediator between private American investors and Latin American governments. The smaller Caribbean states, in the face of the lingering threat of Yankee intervention, had no choice but to yield. But South Americans, suspicious of American motives, never accommodated the persuasive rhetoric emanating from Washington. They accepted foreign banking, mining, and petroleum ventures as means of promoting national development and employment. Halfheartedly they listened to Hoover's strictures warning against loans for the purchase of armaments or some other impolitic diversion of funds.

Hoover and Klein were the last of a line of American economic advisers to Latin America in the tradition inaugurated by Elihu Root at the Rio conference in 1906, continued under John Barrett's direction at the 1911 commercial conference, and pursued more aggressively after World War I. The intent was the promotion of *functional* as opposed to *authoritative* government, a belief grounded in the political wisdom that the duty of government lay in the sustenance of sound economic philosophy carried out mostly by private enterprise. That Latin America's economic and political values were rooted in the centralist philosophies of authoritarian Spanish and Portuguese monarchs—rather than in Adam Smith or John Locke—was not, to Hoover, a matter of great consequence.

In the 1920s Latin American intellectuals largely rejected the business ethic that prevailed in the United States. The movement had begun a generation earlier in the writings of José Enrique Rodó, the Uruguayan writer, who had condemned American materialism. The United States had brought its power, and its wealth, and its technology southward, but despite its professions of godliness, he argued, it had abandoned God in its quest. Abruptly Latin American thinkers who had once written admiringly of the northern industrial democracy began to look more closely at their own cultures as models for the future. They had done precious little for the downtrodden and had little intention of doing much for them in the future, but in vilifying American culture they glorified their own. Rodó spoke of a Latin race that repudiated the unholy combination of Protestantism and materialism. In *Ariel*, published in the aftermath of the American triumph over hapless Spain, Rodó employed Shakespearean images to show that American materialism led to mediocrity. Latin America, by extolling idealism, must reach for spiritual heights.The literary outburst continued with Rubén Darío, the Nicaraguan poet, perhaps the greatest poet in the Spanish language, who spent a dissolute life in Paris but inveighed against Yankees trudging across his native land.

Such an achievement, it seemed, was impossible as long as Latin Americans retained their jealousies of American wealth and power. Rodó's response, echoed by Manuel Ugarte in *The Destiny of a Continent*, held that the United States possessed no culture worthy of admiration. The collapse of Europe in the carnage of the war removed the Old World as a symbol. In the void Latin Americans must construct their own version of civilization. In Argentina the cause took the form of glorification of the nation's turbulent *gaucho* past; in Brazil, the creative forces of a miscegenated people; in Haiti (still in the grip of American power), in the resurgence of negritude, the nation's

African roots; and in Peru, in the country's Incan past. Everywhere the late nineteenth-century positivist credo, which Latin Americans had once embraced from the European and American model, stood in disrepute.[14]

For many Latin American thinkers, the Mexican Revolution represented the collective protest of an oppressed people against American-style order and progress. When it ended, Mexico continued its defiant break with tradition. The revolutionary heirs drove the priests from the schools and dispatched their own educational zealots into the countryside. José Vasconcelos, the educational czar, spoke of the cosmic race. The muralist José Clemente Orozco glorified Mexico's Indian past. Culture and nationalism were fused into a new dynamic, "spiritual nationalism," which transcended the narrow political variety. Out of it the first generation of postrevolutionary leaders fashioned a new political order. They did not create a democratic or an egalitarian Mexico, but they drew on the xenophobic heritage of its people to raise the cultural banner against the outside world and its credos. Throughout the decade of the 1920s Mexico defied U.S. diplomatic pressures to accommodate American petroleum and mining companies, its strategy of charting the course of Mexican finance, and American efforts to mediate the bitter church-state conflict. The nationalism born in the Revolution and its violence no longer tolerated passivity before American power. There were confrontations and threats of U.S. retaliation and rumors of war against "Bolshevik" Mexico, but the country did not lower the flag of defiance.[15]

Just as the image of a democratic United States had deteriorated with the exercise of the police power and the big stick, so, too, had the stature of the enterprising Yankee in the Latin American marketplace. In Mexico the revolution wrought an anti-Americanism that persisted, making not only American business but even tourism a riskier matter. Farther on, the banana companies of Central America, once familial operations, had by the 1920s evolved into powerful challenges to the state. United Fruit, incorporated in 1899 by three Americans, was the dominant economic force in Guatemala and Honduras and had extensive holdings in the tropical lowlands of eastern Costa

Rica. In Honduras, the only reliable sources of government revenue were the Cuyamel, Standard, and United Fruit companies. In Venezuela and Bolivia, American oil companies loomed ever larger on the economic horizon. The presence of American multinationals—the term was not widely used then but accurately reflects the scope of their operations—confirmed leftist suspicions that Latin America was rapidly slipping under American economic domination. But the more ominous challenge of these powerful companies, which in the smaller republics had become the largest employer of "native" labor, lay in their imprint on national culture.[16]

Guatemala's relations with United Fruit illustrated the apprehension its leaders sensed about the penetration of an American economic giant into a stratified society of master and man. At the turn of the century, the country had fallen under the sway of Manuel Estrada Cabrera, who virtually enslaved its Indian masses in a modern labor system. When United Fruit began to shift its operations away from the Nicaraguan east coast, it looked to Honduras and its rich northern coastland and fertile sites in northeastern Guatemala. Unlike compliant Honduran executives, who generally gave the banana tycoons anything they wanted, Estrada was determined to be their partners. He resisted efforts from Washington to transform the country into a financial protectorate but struck deals with Minor Keith, one of United Fruit's founding fathers, to establish banana enclaves in the sparsely populated Guatemalan east. Keith was then permitted to build a rail line into the interior that ultimately expanded into the United Railways of Central America. Estrada made sure that the banana laborers—many of them descendants of black West Indians who had settled on the neglected Caribbean coast two centuries earlier—remained in the protective enclaves around Livingston, Puerto Barrios, and the Montagua River Valley. In such manner the Guatemalan shielded his people from whatever economic and political dynamic such operations generated.

Years before, when he was carving his banana empire in Limón province in Costa Rica, Keith had struck a similar arrangement with the Costa Rican elite in the highlands. He built hospitals and schools for his black laborers and connected the capital to the Caribbean with a railroad. United Fruit governed in the lowlands, but it kept its black subjects from migrating into the highland interior. As did their American counterparts elsewhere in Latin America, the banana companies accommodated the elite. But the manner in which they operated— their organizational structure with its dependence on a managerial elite, along with the profits they generated—offered a tempting prospect of material reward and a social stature that depended on what one did for a living. Latin America's critical intelligentsia may have written off the American intruders as crass émigrés from a materialist culture, but the penniless day laborers under their sway discovered that a few jingling coins in the pocket made one feel less like a peasant.

Yankee Imperialism at Bay

A foreign policy predicated on strategic necessity, economic expansion, and political tutelage can inspire gratitude but only among those subjects who benefit from its presence. Among them it leaves unforgettable impressions of what a great power can do. Unintentionally but inevitably, the intruding country—whether it comes to do ill or, in the case of the United States, to do good—will inspire an opposition. The opposition may take the form of a cultural defiance, in which the people simply pretend to adapt or change their ways long enough to benefit from the largesse of an intruding benefactor. (As the Mexicans say, the American requires self-deception. He must be convinced that he is doing a great deal of good for others even though he intuitively knows he is acting from self-interest.) Toward the end of what most Americans considered a benign intrusion into Latin America, their Caribbean charges were no closer to democracy than they had been in the beginning. American browbeating, interventions, and an occasional occupation government had momentarily gotten them out of the "revolutionary frame of mind." When the American grip began to relax in the mid-1920s, the opposition to

American rule, which had diminished but never disappeared, resurfaced in more violent form.

Shortly after the war ended, the architects of Wilsonian penetration of Latin America found themselves under assault. In 1919 the military narrowly averted a scandal over alleged atrocities in Haiti. A year later, during the heated presidential campaign, the American imperial structure came in for harsh assessment from the most unimaginative of political candidates—Warren Gamaliel Harding, who declared that as president he would not instruct West Indians in the art of democracy with bayonets. In responding, vice-presidential Democratic candidate Franklin D. Roosevelt publicly boasted that he had written Haiti's constitution, which the country had been virtually compelled to adopt by the presence of American marines. It was an impolitic assertion, indicative of the callousness of Wilsonian rule.

The nation's blunders in the Caribbean did not determine the outcome of the election, but Harding's triumph indicated a public weariness with the Caribbean burden his predecessor had undertaken. For Latin Americans the apparent lessening of American will presented both opportunity and a dilemma. It meant, among other things, that the United States was admitting it held no lasting formula for Latin America's problems. At the same time, as had been made clear in Article 21 of the League of Nations convenant, the United States had no intention of retreating from the tradition of regional domination, expressed concisely in the Monroe Doctrine. Most Latin American states, confronted with the prospect of joining the League (and, presumably, accepting the Monroe Doctrine) or remaining aloof from the international organization and thus losing its protective benefits, naturally preferred abandoning the doctrine. One of the more enthusiastic proponents of hemispheric unity, the Uruguayan foreign minister Baltasar Brum, boldly advanced the idea of a Pan-American League of Nations.

After an intensive congressional investigation in 1921–22, Washington declared it was withdrawing its troops from the Dominican Republic and reorganizing the Haitian occupation. In this atmosphere

of retrenchment from Caribbean empire, the fifth Pan-American conference met at Santiago, Chile. Latin American delegates were eager
to tout the League of Nations and denounce the lingering American
empire in the tropics. The U.S. delegation, instructed not to discuss
the League in the wake of the Senate's adamant rejection, listened
gloomily as Latin American spokesmen extolled the Bolivarian dream
of hemispheric unity and assailed Washington's domination of the
Pan-American Union. They championed the efforts to codify inter-
American law—which, to be sure, the United States had sustained
since the Commission of Jurists had been established at Rio de Janeiro
in 1906—and insisted on discussing "political" questions. In the end
the Americans declared that the United States preferred a Pan-American system distinct from the League and that the Monroe Doctrine,
which Wilson had advanced momentarily as hemispheric policy, had
reverted to a unilateral policy of the United States.

The willingness of the Americans to listen to Latin American complaints probably countered the rhetorical assault of the Argentines,
who desperately sought a hemispheric declaration on naval armaments to check Brazil's rapid expansion in shipbuilding. Of greater
significance was Latin America's participation in both the Pan-American system and the League of Nations, thus demonstrating, apparently, that it was possible to belong to the Western Hemisphere and to
the world. A recurring theme in Latin America's protestation was
U.S. intervention in hemispheric affairs and the manifest need for the
Pan-American system to avow the principle of nonintervention and
reaffirm the rights of states. Until the end of World War I, when the
European threat to hemispheric security had subsided, the American
response held that the Pan-American system had neither produced
an effective hemispheric security structure nor codified a hemispheric
law that all the states supported. Latin American delegates—especially the Argentines—continued to speak of the rights of states;
their American counterparts, of the "rights and duties" of those
states. Unless the Pan-American system required the second,
declared a succession of U.S. secretaries of state, hemispheric govern-

ments could not reasonably expect to enjoy the full benefits of the first.

Behind the formal sessions another drama unfolded. As so often for the United States in its hemispheric endeavors, the irritant was Mexico. Denied American recognition because of disputes over Mexico's 1917 constitution, which boded ill for U.S. companies still operating in the country, the Mexican government had refused to send a delegation. But every day a number of Latin American participants trooped over to the residence of the Mexican ambassador to Chile to discuss Mexico's position on this or that matter. More embarrassing was the sight of a mute Henry Fletcher, chief of the American representation, under express instructions *not* to respond to the effusive praise of Woodrow Wilson delivered by the president of Paraguay.[17]

Later that year, Secretary of State Charles Evans Hughes, in a centenary address on the Monroe Doctrine, reaffirmed its anti-European intentions. The United States was retreating from empire, it recognized the juridical equality of Latin American states, but it would not join them in a regional security pact. At the same time the United States was boldly reasserting its primacy in Central America in a series of treaties aimed at containing isthmian discord by the expedient of recognizing neither revolutionary governments nor anybody related to a revolutionary who gained power by the electoral process. The restriction was even more severe than that laid down by Theodore Roosevelt in 1907. In its determination to chastise Nicaragua for its meddlesomeness, the American government had ignored that treaty and invaded the country in 1910.

In late 1926 Nicaraguan disturbances brought yet another intervention. The United States had no Platt Amendment with Nicaragua, as it did with Cuba, but since 1912 Nicaragua had been a virtual protectorate with a marine legation guard symbolizing the reach of American power. In the mid-1920s the State Department quietly withdrew them, but a few weeks later the country was plunged into a political crisis. The new president had tried to placate the opposition party with jobs; his efforts only served to irritate his own political family.

The leader of the disgruntled was Emiliano Chamorro, called affectionately the General, who had helped the Americans crush the revolt of 1912. Through intrigue and intimidation he drove the president from office and maneuvered himself into the executive chair. His putative friends in Washington either had to accept him or find some alternative. They chose the latter.

Technically, Chamorro had violated the 1923 treaties, which the United States was bound to uphold. But Chamorro's seizure of power had precipitated a revolt in the name of the ousted vice-president, Juan Sacasa, who had assembled a dozen revolutionary groups vowing to place him in the presidency. Whatever its displeasure with Chamorro, Washington was not prepared to tolerate Nicaraguans settling their own affairs in a revolution that threatened its interests. In late 1926 the American minister pushed Chamorro out. In his exit the General was able to prevent Sacasa from taking power. The national assembly, with the blessing of the American government, selected Adolfo Díaz, Washington's choice, in 1912. Shortly afterward, American troops began landing on Nicaragua's eastern coast, ostensibly to safeguard the considerable foreign business there but in reality to influence the outcome of Nicaraguan politics. A considerably larger intervention occurred on the west coast and, in spring 1927, Henry Stimson arrived, urging mediation and pledging fair elections. All save one of the rebel leaders struck a deal. The holdout, Augusto César Sandino, raised an army of men, women, and children and declared, in words of defiance heard as far away as China, that Nicaraguans possessed the right of self-determination.[18]

Policy in Central America made no provision for such a claim, nor could Americans understand how Sandino could mold a revolutionary army on such a slogan. But in time Sandino had volunteers from all but one Latin American republic. To Americans, he was an improbable leader: he would not stand and fight, he ran into the mountains, and (when the marines pursued him) he ran off to Honduras or Mexico. Yet somehow he managed to acquire a following and a vaunted hemispheric fame. His ability to do so is a feature of Latin American politics that outsiders have rarely understood—the "good leader" does not acquire his reputation so much by action, accomplishment, or managerial skills as by articulating universal truths he only vaguely understands. These he deftly meshes with appeals to spiritualism. He goes off into the mountains, communes with the gods, and returns with proclamations of truth and denunciations of all those from the outside who deny national self-determination and the people's will. It does not matter that the nation cannot achieve the destiny its leaders prescribe. Man, after all, cannot be perfected, but he must be redeemed. It did not matter that Nicaragua in the 1920s was not a nation in any meaningful sense and that Sandino was not going to make it over into a nation. He expressed the sentiments of nationhood to a people who did not expect him (or any other leader) to overcome history's and nature's legacy to Nicaragua by making it into a nation. What counted was the spiritual force of his words and the images of what he represented. To reverse the American saying, words speak louder than actions.

Dutiful to its pledge, the United States supervised an indisputably honest election in 1928. When Sandino denounced the American presence as imperialism, President Calvin Coolidge dispatched five thousand marines to roam the Nicaraguan north in a vain search for a man their commander derisively called a "mule thief." The Sandino chase was denounced throughout the hemisphere, in the U.S. Senate, and in the press. Senator William E. Borah of Idaho, alluding to Coolidge's statement about "our special interests" in Nicaragua, decried the intervention as an "oil and mahogany policy." In truth, the American commitment posed a more troublesome issue than safeguarding foreign property in Nicaragua. There were indisputable security interests in Nicaragua; the issue lay in the means of maintaining them.

Roosevelt's notion of intruding into unruly societies in limited interventions, exercising a police power, had yielded to the Wilsonian view of intervening more intensely to "teach them to elect good men" and inculcate a respect for political order. That policy was now failing. It suffered not from the failure of American military strength but from the lack of will to sustain it against even a poorly equipped foe. The civilians had given the task of community building in the Caribbean to the soldiers more than a decade before. But they could not govern until they had intervened, and where they had dispatched troops—in Veracruz, in Hispaniola, and now in Nicaragua—they could not easily escape the burden of the colonizer. Even at its height, the British Empire had strained under the continual burden of policing its outposts. Americans had always believed the United States could avoid this dilemma by largely rejecting colonialism and exercising its influence through informal but effective political measures. What Americans did not understand was that for Latin Americans the distinction Americans made between their purpose and those of Europe's formal empires was not that important. What mattered was U.S. actions and, more important, the American presence on their soil.

The jungle war in Nicaragua convinced a generation of civilians in the State Department that they must retake command of Latin American policy. Nicaragua provided the opportunity. At the height of the intervention, the sixth Pan-American conference convened in Havana. Coolidge himself led the American delegation, arriving in a U.S. warship. He was greeted at the dock by Cuban president Gerardo Machado, the cattle thief turned businessman who had clamped down on dissent and promised the nervous Americans an uneventful meeting.

Urged on by Mexico and Argentina, the Latin Americans were determined to debate Nicaragua. Coolidge delivered a predictably uninspiring address and looked to former Secretary of State Hughes to hold back the verbal tide. Expecting platitudes about political order and the security of the Panama Canal, the delegates heard instead mild assessments of the U.S. position. When the final plenary session took up the issue of intervention, the rhetoric escalated. Anti-American diatribes rang throughout the hall. Hughes responded with a defense of the Monroe Doctrine as a protective shield for Latin Americans. States have an obligation to protect their citizens in countries that cannot safeguard their lives and property. This was not intervention but "interposition."

It was a euphemism, perhaps, but Hughes's choice of words

momentarily salvaged American prestige. The Argentines had tried to get an absolute ban on intervention but failed and stalked out. Hughes electrified the audience, won praise for confronting the issue, and returned to the United States realizing that some other basis for protecting American interests must be found. In 1930 the solictor general of the State Department, J. Reuben Clark, declared the Roosevelt corollary an unsound and impolitic legal basis for intervention. Roosevelt had transformed the Monroe Doctrine, he said, from a policy of United States versus Europe to United States versus Latin America. There was an immediate outcry about retreating from responsibilities, and the "repudiation" of Roosevelt's corollary was abruptly repudiated,[19] but there was no turning back to the large-scale interventions of the past. The following year Stimson, now secretary of state, announced that American property owners in Nicaragua must look to Managua and not Washington to safeguard their interests. As for U.S. strategic interests in the region, international law provided the nation with sufficient foundation to safeguard its interests, by intervention if necessary. Washington wanted a "special relationship" with Latin America; it would not relinquish its historic, unilateral interests in the Caribbean without a firm commitment that the smaller countries of the region would safeguard them.

It found such an assurance in a generation of Caribbean strongmen, leaders it did not really want, did not particularly like, and ultimately disowned. It accepted them, frankly, because their interventions in U.S.-crafted governments had achieved military security for the United States in a region vital to its interests and opportunity for private American capital and companies. It accepted them, finally, because the cost of a policing role in the Caribbean had gone beyond U.S. willingness to pay for the service with American troops. Democracy and the American Dream, the inspirational goals of United States intervention and the hallmarks of American culture, were casualties. In fragile and unstable small countries the United States confronted backward but changeable economies and political systems but resilient cultures with their own priorities, their own ways of doing things, and their own unappreciated strengths.

6   Good Neighbors

The American performance at Havana validated Latin American intellectuals' generally contemptuous assessment of U.S. cultural unworthiness and innate aggressive instincts. The Mexican Isidro Fabela had expressed a widely held sentiment two years before: "Every dollar that crosses our frontier not only has stamped on its obverse the North American eagle but carries also in its hard soul the flag of the stars and stripes, which is today the most imperialistic in the world."[1] From the Mexican border towns to Patagonia, the continent's philosophers railed against a crass United States inflicting its Protestant materialism on a hapless but proud culture.

Some, like the Argentine philosopher José Ingenieros, called for the "moral union" of Hispanic peoples against the menace of Wall Street. Others, inspired by a Chilean proposal, urged a Latin American league to supplant the spiritless Pan-American Union of Yankee domination, a cause advanced before the League of Nations in 1930. There was a limited but publicized Hispanic countercultural invasion in the defiant work of the Mexican muralists Diego Rivera and José Clemente Orozco, who parodied American capitalism in their artistry on public buildings from California to New York. Less subtle in his assault was the Peruvian socialist Víctor Raúl Haya de la Torre, who had visited New York in the mid-1920s and sailed away thinking how Wall Street had overtaken the Statue of Liberty as America's conscience. He returned to Peru and began preaching another creed. The real Latin America, said Haya, must rediscover its Indian past and reject the domination of U.S. business. He formed the American Revolutionary Popular Alliance (its Spanish acronym is APRA), which preached hemispheric unity, internationalization of the Panama Canal, neutrality, and socialism appropriate to Indo-America.

Such condemnations had become an issue in American politics and within the American government. In 1928 Franklin D. Roosevelt, who had played a minor role in shaping the Wilsonian empire in the Caribbean, confessed that the United States had few supporters among the Latin American states. His discovery was not limited to Democratic aspirants. The Coolidge administration had already confronted an obstinate generation of revolutionary leaders in Mexico. The president's college friend Dwight Morrow had descended on Mexico City professing to "like" Mexicans, which had prompted the Mexican president, Plutarco Elías Calles, to ease somewhat the government's pressures on American oil companies in Mexico. But when Morrow tried to get the Mexicans to accommodate U.S. suggestions in their financial planning (a not uncommon practice of American diplomats in the 1920s) he encountered Mexican resistance. Under pressure from American Catholics, he tried to mediate between church and state in the bitter aftermath of the Cristero revolt, when priests displaced by government teachers rallied peasants in central Mexico against them. The government retaliated with harsh anticlerical laws. Morrow placated them, and the churches reopened, but the revolutionary decrees remained on the books.

The massive show of military strength in Nicaragua had amply demonstrated American domination in the hemisphere. Yet, unexpectedly, the frustration of the Sandino chase, the inability to chastise the Mexicans, the frustrated withdrawal from the Dominican Republic, and American defensiveness at the Havana Pan-American conference had collectively exposed the inherent disability of U.S. policy in the Caribbean after the triumph over Spain. Even Herbert Hoover, who as secretary of commerce had orchestrated a Latin American policy of commercial and financial enlightenment through the Bureau of Foreign Trade and Commerce, sensed the limitation of American influence. Shortly after trouncing Al Smith in the 1928 presidential election, he embarked on a goodwill tour of Latin America, disavowing any intention to play "big brother" in the hemisphere.

The Crisis of Democratic Capitalism

The decline of public enthusiasm—especially congressional support—for the Nicaraguan intervention and the onset of the depression were practically simultaneous. The cost of intervention made its political acceptance even less palatable. Condemned at home, the capitalists found few sympathizers for dispatching the marines to safeguard their investments in the tropics. In 1931 the House Committee on Appropriations listened gloomily as the quartermaster general explained that marine operations in Haiti, the Dominican Republic, and Nicaragua from 1915 had consumed $9 million of public money. The anti-interventionists, predictably, considered this a heavy charge for the cause of expanding democracy in the tropics and of "teaching them to elect good men." From those who had identified the country's strategic interests in the Caribbean as a justifiable motive for interventionist policies, there was a reluctant admission that some means other than the use of military force had to be found to carry out U.S. policy.

As the depression sank in, even true believers in the country's democratic mission began to question the practicality of interventionist policies. In 1930 six civilian governments in Latin America, among them Argentina, Peru, and Brazil, fell under military rule. In South America the demise of professedly democratic governments brought scarcely a murmur of American disapproval. But even among nominally compliant Central American republics American tolerance of antidemocratic elements proved surprising. In Guatemala and El Salvador revolutionaries shot their way into power, in defiance of the 1923 treaties that forbade recognition of coup d'etat governments, persisted, and eventually won U.S. recognition. In subservient Panama, where a public outburst had killed a revision of the hated 1903 canal treaty, a middle-class reform movement tossed out an aristocratic president in a bloodless coup and escaped American interference—despite cries of threats to canal security.

In Nicaragua the numbers of American troops began to decline sharply after 1929, and a dispirited American military shifted its policing and the American government its political burden to Anastasio Somoza García and the National Guard. In 1930 a political crisis (and a hurricane) provided Rafael Leonidas Trujillo with the opportunity to inaugurate a thirty-one-year tyranny in the Dominican Republic. To Cuba, Roosevelt dispatched a special emissary, Sumner Welles, whose task was to persuade Gerardo Machado to step down as president. Already, however, a generation of Cuban professionals and youthful idealists, who had been fighting Machado for several years, had raised the flag of rebellion. Machado resigned and, following several hectic weeks, a reformist junta under Ramón Grau San Martín took power. For five months, the revolution of 1933 held sway—altering Cuba's political, economic, and social culture—as a nervous Roosevelt watched. Roosevelt named Welles ambassador, gave him extraordinary latitude to operate in the confusing Cuban political scene, and surrounded the island with the menacing firepower of the U.S. Navy. In the meantime his secretary of state was in Montevideo pledging the administration to a policy of nonintervention, limited only by the obligations of treaties and the rights of nations under international law. The Pentarchy of Grau instilled a momentary revolutionary triumph among a generation of young Cubans who had plotted against the Machado dictatorship and suffered the indignities of the Platt Amendment. But in the end, it fell—the victim, many Cubans still believe, of American nonrecognition and the plotting of Welles and Fulgencio Batista.

All three received Washington's reluctant approbation. Inevitably, when their rule degenerated into sordid familial tyrannies, the Good Neighbor policy espoused by Roosevelt and his generation would be lambasted as evidence of American sustenance of Caribbean dictatorship.[2] But this was not a choice easily made. The changing priorities of American policy toward the hemisphere are often over-. looked. Until the 1920s, American security interests had taken precedence, followed by promotion of U.S. trade and investments, which had escalated after World War I. The Nicaraguan intervention severely damaged U.S. political standing in the hemisphere, which Hoover and especially Roosevelt sought to correct by more than symbolic gestures. Just as potentially harmful was the collapsing American economic stake in Latin America, which followed closely in the wake of Latin America's virtually united condemnation of U.S. policy at Havana. From 1929 until the eve of Roosevelt's inauguration, American exports to Latin America declined in value by more than 75 percent, its imports from the republics by 68 percent. Bond creditors heard equally grim news. In the 1920s American brokers had merrily sold American investors bonds on Latin American governments and municipalities. In the global repudiation of debt after the collapse of the American economy, Latin America was in the forefront.

Embarking on a program of economic nationalism at home, Roosevelt and especially Secretary of State Cordell Hull recognized that restoring hemispheric trade was crucial. For Hull, an unreconstructed Wilsonian, the means to accomplish this lay in a vigorous reciprocal trade program. If the United States lowered its tariff, imported more from Latin America, and signed regional and bilateral commercial agreements that opened up the hemisphere to American products, he believed, trade barriers elsewhere, especially in the more desirable industrial markets of Europe, would tumble. Latin America provided the opening because its economies had been historically more responsive to pressures from the industrial economies of Europe and the United States. Pan-American economic cooperation thus became a State Department slogan from the beginning of the Roosevelt administration. When the Reciprocal Trade Agreements Act became law in 1934, the president could expand American exports to Latin America and jeopardize neither domestic industry, which faced no competition from the south, nor domestic commodities because the covered imports were materials such as rubber, bananas, bauxite, and platinum, which Americans did not produce.

The Good Neighbor credo was "nonintervention, noninterference, and reciprocity." Roosevelt pledged not to send marines to chastise Latin Americans, and not to browbeat their governments with heavy-handed policies, but he asked them to reciprocate by accommodating his international economic program. In practical terms, this meant that he expected the smaller republics in the Caribbean to acquiesce in Washington's economic priorities but was willing to make concessions that cost very little. The Panamanians, for example, still chafing under the 1903 canal treaty, negotiated the end of the humiliating protectorate and won a few economic concessions but had to accept responsibility for defending the canal. More indicative of the ulterior purpose of the Good Neighbor was not Roosevelt's willingness to relinquish the Platt Amendment, which had made Cuba a protectorate in 1902, but the steadfast opposition to a revolution that threatened American sway over the island's economy. In Cuba, always a special case in its calculations, the United States tossed aside the general principle of an economic open door, thoroughly subordinated the Cuban economy to its own, and kept it largely closed to any save American products. When Batista, who spent the 1930s as president-maker of Cuba, began espousing a Cuban variation of economic nationalism, American investors grew wary and looked to Washington for support. Batista resisted. In 1940 he ran for president on a constitution that pledged social and economic reforms and committed Cuba to a constitutional democracy. But the powerful American investment community understood what he really wanted—and willingly paid it.[3]

In these spirited endeavors to promote inter-American economic solidarity the United States discovered again that Latin American governments have their own timetables and political priorities. Argentina's role at the seventh inter-American conference at Montevideo in 1933 and again at the special hemispheric meeting for the Maintenance of Peace at Buenos Aires in 1936 demonstrated how one government could frustrate the best of American intentions.

Argentina, not the United States, appeared to be the mediator of peace in the Southern Cone. In the year before the seventh inter-American meeting convened, the Argentines were in effect conceded by a dispirited Brazil and Chile the opportunity to decide whether there would be peace or war between Bolivia and Paraguay over the Gran Chaco. The impoverished Bolivians, fired by an impulse to break out of their isolation by obtaining access to the Atlantic, unleashed their attack on underpopulated Paraguay in June 1932. Paraguay could not resist unless it had Argentine support; its status as an economic appendage of Argentina virtually assured that Buenos Aires had the power to determine whether the nationalistic Paraguayans would be victorious or suffer a humiliating defeat.

With diplomatic legerdemain the Argentine foreign minister, Carlos Saavedra Lamas, skillfully exploited this crisis, which rapidly escalated into a gruesome war, to achieve Argentine mastery over Southern Cone international politics. A few months after Hull launched his trade program, the Argentines signed a commercial pact with the British, which provided Buenos Aires with an economic status roughly akin to a dominion in the empire. Saavedra Lamas publicized an antiwar treaty linked to the League of Nations. Then Argentina insinuated itself into command of a commission to mediate the Chaco dispute by obtaining a hastily arranged membership in the League of Nations, which meekly deferred to Buenos Aires' direction in the settlement. When the compliant Hull arrived in Montevideo, ready to yield on Latin American demands for an absolute prohibition on intervention, the Argentine press unleashed a virulent anti-American propaganda campaign. Saavedra Lamas was ingratiating: the United States and Argentina, the Argentine told his American counterpart, will "become the two wings of the dove, you the economic, and we the political."[4]

In reality the Argentines were carving out their own economic arrangements that defied Hull's reciprocity program, and Saavedra Lamas's cynical exploitation of Latin American and the League of Nations' despair over the Chaco soon made clear that there would be no peace between Paraguay and Bolivia unless the Argentines wanted it. The Brazilians complained of Argentine manipulation of the conflict; the Chileans, frustrated over their inability to support the ravaged Bolivians, blamed Buenos Aires for the failure of peaceful negotiations by the League. When the Chileans tried to negotiate a commercial treaty with Peru in the spirit of Hull's reciprocity program, the Argentines (who furnished 50 percent of Peru's wheat imports and stood to lose by the arrangement) vigorously complained. The American government could not afford to offend Buenos Aires. The Bolivians finally grew so exhausted with their war that they were compelled to turn to Argentina, clearly the only country in the hemisphere that could determine peace in the South American cone.

Peace did not come in the Chaco until January 1936.[5] The Americans had throughout yielded to Argentine pretensions as the political arbiter in the Southern Cone and gotten little in return. With Hull his most enthusiastic supporter for the honor, Saavedra Lamas was accorded the Nobel Peace Prize. In the meantime the Argentine economy, fueled by a 150 percent increase of its exports to the United States (which was unable to break the 12.5 percent duty on American products entering Argentina) prospered while that of its South American neighbors stagnated. The docile Peruvians had to accept Argentine wheat on the same terms as Chilean or pay a hefty surcharge for selling its petroleum to Buenos Aires. From Washington came praise for the Argentine success in bringing peace to the Southern Cone and recognition of its economic accomplishments in the face of adversity. As the encomiums poured forth, the Argentines ordered seven warships from Great Britain. Saavedra Lamas was named president of the League Assembly and at the direction of Adolf Hitler received the Star of the German Red Cross for his pacific diplomacy in the Gran Chaco war.

The Clouds of War

Despite the Argentine diplomatic triumph over the United States and its defiance of Hull's trade program, Washington persisted in wooing Latin America to the Good Neighbor. Roosevelt himself led the diplomatic challenge at the Conference for the Maintenance of Peace, which convened in Buenos Aires in late 1936. The president sailed for the meeting aboard a U.S. warship—not as conqueror but as the true good neighbor who had purged American policy in the hemisphere of its odious tradition of interventionism and dollar diplomacy. He was saluted everywhere. Stopping in Rio de Janeiro he was greeted by schoolchildren waving the American flag and singing the U.S. national anthem. Getúlio Vargas, who in the following year announced the "New State" in Brazil (which to democrats bore an unsettling similarity to European fascism), declared a national holiday to honor Roosevelt.

Not to be outdone, the Argentines promptly followed with their own national holiday to commemorate their distinguished visitor. Roosevelt and Hull reaffirmed the commitment of the United States to absolute nonintervention, and the Latin American delegates cheered the "Pan-Americanization" of the Monroe Doctrine. Then they promptly followed the Argentines in demurring on any strong commitment to bind the hemispheric republics in an alliance against German penetration. Spruille Braden, U.S. ambassador to Argentina, was so irritated with the intransigent Saavedra Lamas that he personally appealed to the Argentine president, General Augustín B. Justo. But Saavedra Lamas had the satisfaction of final defiance. He not only torpedoed Hull's laborious efforts at the conference but submitted the secretary of state a parting indignity by declining to say good-bye when the American delegation left for Washington.

In this and other experiences with Latin America in the coming years the American government learned a painful reality about what can happen to a dominating power that with considerable publicity alters its interventionist habits in the affairs of its more vulnerable neighbors. Correctly anticipating a menace to its own security in Latin America's vulnerability to European fascism, the United States ventured into these conferences preaching hemispheric unity to confront a world that was rapidly falling under the sway of the economic and political models symbolized by European fascism. Among Latin American leaders intellectually disposed to the notion of the "organic" or "corporate" state—in which the government served not as "broker" but as unifier (and dominator) of the nation's diverse social, political, and economic sectors—the German and Italian examples were inspirational. But until the fall of France and the Low Countries in summer 1940 (which signaled a German opportunity to acquire the West Indian dependencies of the defeated countries) U.S. protestations about the "fascist menace" fell largely on Latin American governments more concerned about maintaining their economic links

with Europe. The United States had necessarily chosen economic nationalism in 1933, Latin American leaders contended, and so, too,
must they.[6] Germany, Italy, and Japan no doubt posed a threat, but to
most of Latin America the more visible peril was American meddling
or hypocritical preachments of economic liberalism in an era when
their European connections offered more immediate economic rewards. American diplomats extolled the "democracies" of the hemisphere, but the political reality was a string of republics stretching
from Mexico to Argentina, with governments more closely resem-
bling (in content if not in form) the authoritarianism of Italy or
Germany.

Authoritarian governments in Latin America were, of course, not
entirely repugnant to American policy makers, especially if they offered a realistic alternative to the uncertainties of the revolutionary
nationalism that had exploded in Cuba in 1933. The danger lay in the
obstacles to Washington's efforts to solidify the republics in a common
defensive network posed by regimes wary of American intentions
and presumably responsive to aggressive German economic and political overtures. By the time the eighth Pan-American conference met
at Lima in 1938, Germany had mounted an impressive trade program
in the hemisphere that had wrought political dividends. It had not
only recovered to the levels of its pre–World War I trade with Latin
America but had become a more important supplier than Britain. German firms, relative newcomers, were less resented in those countries
where the British had long been accustomed to dealing with their
Latin American customers in a domineering fashion. Even in Central
America, for years under the political shadow of American power,
German economic penetration (especially in Guatemala and Costa
Rica) had achieved impressive levels.

With the surge of German commerce (and of the Japanese in Ecuador and Peru) the United States understandably associated a more
vigorous German cultural and political pressure. In Chile, where a
leftist government (the Popular Front) narrowly won a victory in 1938
over the National Socialist party, German settlers who lived on the
frontier and had their own schools were, the government presumed,

vulnerable to German propaganda. Across the Andes, the British reach still prevailed, but throughout the Southern Cone, the Germans had made great headway. The German colony in Buenos Aires numbered 250,000 and, though not united in its support of German ambitions in Argentina, was viewed by the Auslandsorganisation (the network of German nationals in foreign countries) as a useful political and cultural tool for German interests. The Argentines were alert to the danger of foreign ideologies, whether of Right or Left: the government outlawed the Communist party and, when Nazi agents began circulating among the German community urging the teaching of Nazi propaganda and the Nazi salute in the schools, resentful Argentines called for an investigation. In 1939 they heard frightful (and untrue) stories about a German conspiracy to seize Patagonia. Under public pressure the Justo government outlawed the Nazi party, but another German organization rose in its place. Argentina's strong economic ties with Germany dictated a policy of accommodation, not confrontation.

In Brazil the German population reached almost a million, of whom a tenth were putative Nazis—ready, it was presumed, to advance the German cause in the vulnerable northeastern bulge of South America. Vargas, who had seized power in 1930 in the wave of military coups that had swept Latin America, perceived enemies on both the Left and the Right. Declaring that the communists were plotting to seize power, he dissolved the national congress and ruled virtually by decree. Proclaiming the New State (Novo Estado), a Brazilian variation of fascism, he dispatched "intervenors" into the Brazilian states and banned political parties. In Washington there circulated fearful rumors of a German fifth column in Brazil, sustained by the Integralistas, a movement organized in 1932 by a novelist and political ideologue, Plinio Salgado. Quite unexpectedly, the Integralistas attempted a coup in May 1938, surrounding the national palace. Vargas managed to hold them off until troops arrived. The Integralistas spoke of "Brazil for the Brazilians"—as did Vargas, who more than Salgado expressed his displeasure over German efforts to divide the loyalties of Germans living in the Novo Estado and undertook repressive measures against political and cultural organizations with foreign connections. He closed German schools and commanded his soldiers, armed with German-made weapons and trained in the German tradition by German-speaking officers, to speak Portuguese. Thousands of Germans departed for the Fatherland, but Vargas did not sever the German supply line of Krupp arms.[7]

How did Roosevelt perceive the ominous warnings from the south about the Nazi menace? There was no dearth of sensational literature, from both American and Latin American writers, about the German intrusions. The writer Carleton Beals (who had been the bane of American interventionists in Nicaragua in 1927), with predictable but credible hyperbole, warned in *The Coming Struggle for Latin America* that the continent was awash in fascism. Only an American government sufficiently committed to social justice for Latin America's downtrodden could hold back the German tide. Within the State Department Beals was largely written off as an alarmist, but not a few of the department's hemispheric observers, including Adolf Berle, were issuing similar warnings to Roosevelt. Ironically, as the American government was grimly assessing the Nazi penetration in the hemisphere, the German foreign office had come to similarly morose judgments about the American challenge to German ambitions in Latin America. The Nazi ambassador to Argentina was called to Berlin, informed that the German image in Latin America had suffered from its high visibility, and returned to Buenos Aires with a stern message for the Auslandsorganisation minions.

More disquieting for Roosevelt were stories emanating from Latin American capitals about German sympathy among the *nacistas* of Chile, who, in an especially bitter political campaign in 1938, attempted to overthrow the conservative government of Arturo Alessandri. When the Integralist putsch failed in Brazil, it was widely believed, the German agents had shifted their attention to Chile. The rebels took control of two government buildings and called for help from Chileans fearful that Alessandri would choose his successor. Alessandri's troops brutally crushed the uprising and the vengeful president ordered sixty-two of them executed. His reaction probably guaranteed the victory of the Popular Front candidate a short time later.

This and other dreary tales about the precarious state of Latin American democracy, coupled with credible warnings about German political opportunism, inspired reassessments about the place of the hemisphere in American strategy. What elevated Latin America to a position of high priority among policy makers was the certainty with which Americans professed their determination to avoid involvement in another European war—even during the tense days of the Sudeten crisis—but their obvious willingness to shore up American security in the Western Hemisphere. In *The Ramparts We Watch*, Major George Fielding Eliot wrote confidently that Britain, France, and the Soviet Union could deter Germany in central Europe, but fascism, soon to be installed with Francisco Franco's triumph in Spain, would spread to Portugal, then across the Atlantic, and ultimately corrode the political cultures of Latin America. That notion was farfetched, admittedly, but it carried sufficient credibility to inspire the analysts in the War Department to amplify their requests for defense sites in Panama with scenarios about fifth columnists and saboteurs and the vulnerability of the canal to attack from aircraft carriers at sea.

The Mexican oil expropriation crisis, which had begun earlier in the year with the abrupt decision of the Lázaro Cárdenas government to nationalize foreign oil properties (mostly British and American) now assumed strategic importance. In the beginning, Hull, reinforced by an outraged British government, had put heavy pressure on the Mexican government to make a settlement the companies found agreeable. Confronting the harsh rhetoric from the north, Cárdenas resisted. When the Americans and British refused to buy or transport Mexican oil, he struck a deal with the Germans (who privately regarded him as a socialist and an enemy of the Reich but nonetheless sensed an opportunity to undermine American interests) to exchange oil for aircraft. From Mexico City, Josephus Daniels, Roosevelt's boss in the Wilson administration and now his ambassador, toned down the abusive instructions coming from Hull—and thereby risked being recalled. Secretary of the Treasury Henry Morgenthau, Jr., apparently persuaded the president that strategic interests in Mexico were being jeopardized. Hull got the message. By the time the foreign ministers met at Lima later in the year, he had acquiesced in Cárdenas's decision not to meet the companies' demands.[8]

Roosevelt dared not challenge the isolationists and their determination to keep the United States out of European conflict, but he accurately sensed the insecurity the country felt about its position in the Western Hemisphere. The Munich crisis did not dispel isolationist sentiment, but fear of German penetration in Latin America provided a credible rationale for undertaking more ambitious defensive policies with the other American republics. The grander design, which Adolf Berle called the "north-south axis," anticipated not only economic but political commitments—the first designed to knit the hemisphere in commercial and investment ties and the second, equally vital, to sustain vulnerable governments from the powerful influences of pro-Axis movements. There must be no Axis undermining of Latin America, Berle said, by a fascist Trojan horse. On the eve of the Lima conference, scheduled to meet in December 1938 in a country with strong ties to Benito Mussolini's Italy and newly signed commercial pacts with Germany, the Division of the American Republics in the State Department grimly anticipated more troubles from pro-German elements everywhere in Latin America.

Roosevelt's detractors, predictably, and even some of his defenders have portrayed these frenzied political efforts in the inter-American system in the years before World War II as yet another example of duplicity in his approach to the global crisis. Clearly, Roosevelt exploited the apprehension about German intrigue in the hemisphere, and certainly Hull realized that a policy of globalism stood no chance against the entrenched strength of isolationism unless the United States followed the hemispheric defensive strategy Roosevelt's military advisers were calling for. As in the first two decades of the twentieth century, when German imperial ambitions in the Western Hemisphere, particularly in the Caribbean and Mexico, appeared more a menace to American interests than subsequent analyses revealed, so did Washington's interpretations of Hitler's intentions perhaps exaggerate Germany's capabilities to undermine Latin American governments. But the cumulative impact of irrefutable statistics of German and Italian economic and military ties with Latin American governments coupled with the undeniable philosophical appeal of corporatism (the euphemistic name for the political and economic structure fascism and Naziism symbolized) made for a disturbing assessment of the Latin American condition in the aftermath of the Munich crisis and the prospect of a Falangist victory in Spain. Hitler was a continentalist, but he was determined to restore German influence in the world. The conquest of South America, he told a confidant, would not require German troops but could be attained on the strength of German settlers, the better social classes, and fifth columnists.[9]

The thought may have been fanciful, but analyses of Berlin's limitations in Latin America could not dispel the somber data about German intrigue. When Hull arrived in Lima, gloomily anticipating another scrape with the Argentines, German agents and Italian propagandists had already implanted stories of the threat to Latin America's "Latin and Mediterranean conscience" by this disciple of "atheistic, brutal imperialism" from the north. Again, the Argentines remained committed to a transatlantic perspective. On the opening day of the conference, José María Cantino, the Argentine foreign minister, paid faint praise to hemispheric unity, then proudly reaffirmed, "If to the mother country [Spain, Portugal, or England] we owe the basis of our literature, then to French culture we owe the basic formation of our intellectual life, and to Italy and Germany all the vital aspects of our evolution."[10] Then he departed, delegating responsibility to an underling and leaving Hull again infuriated at the craftiness of Argentine diplomacy and the American entourage fearful of being isolated in a hemisphere the United States was striving to unite.

Sumner Welles, left behind because he tended to dominate in negotiations with Latin Americans, had argued that if the United States must accept a less satisfactory hemispheric pact to get Argentina's participation it should do so. Often in disagreement over tactics in hemispheric policy, Hull and Welles believed unanimity was uppermost in American strategy at Lima. The American delegation, noticeably annoyed with Buenos Aires' refusal to break the European connection, confronted in the Mexican and Colombian governments a seemingly unshakable determination to defy the fascist menace with a unifying pact more provocative than Washington thought was necessary. In the end, Hull got less than he wanted, but the American delegation went home with the satisfaction that the Declaration of Lima, which extolled "continental solidarity" and promised "consulation" in the event of a threat to it, had been approved by all the republics. Samuel Guy Inman, who had brought to the inter-American cultural program and the Good Neighbor policy the missionary's zeal, proudly declared that the Monroe Doctrine had now been Pan-Americanized into a "fighting platform for American democracy."[11] In truth, the "platform," like the dream of hemispheric unity, was more a spiritual than a tangible military foundation—but at least it was a beginning in the American determination to confront the European peril by following a Latin route.

The Western Hemisphere at War

World War II enabled the United States to accomplish in Latin America what intervention and a vigorous expansion of the American export economy had failed to achieve—the incorporation of the hemisphere into its global strategy. In mid-1939, on the eve of Hitler's attack on Poland, the Roosevelt administration had not broken the transatlantic cultural and economic bonds between South America and European fascism. In the inter-American political arena, American diplomats had wavered under Argentine determination to prevent a stronger declaration at Lima, and Hull's spirited promotion of American exports had not shaken South America's faith in its own credos of economic nationalism.

Even the larger South American republics, traditionally resentful of U.S. pretensions, perceived the need to accommodate the American government. At Panama, where the foreign ministers convened only a few weeks after the outbreak of hostilities, the American delegation reaffirmed U.S. intentions to aid the republics in overcoming the debilitating economic impact of ruptures in hemispheric trade with Europe. They adopted Roosevelt's notion of a hemispheric "safety belt," an imaginary (and indefensible) line three hundred miles outside the United States and Latin America, and forbade the European belligerents from waging war inside the "neutral" hemispheric waters. Most considered the safety belt unenforceable and even laughable but recognized that economic exigencies warranted their acquiescence. They renewed their efforts for an inter-American development bank, which the State Department pledged to take up with the Inter-American Financial and Advisory Committee. The committee dispensed questionnaires and by May 1940, despite some reservations about their ability to help fund the bank, eight of the republics had signed the charter. When the administration went to Congress for funding, however, it encountered strong opposition from conservatives, who saw the bank as another barrier to the country's economic strategies.

American economic strategists were now arguing that the outbreak of war in Europe dictated a shift away from Hull's free trade philosophy and toward a hemispheric economic policy that reinforced American security. The Export-Import Bank, not the reciprocal trade program idealized a few years before, charted the nation's course in a world economy in which the Wilsonian ideal of free trade, a policy of dubious success in a world economy devastated by the depression, now was imperiled by war. In the two years of hemispheric neutrality, the American government had placed far greater emphasis on stockpiling strategic materials, withholding vital supplies from export, and attaching political stipulations to its loan and investment policies for Latin America. From 1938 to 1940, Latin America not only lost much of its trade with continental Europe but found itself locked out of the British imperial economy. Latin Americans bought from Americans at less competitive prices; they sold to Americans at lower prices. In these two years, the United States increased its imports of Latin American products by 37 percent and its exports to the hemisphere by 45 percent. When the American government proposed an inter-American trading corporation to act as purchaser of Latin American products for resale in Europe, the larger countries of South America, led by the defiant Argentines, resisted the plan as yet another effort to subordinate the Latin American economies to the United States.[12]

The European belligerents promptly violated the Panama safety belt in a dramatic and potentially dangerous naval battle between three British warships and the German pocket battleship *Graf Spee* off Uruguay in late 1939. The commander of the German ship took refuge in Montevideo, Uruguay, was ordered out of the port by a tentative Uruguayan government, and scuttled his ship in international waters. Argentina took his crew in internment. Throughout the Americas the incident demonstrated the vulnerability of South America south of the Brazilian bulge and the inability of the U.S. Navy to safeguard hemispheric waters.

The following June, when the fall of France precipitated yet another hemispheric crisis, Roosevelt had already resolved to press the issue of hemispheric security, but the American public and the American military were more concerned with the Caribbean, where the northern republics of Latin America had become alarmed over German submarine patrols and the disquieting prospect that France and the Netherlands, now under German domination, would cede their Caribbean possessions to the fuehrer. Among the U.S. military the need to acquire bases in Panama, which a nationalistic government under Arnulfo Arias was resisting, became necessary to safeguard the canal, and in the War Department arguments for defense facilities in Venezuela, the Dominican Republic, Colombia, and Brazil were strengthened. Frank Knox, a Republican critic of the president, who joined the cabinet as secretary of the navy in these troublesome days, had earlier advocated seizure of the European possessions in the West Indies to prevent their falling under German control.

Shortly after the fall of France the foreign ministers convened again at Havana. The discussions were more somber, the resolution to protect the vulnerable European possessions from German control more determined. Still, as in earlier Pan-American meetings, the Latin

Americans were seemingly more concerned with traditional national interests than with hemispheric unity. In the United States fretful observers called for seizure of Europe's hemispheric possessions. The British, responding to a Dutch appeal, landed marines in Aruba and Curaçao to shield Venezuelan oil facilities. Already the U.S. Congress, echoing an 1811 resolution that had prohibited the transfer of Spanish Florida to another European power, resolved not to recognize the transfer of any European colony in the West Indies to Germany and empowered Roosevelt to enforce it. When the German foreign office denigrated the resolution, the State Department responded with an even broader commitment to a Pan-Americanized Monroe Doctrine. Again, the Latin Americans exacted their price for acquiescing in American strategic priorities. Guatemala, Venezuela, and especially Argentina (which had claims on British Honduras, British Guiana, and the Falklands, respectively) wanted special consideration for their support. Eventually they gave in when Hull pledged to meet their peculiar economic needs with Export-Import Bank loans. Under American pressure the Argentines had capitulated but not without grumbling about renewed U.S. penetration of the Caribbean. Even so, the pro-Nazi government in Vichy, France, so alarmed the American military with its yielding to German pressures that Secretary of the Navy Knox recommended seizure of the French West Indies, which the Act of Havana, if broadly interpreted, permitted. As things worked out, French officials in the West Indies, recognizing the vulnerability of the islands, declared their neutrality and thus avoided American occupation.[13]

Pearl Harbor did not elicit a commitment to a hemispheric defensive alliance, but it did break the Argentine hold, especially on the northern republics. On the same day Roosevelt spoke of a "day of infamy," Guatemala, Costa Rica, Honduras, El Salvador, Haiti, the Dominican Republic, and Panama declared war on Japan and, a few days later, joined by Cuba and Nicaragua, on Germany and Italy. But on the South American mainland there was hesitation: Colombia and Venezuela broke diplomatic relations, and the other republics, reluctant to offend the Axis powers without the reassuring presence of

American or British naval protection, maintained a discreet neutrality. When the foreign ministers gathered at Rio de Janeiro in January, Welles pressed the case for severance of diplomatic relations as the only effective means for harassed governments to deal with German subversives. The Colombians, Mexicans, and Venezuelans championed the American cause, but, as before, the Argentines were predictably hesitant, and the Chileans demurred on the credible grounds of their vulnerability to Japanese naval supremacy in the Pacific and the inability of the Americans to safeguard their long coastline. In the end, despite Hull's wishes for harsher pressures on the recalcitrant Argentines, Welles retreated, accepting a resolution that recommended rather than demanded a severance of relations. But the diplomatic battle triumphed in other ways; before the conference ended Brazil, Paraguay, Ecuador, Uruguay, Bolivia, and Peru severed relations with the three Axis countries.

The Good Neighbor at war strived to accomplish what in retrospect was a laudable but gargantuan task—to forge a unified hemisphere of democracies in a war against totalitarianism out of disparate cultures and political traditions. Philanthropic endeavors of the 1920s were transmuted into policies of the Division of Cultural Affairs of the Department of State, whose ideologues (some of them harsh critics of gunboat diplomacy in the old days) now spoke of understanding and the bonds of democracies at war. In the Office of the Coordinator of Inter-American Affairs, a budget that escalated from $3.5 to $38 million in two years enabled its energetic chief, Nelson Rockefeller, to launch a highly publicized propaganda campaign of "America for the Americas" to combat Nazi subversives, extend U.S. technical assistance, discourage revolutions, and expand American exports. The true believers—like Inman, the former missionary, and the disciples of the historian Herbert Bolton, who had spoken so eloquently of the "epic of Greater America" and a unified Western Hemisphere— sensed no insurmountable obstacles in the path of cultural unity. Others, such as Samuel Flagg Bemis, who published his *Latin American Policy of the United States* in 1943, and the Yale political scientist Nicholas Spykman, who startled the hemispheric unionists with his

America's Strategy in World Politics, were politely disdainful of the prospects for a defensive alliance built on cultural sympathy rather than the realities of international politics.

American rhetoric, expressed in radio transmissions, advertisements in pro-American newspapers, slick publications such as *On Guard*, movies and cartoons geared to a Latin American audience, and the description of the Monroe Doctrine as a statement of collective hemispheric defense, among other things, conveyed one message to Latin Americans. But U.S. actions, it was alleged by formerly critical observers such as the Peruvian Haya de la Torre, gave quite another of American intentions. To counter German military influence in the hemisphere, particularly in South America, the American government increased the number of its military missions from a paltry five in 1938 to one in each of the republics two years later. In 1940 the War Department expended $500 million on the program. Junior Latin American officers were trained "in the American way" in the United States, and the Latin American militaries began receiving war matériel at cost before Lend-Lease became law. The goal was not only to discourage Latin American military ties to Europe but to validate American purpose in the defense of democracy and the belief that a modernized Latin American military could more ably confront the inner menace of Nazi agitators and fifth columnists. The legacy, though unintended by a beneficent American government, was to reinforce the strength of the Latin American military as a political instrument.[14]

Dictators lined up with the United States in defending democracy in a totalitarian world, and in their own countries they accommodated American strategic priorities by permitting U.S. agents to fashion counterespionage networks and cracked down on Germans, some of whom were guilty of nothing except being German. Throughout the Caribbean, Mexico, and Central America, entire economies were drawn into the wartime economy of the United States. American health and sanitation officials and engineers descended on the republics to combat disease, lay sewage lines, and construct roads— probably the most significant accomplishment of American proconsuls in the tropics earlier in the century. The war effort required agricultural and industrial labor, and Mexicans entered the U.S. work force. Monocultural economies lost their European markets for sugar, coffee, and bananas; Americans bought those items. When their productive energies went into vital products and they could not grow enough food for their population, the United States provided it. When their country people began drifting in from the outback to the cities looking for work and were unable to find it, the American government promoted public works programs to employ them and urged the extension of the vote to instill the American conception of "democracy." In Brazil, America's most important wartime ally, the United States helped build Volta Redonda, the steel mill symbolizing the Brazilian industrial future, just as in Mexico it provided economic sustenance for the future Mexican steel industry at Monclava.

The smaller countries rushed to acknowledge their commitment to the American hemisphere by declaring war, but the larger countries—Mexico and all South America—hesitated. Willing to break diplomatic relations, they were reluctant to plunge into the global struggle with an American government unable—or unwilling—to accommodate their priorities. Mexico hesitated until the sinking of a Mexican vessel off Florida unleashed an outburst of anti-German sentiment and gave the Avila Camacho government an excuse. With the declaration of war Mexican authorities "intervened" in German (and later, Italian and Japanese) businesses, cracked down on German social clubs, and used the outpouring of antifascist sentiment to smash the Sinarquistas in central Mexico. Even the Mexican Left, symbolically represented by former president Lázaro Cárdenas and the chieftain of Mexican labor, Vicente Lombardo Toledano, joined in the government's program to unite Mexico with the Allied cause. Mexico supplied vital raw materials, dispatched an air unit to the Philippines, and demanded (and ultimately received) sufficient economic and technical assistance to facilitate the Mexican economic miracle of the postwar era. The social price was high: Mexican productivity was geared to the American economy, and the prices for consumer goods and foodstuffs escalated by 400 percent from 1939 until the last year of the war. By then the urban population confronted serious shortages of even basic foodstuffs, and a black market expanded in such items as coffee, fruit, and vegetables. Wages rose, but prices outstripped them.[15]

Vargas, the "proto-fascist," as a few American cynics called the Brazilian leader, broke diplomatic relations with the Axis but stopped short of declaring war. Brazil, Vargas told confidants, would "stand or fall" with Washington. He began cracking down on German aliens, disbanded the remaining German social and political clubs, and closed German schools. Though Brazilians grumbled about obnoxious American servicemen and the tightening economic grip of Washington, Vargas cleverly exploited Hull's scarcely disguised hostility to the Argentines and demanded greater amounts of military aid. And despite Washington's hesitation in accepting Brazilian troops for the European campaign (lest the other South American countries demand equal treatment, thus necessitating an even larger dispersal of vital war equipment), the Brazilian generals, declaring that they did not intend to be "spectators," pressed for a direct role in the crusade against fascism and dispatched troops for the Italian campaign. Brazil as a participant, Vargas realized, augured well for its future international status.[16]

Under American prodding the other South American republics— save Argentina—fell into line. Midway in the war it had become obvious to most of them that breaking diplomatic relations with the Axis countries was insufficient if they were to play a role in the collective alliance of antifascist belligerents fashioned in 1942 and in shaping the peace. Venezuela concluded a peaceful adjustment with the oil companies that differed significantly from the Mexican example and declared war, contributing its vital petroleum to the Allied cause. Colombia had little oil to contribute, but since 1939 (when the government had rid its airlines of German and Austrian nationals), it had, like Venezuela, identified strongly with the United States. After Pearl Harbor, the American military had access to strategic sites in the country. When the Germans sank several Colombian vessels in late 1943, the government declared war and formally adhered to the

United Nations. In Bolivia, Enrique Peñaranda, who ruled largely at the behest of traditional oligarchical interests, committed the country to war after a succession of agreements with Standard Oil (whose properties had been nationalized by a socialist military regime in 1937) and the Export-Import Bank. He was promptly tossed out in a "national socialist" coup headed by a discontented military officer, Gualberto Villaroel.

In Washington (and elsewhere) it was generally assumed that the rightist coup in Bolivia was the work of the Argentines, who persisted in ignoring the declarations of the Rio conference, maintained their ties with Berlin, and casually tolerated a visible German presence in Buenos Aires. In neighboring Paraguay, General Higínio Moríñigo, ruled in a scarcely disguised authoritarian state that was economically (and, it was alleged, politically) beholden to Argentina. Good Neighbor diplomats descended on Asunción with pledges of economic and military aid in the expectation that Moríñigo could be weaned from his proto-fascist convictions. When the Brazilians joined in the overtures, the suspicious Argentines, ever alert to the dynamics of Southern Cone international politics, responded with their own commitments to the suddenly courted Paraguayans. Yet throughout the region the carrot-and-stick policies of Washington isolated the Argentines.[17]

In 1943 the wrath of Sumner Welles fell on Chile, whose government was accused of ignoring the resolutions of the Rio conference about cutting economic ties with the Axis and cracking down on German-owned businesses and Nazi propagandists. To the Chileans, the Germans were not goose-stepping Huns but the hardworking (and largely anti-Hitler) German farmers who had settled in the south. Under pressure to fall in line, the Chileans broke diplomatic relations with no strong intention to go further, but in late 1944 came the unsettling announcement (provoked, it was said, by Soviet insistence) from Washington that only belligerents could take part in the forthcoming United Nations conference. In early 1945 the "associated states" of Ecuador, Peru, Venezuela, Uruguay, Paraguay, and Chile, unwilling to risk U.S. disfavor, declared war.[18]

Argentina now stood alone. After the Rio conference it had defied

Washington by maintaining its ties to Germany. Brazil had accommodated Washington and its military stockings were filled by the grateful Americans, who declared that a corresponding generosity for Buenos Aires would come only if Argentina severed its ties with the Axis. The Ramón Castillo government promptly turned to Berlin. In mid-1943 a military coup spearheaded by a rightist coalition, the Group of United Officers, drove Castillo from office. Its seizure of power commenced a three-year confrontation with the Americans that ultimately culminated in the political triumph of one of its disciples, Juan Domingo Perón, in 1946. Castillo's war minister, General Pedro Ramírez, assuming executive power, dispatched a naval reserve officer to Germany to procure armaments. The emissary was arrested en route by the British and under questioning confessed he was a German spy. With this information and details of Argentine involvement in the Bolivian coup, Hull, ever determined to bring the Argentines to heel, increased the pressure on Buenos Aires. In January 1944 the embarrassed Argentines suddenly announced a break with Germany and Japan. The next month, Ramírez turned over the presidential seal to his vice-president, General Edelmiro Farrell.

Hull was not yet convinced of Argentine compliance. For a year Washington withheld diplomatic recognition on the grounds that Argentina's commitment to hemispheric unity against the Axis was shallow, prompting the Argentines to look again to the Germans for military supplies. By this time the Germans had little to provide. Hull remained unrelenting in his stalking of the recalcitrant Argentines, prompting increasingly vocal criticism (from the Latin Americanists within the department and from Welles, whom Hull had driven from power) and warnings that his policy of isolating Buenos Aires was harmful to hemispheric unity. But the secretary, reinforced by Berle, clung tenaciously to his charges of Argentine perfidy. When Buenos Aires appealed for understanding to the other Latin American governments, Hull publicly denounced Argentina for "openly and notoriously . . . giving affirmative assistance to the declared enemies of the United Nations."[19]

The Argentine plea did not go unheeded among other Latin American governments. Again, as in earlier inter-American confrontations, the Mexicans stepped into a bitter diplomatic battle between Washington and Buenos Aires. At the Inter-American Conference on Problems of War and Peace, which convened at Chapúltepec Heights in Mexico City a month before Roosevelt died, the gestures of good neighborliness culminated in Argentina's declaration of war against the Axis. Argentina gained admission to the United Nations, American Lend-Lease supplies entered the country, and the Farrell-Perón coalition made concessions to hemispheric unity by blacklisting German firms. Most of the Latin American governments understood the Argentine position: they saw it as a reflection of political and economic reality. But the Americans remained unforgiving.[20] A few months after Chapúltepec, Spruille Braden, who had clashed with the Argentines before, publicly declared on his arrival in Buenos Aires that his mission was to promote democracy in a putatively undemocratic state. He threw down the gauntlet to Perón, who had already announced for the presidency, by demanding surrender of the German assets in the country. Perón responded with his own barrage in the Argentine press. It was a battle he won in 1946, after Braden had issued the tactless *Blue Book* detailing Argentine perfidy during the war. Perón's response was an ingenious appeal to Argentine nationalism: "Whom do you choose—Perón or Braden?"

By then American priorities in Latin America had already begun to shift to Washington's global calculations. Roosevelt, who had spoken often of the Good Neighbor and "giving them a share," had altered the American image in the hemisphere, but the Good Neighbor policy indisputably expanded American military influence in Latin America as the only realistic and politically acceptable way of defeating isolationism and bolstering American defense efforts. This meant, inevitably, that Latin Americans confronted political and economic realities seemingly beyond their control. As in the past, American security interests required stable governments; global economic patterns, disrupted by the war, meant dependence on the external market.

The Good Neighbor had sought to bridge the gap between North and South in the Americas and had succeeded in ameliorating their historically troubled diplomatic relations, forging economic bonds that had not existed before the war, and fashioning a cosmetic cultural understanding. The wartime alliance offered opportunity but required Latin America's accommodation to Washington's priorities. The United States provided loans and grants, bought strategic and surplus commodities, and tried to improve Latin American transportation, agriculture, and industry. Through financial agreements and technical assistance, Washington had shielded Latin America from some of the harsher impacts of the war. The balance sheet was uneven. The postwar Mexican economic miracle depended heavily on its wartime economic relationship with the United States; Mexican economic dependence has its origins in the same place. Brazil, Haiti, Bolivia, and Ecuador gained less from the American development projects than promised. Argentina fared better in the war, and its defiance of the United States is often cited as justifiable as a way to avoid economic dependence, yet in the postwar years the Argentine economic record was not as impressive as Brazil's or Mexico's.[21]

The Good Neighbor did not perish with Roosevelt, but the experience of war altered America's hemispheric priorities. As Spykman had prophesied, the world that mattered politically, economically, and culturally turned on an east-west, not a north-south axis. Latin America, in this scheme, now seemed less vulnerable to a threat from abroad. Spykman was arguably correct about American global interests and Latin America's place in U.S. strategic thinking, but he and many other Americans profoundly underestimated the revolutionary potential latent in Latin America's political and social structure.

Lamentably, something else was lost in the triumph of democratic capitalism—the momentary vision of American intellectuals such as Waldo Frank of an inter-American harmony based on mutual respect of differing cultural identities. Hundreds of West Indian Canal Zone laborers, promised U.S. citizenship, had volunteered for military service. Thousands of Latin Americans had appeared at U.S. embassies to join America's struggle against the Axis. In the wartime alliance Americans found in the Latin American (largely Hispanic) sense of cultural preference—of friendship over work, of quality over productivity, of spiritual rather than material well-being—more admirable symbols. There was an innocence in this view, Fredrick Pike has observed, but the Americas, north and south, had profited, spiritually if not economically.[22] In retrospect, such cultural bonds would have better served American interests in Latin America than Washington's future prescriptions for hemispheric unity.

7 The Cold War in the Americas

The United States emerged from World War II as the most visibly dominant economic and political power in the world. To wage the conflict that had brought this stupendous victory it had integrated Latin America into its global strategy. It had accommodated dictators and democrats, it had challenged and defeated the German economic and political threat to its sway throughout the Americas, and it had cultivated a new image among Latin Americans. It had sought and largely achieved the integration of the Latin American economies into its international economic strategy. It had sought and largely achieved the dependence of the Latin American militaries on American tutelage of its officers. It had sought and largely achieved the creation of a postwar inter-American system that did not conflict with its global political strategy or require primacy in its foreign policy priorities.

Yet for all these triumphs, the efforts to forge an American hemisphere of common political, economic, and cultural aspirations had already begun to disintegrate. Latin Americans expected a more just economic, social, and political order, but they could not agree on the means or, ultimately, on the social and political price they were willing to pay to achieve it. Awed by American power and material bounty, they retained traditional convictions that they were morally if not materially superior. Their wartime ally both attracted and repelled them. The country they had once condemned as a predator had gone to war against predatory fascism in the service of humanity. With an unexpected generosity it had shared its scientific and medical knowledge to assist ravaged peoples, had linked isolated communities throughout the Americas, and in these and other tasks had conveyed that Yankee enthusiasm for getting things done—all without the inspiration of the profit motive. But often Latin American wartime visitors to the United

161

States, overwhelmed by the factory transformed into an arsenal, were taken aback by American superficiality, conformity, and stultifying lifestyle. And in Latin America, the Yankee too often exhibited the worst characteristics of the intruder who believes the only things that count are those that can be counted. The wartime experience had thus produced cultural shock, which Latin Americans in time would be able to accommodate, but the modern society America symbolized and whose benefits they wanted required from them a fearful social price. The United States had built its modernity not by disowning but by building on its past. Latin America did not have that choice.

The Legacy of War

What Latin America wanted after the war was development, which the United States applauded but would neither adequately sustain nor safeguard against American economic penetration or the uncertainties of a world market. At the Chapúltepec conference, called abruptly by the Mexicans to reconcile the Argentine and American governments, the U.S. delegates spoke eloquently about the United Nations while the Latin Americans spoke about their preferences for a regional system to safeguard the peace and address their economic problems. In what the Americans regarded as a concession, the hemispheric alliance was validated in Articles 51 and 52 of the U.N. Charter. Of equal concern to the Latin American delegates was their own economic charter. A State Department official had forthrightly expressed the justice of their case: "We asked for and obtained the help of Latin America in the prosecution of the war—Latin America will ask, and we must give, help in the transition from war to peace."[1]

The high expectations Latin Americans had developed during the war meant that the cost of postwar aid was not only high but, more important, beyond the ability of the United States, given its global commitments, to offer. Latin Americans had suffered economic deprivation during the war; they believed American commitments of postwar assistance would not only be honored but channeled according to their developmental preferences. American assistance had been critical: bereft of a world market for their primary products, they had found in the United States a purchaser at a guaranteed price. They had built up huge dollar reserves ($4.4 billion in foreign reserves) and an unsatisfied appetite for American consumer goods. Now, at war's end, they believed the relationship must continue. In the protective economic shield of the inter-American system lay their best prospect for catching up with the industrial nations of the north and escaping the nineteenth-century economic order that still encumbered the republics. Latin America could do so only with massive credit and assistance. Instead it encountered a postwar United States that raised prices for its commodity exports and devalued the dollars Latin Americans held. From 1945 until 1948, the higher costs of American products consumed $2.7 billion of their reserves. Of more consequence, they confronted a United States that directed its primary attention to the shattered economies of Europe and Asia.

With the broader objectives of the Latin Americans—continued use of resources until victory over the Axis was achieved, a stable and orderly economic transition to a peacetime economy, and a long-range development goal for industry and agriculture—the American government was in agreement. But it demurred on the question of economic nationalism and the Latin American insistence on using the state to promote economic development and shielding national economies from the competitive forces of the more advanced industrial countries. On this matter the usually suppressed cynicism of the Latin American delegates erupted in sarcastic comments about a nation that protected its own industries and agriculture but refused to concede the same advantage to others. The American draft of the economic charter spoke of tearing down barriers to trade and establishing safeguards for private investment—a point of view considerably distant from the Latin Americans' predilection for closely supervising the investment dollar. At the U.N. organizational conference at San Francisco in May the Latin Americans renewed their pressures for a regional pact, voicing their own apprehensions about Soviet ambitions in Latin America, and eventually wringing from the Americans a commitment for an inter-American defense pact.

It was a pledge not fulfilled until two years later at Rio de Janeiro, when the American government had crafted the containment doctrine and made Latin America's economic development secondary to American security in the Western Hemisphere. In the meantime Washington directed its hemispheric energies to harassing the defiant Argentines by preventing the election of Juan Perón. To this end Spruille Braden, who had left Buenos Aires to become assistant secretary of state for American republic affairs, induced the Uruguayan foreign minister, Eduardo Rodríguez Larreta, to issue an appeal for collective intervention to ensure democracy and respect for human rights in the Americas. With no particular enthusiasm for Perón's cause, the other Latin American republics politely rejected the idea as a violation of strict nonintervention. Perón triumphed and launched his own brand of economic nationalism that he called *"justicialismo,"* which Braden interpreted as fascism. In the mind-set of Washington in 1946, *justicialismo* laid the groundwork for communism in the Southern Cone. A few—Rockefeller, who reflected Wall Street's sentiments when he pointed out that Perón's domination of highly political Argentine labor offered a buttress against communist intrusion; Arthur Vandenberg, the Michigan Republican who had taken a special interest in Latin America's incorporation into the United Nations; and George Messersmith, who replaced Braden in Buenos Aires—saw in Perón's politics an effort to shape a modern Argentine economy and political culture in a country where the traditional landowning classes and the military had lost their credibility. But in these years when the hemisphere remained vulnerable to American pressures and could be subordinated to its strategic priorities there was lessening tolerance in Washington for the policy maker with a "regionalist perspective." Rockefeller was eased out in 1945. Two years later, with Vandenberg calling for the long-delayed Rio meeting (which Braden had opposed), Braden himself fell from grace, largely at the Michigan senator's insistence. For his unwilling retirement Braden exacted as price the fall of Messersmith, who had been decorated by Perón for his efforts to promote American-Argentine cordiality.[2]

In an atmosphere of uncertainty, confusion, and sometimes bitter departmental conflicts, U.S. postwar hemispheric policy evolved. Latin American aid was assigned a secondary status to that apportioned to Europe, a not unexpected decision, but Roosevelt's words about "giving them a share" and the wartime enthusiasm for hemispheric economic development rapidly dissipated. The Brazilians, for example, expecting much larger amounts of U.S. aid after the war, were given less and politely informed that the United States had other commitments for its public funds. Latin American countries that depended on raw material exports for their economic well-being wanted industrial equipment and technology from the United States but needed a higher price for their exports to pay for them. American manufacturers passed on rising costs to their Latin American purchasers; with the support of their government they kept down the prices they paid for Latin American imports.

If there were genuine fears of internal communist subversion or involvement by Perón, as in Chile in the last years of the Popular Front, Washington provided a minimum of financial assistance and its political support to a beleaguered government. In Chile the stake was deemed high enough to invest: a government with a working arrangement with the communists, but confronted by a labor strike in American-owned copper mines and in the coal mines had to acquiesce in American demands to crack down on the miners to survive. Ambassador Claude Bowers identified the crucial issue: "The strike is Communist and revolutionary and [as a] result will have inevitable effect throughout South America. . . . In view of the world contest between Communism and democracy it seems incredible that we should be indifferent to the major battle Communism is waging in Chile. . . . Unless we can and [will] do [more] we may prepare ourselves for a grave Communist triumph in our backyard . . . which will spread to other American nations."[3]

In the increasingly simplified context in which Washington gauged Latin America's place in its global perspective, the hemispheric delegates met at Rio de Janeiro in March 1947. A makeshift truce had been arranged with Perón, who had already voiced concerns about the Soviet peril in the world, had requested arms to confront it, and had begun receiving them. A surface cordiality reappeared when discussions focused on the safeguarding of the Western Hemisphere. The United States obtained the first of several Cold War alliances that followed in the next half dozen years. The Inter-American Treaty of Reciprocal Assistance restated the principle that an attack against one hemispheric nation obligated the others to come to its defense in a succession of responses culminating, if necessary, in war. Senator Vandenberg, who had served as delegate, returned with a glowing description of the defensive alliance as "sunlight in a dark world," a subtle reference to Soviet expansionism. A year later, at the ninth inter-American conference in Bogotá, the State Department dispatched with its representatives a guide entitled "U.S. Policy Regarding Anti-Communist Measures Which Could Be Planned and Carried Out within the Inter-American System" but suggested that they should avoid anticommunist agreements with the other republics and concentrate on anticommunist resolutions.

In both conferences, the United States generally got what it wanted; the Latin Americans did not. Washington fashioned the Rio treaty and the Organization of American States (OAS) charter, the first a hemispheric defensive alliance and the second a hemispheric institutional structure, to conform to its own priorities and—as the United States had done in its prewar commitments to Latin America—to provide a military and political example for its global anticommunist network. At Bogotá there was an ominous prelude. A popular Liberal, Jorge Eliécer Gaitán, who had, it was alleged, committed an unpardonable political (that is, social) error with fervent appeals to the masses, was assassinated on the street. A wave of riots and destruction followed, with the government blaming the communists for much of the damage. Secretary of State George Marshall arrived in Bogotá with a warning about international communism, and the delegates responded with a resolution declaring that "international communism or any totalitarian doctrine is incompatible with the concept of American freedom."[4] As a mark of its consistency with the global implications of Latin American policy, the Department of State, initially lukewarm to the rearming of

Latin America's militaries (on the credible thinking that they consumed too much of depleted public treasuries), reversed its position and moved to revive the moribund Inter-American Defense Board, reinforcing its recommendation with the comment that Latin Americans had their own priorities for their militaries and if the United States provided the arms it would increase its influence among them.

In retrospective and occasionally scathing evaluations of the course the United States chose in Latin America after the war it has been often argued that Latin America deserved more than it got from its wartime ally. Further, if Latin America had received the developmental assistance its beleaguered economies required, if the United States had given its support to the proposed inter-American development bank, if (as the ambassador to Brazil William Pawley suggested) the United States had sustained a "Marshall Plan" for Latin America, then communism would not have been the threat Marshall and the hard-liners in State warned about. Almost casually, President Harry S. Truman at Rio de Janeiro and Marshall at Bogotá spoke of European priorities and the expectation that private sources offered the Latin American mendicants their only realistic alternative. This meant, inevitably, Latin America's acquiescence in the American developmental model, which did not meet the hemisphere's needs because it conformed to American and not Latin American priorities. In denying Latin Americans the aid they solicited, Truman spoke of the differing problems confronted by Europe and Latin America. The task in Europe was reconstruction, which could be achieved by public aid. "The problems of countries in this Hemisphere are different in nature and cannot be relieved by the same means and the same approaches."[5]

His comment anticipated, doubtless unintentionally, the severity of solutions to Latin America's problems that has persisted ever since. The United States had industrialized and in the process had raised the standard of living for its peoples. More important, America had done something that Latin America, despite its professed commitments to modernization, had not yet accomplished. Latin Americans only begrudgingly permitted the social order to expand; that is, they were reluctant to measure the social status of the individual by his economic advancement, nor were they eager to broaden the political base to incorporate those previously left out. What Latin America required, it was feared, was not reconstruction but restructuring of its economy and politics. Such an undertaking would mean, inevitably, a restructuring of the social order. This was a choice the *United States* had not been required to make in its own history because *America* had done so. But it was a choice that Latin America made only at its peril.

Two Revolutions, One Civil War

After the *bogotazo*, the riots that followed the assassination of Gaitán, Colombia sank into *la violencia*, which consumed two hundred thousand lives in a decade and was an ominous indicator of the atrocities that can result from the shaking of the social order. The implicit American view of the Colombian turmoil, which not only produced random violence but opened the country to an odious dictatorship, held that an unenlightened elite had failed to modernize the economy or provide satisfaction for the "revolution of rising expectations." Gaitán had violated a cardinal tenet of the governing social order by appealing to the latent violence of the crowd. The unleashing of social force was a frightening specter that was only marginally explained by the absence of "economic development" or "democracy."

In 1948 Latin America suffered six coups, none of which offered reassurance of the survival of democracy in the hemisphere. Nor, ironically, did a resurgence of dictatorship, uniformly anticommunist, indicate that Latin America was more fully integrated into the U.S. global anticommunist design. Troubled by such critics as the Argentine economist Raúl Prebisch of the U.N. Economic Commission for Latin America (who held that Latin American poverty originated in the industrial prosperity of North America and Europe, which drained the continent of its raw materials) and the broadening appeal of statism, symbolized by Perón's Argentina, the American government altered its tactics in dealing with hemispheric governments.[6]

The architect of the new style in Latin American policy was Edwin Miller, an aggressive but *simpático* careerist who became Dean Acheson's point man on the hemisphere in 1949 as assistant secretary of state. He barnstormed the Latin American capitals, preaching the anticommunist message but with greater understanding of Latin America's resentment over the U.S. tendency to "impose" its own "political system" on the hemisphere. With Louis Halle as kindred spirit, he took on George Kennan, the architect of containment, who had made it clear that in Latin America the United States must seek security first and economic development second in containing the communists. Emulating Kennan's authorial secretiveness, Halle summed up the new wisdom. The recent instability that plagued several countries was distressing but a reality the United States had to accept. Economic development was necessary for the flowering of democracy in the hemisphere. Latin America was evolving toward the political model that flourished north of the Rio Grande. To implant democracy by intervention, as the American record in the Caribbean had amply demonstrated, would not bring Latin America closer to "maturity."[7]

Dictatorship or revolutionary government, though repugnant, would be offered recognition but would not have U.S. blessing. When Somoza installed himself in the Nicaraguan presidency by unconstitutional means in 1947, Washington complained but ultimately recognized his government. A similar logic prevailed elsewhere with other dictators. They were naturally appreciated as being solidly anticommunist, but their political credentials did not automatically guarantee U.S. approbation. The intention was to accept their legitimacy as a means of exercising influence in the hemisphere and simultaneously strive to wean them from their dictatorial ways through economic assistance and inter-American cordiality. But Kennan the hard-liner intruded with his precise strategic calculations about Latin America's place in the global agenda. Given the political disparities between the United States and the hemispheric republics, he doubted the efficacy of the inter-American system as a conduit for achieving

American goals. Latin America produced governments we liked and governments we didn't like: the crucial issue was not hemispheric political or cultural compatibility but whether or not we had "satisfactory relations" with them.[8]

Perhaps Kennan was right about the expedient way to achieve a secure hemisphere. Early in the war, Spykman had argued similarly that power and not cultural understanding determined influence. But Miller pressed ahead, citing Latin America's lukewarm response to American pressures to identify with the U.N. commitment in Korea. He encountered again the globalists, their arguments about the communist threat reinforced by the Korean War, who fashioned a dozen military pacts with Latin American governments. Ironically, Miller's advocacy of increased economic aid to the hemisphere, his polite tolerance of dictators, and his insistence that Latin America be integrated into American Cold War policy facilitated Kennan's approach. Certainly, the bilateral military assistance pacts offered the Defense Department an immediate reassurance that something was being done to contain communism in the hemisphere.[9]

If such a policy translated into coziness with dictators—even decorating a few of them with U.S. medals—or inured the United States against social or political change, it was an unpleasant and, in retrospect, a distasteful choice. At the time it seemed to be the only realistic choice. When military security is the goal of policy, success in results is more highly valued than the political or moral character of the ally. More disturbing, perhaps, was the unmistakable reluctance of the Latin Americans to identify American priorities in the Cold War as their priorities. They took American aid, received American military hardware, and voted with the Americans in the United Nations on Cold War issues, but their accommodation revealed less a genuine commitment than a realization that they had little alternative unless they were willing to pay the price of defying Washington.

Two revolutions and a civil war—in Costa Rica, Bolivia, and Guatemala—delimited American priorities and American responses in the embattled postwar hemisphere. In each, communism became a portentous issue for those who ruled, those who sought power, and those who identified American political and economic influence as a decisive force in the future of the country.

The Costa Rican civil war of 1948 erupted after the breakdown of one of Latin America's most admirable electoral systems, when disgruntled landowner José Figueres raised the flag of rebellion against a government that had wrought impressive social reforms but had depended on the communists to attain them. The alliance had taken shape during the war when popular front images of the communists were common throughout Latin America, a political cooperation presumably approved by Washington. When the American alliance with the Soviet Union was sundered at war's end, Costa Rica's "creole communists" found themselves increasingly isolated.

The landowning elites of Costa Rica, dislodged from power during the war, were determined to reclaim the political authority the conquerors had bequeathed them. In Figueres they found the mythical Hispanic from the interior who challenges central authority and leads the rebellion against it. He belonged to none of the formal social and political unions of the country; each of them laid claim to him. During the war, when Figueres had criticized the government for seizing German property, the president sent him into exile. He returned to a triumphant reception in a Costa Rica bitterly divided over the communist issue. The communist leader, Manuel Mora (already something of a legendary figure in Costa Rican life), tried to soften the party's image among an increasingly suspicious population, but the opposition was unrelenting. The campaign extended into the United States, where ominous warnings about a Russian beachhead in the isthmus found their war into the press. Within Costa Rica, the Social Democrats, the government's most formidable opposition, maintained their anticommunist journalistic assaults against a government whose spokesmen were unambiguously pro-American on the international issues of the day.

To Washington such conciliatory gestures were unconvincing; to Figueres, who had conspired to overturn the government since his return from exile, they meant nothing. "Don Pepe," as the disciples of National Liberation called their leader, had already laid plans to drive from power those who had lost, as Latin Americans often say, their "legitimacy" to govern. Figueres had not only a national but an international network of conspirators and supporters. The Caribbean Legion, dedicated to the overthrow of crass despots in the tropics, supported him. Juan José Arévalo, the leftist president of Guatemala since the tumultuous days of 1944, when dictators had fallen in Guatemala and neighboring El Salvador, pledged arms and troops. Figueres needed only an issue to raise his volunteers against a government whose successive leaders from 1940, Rafael Calderón Guardia and Teodoro Picado, had brought social reforms and with them governmental corruption and ideological conflict into national politics.

The contested election of 1948 provided Figueres with the opportunity to launch his rebellion.[10] In a bitterly contested race a social conservative, Otilio Ulate, had apparently triumphed, but the national congress, dominated by Calderón's followers, declared the election void because of irregularities. Calderón himself, it was widely assumed, would now be designated as president. Throughout the central valley that dominates Costa Rican social and political life, Don Pepe's prediction four years before that Calderón would never relinquish power unless forced to do so seemed prophetic. Figueres now had his long-awaited opportunity. He had gambled that the government would not readily accept the transfer of power to someone whose political views were anathema, and his enemies had not disappointed him. From his farm, appropriately called La Lucha ("The Battle"), the War of National Liberation began on 10 March 1948. Don Pepe dispatched units to cut the Pan-American highway and to seize San Isidro, where three DC–3s belonging to TACA Airlines fell to the rebels. For the next forty days, as the war raged in the countryside, the planes flew nineteen missions to Guatemala and returned with the arms and men that ultimately proved decisive in the war for national liberation.

Pressed from without, the government began to crumble from within. With only a token army it was compelled to rely on Mora's San José legion of workers to defend it. Every gesture of Picado toward the communists brought down the wrath of the opposition, predictably, but also the vocal displeasure of such hemispheric socialists as Haya de la Torre, who warned of "another Czechoslovakia" in the

Americas. In desperation Calderón called on Somoza in Nicaragua to intervene in the struggle against Figueres, who had vowed holy war against him. Costa Rica was spared the larger and even bloodier conflict that might have resulted. Somoza dispatched units across the border and took Villa Quesada but pressed no farther. From his lair Figueres called for negotiations but rejected any settlement that left the Popular Vanguard, the communist militia that held San José, with its arms. He vowed to march on the city if the communists resisted.

His declaration came a week after the *bogotazo* and its frightening portent of urban violence carried out by communists. San José, Costa Rican president (and Calderón ally) Picado decided, ought not to suffer a comparable fate. In an admirable gesture of conciliation he saved Costa Rica from national disintegration. Calderón and Picado took immediate advantage of the terms hammered out between the diplomatic corps and Don Pepe and went into exile in Somoza's Nicaragua to plot their revenge. Within a week Figueres and the National Liberation were parading in the capital. The nation, he declared, had been saved from the communist scourge. This pleased American officials, some of whom had casually referred to Don Pepe as a Nazi only a few years before. In his defiance of the political order, Figueres had assured the restoration of the Costa Rican landed elite in national life. National Liberation had also validated the primacy of the social order, not ideology, in the political culture.

In Costa Rica and elsewhere in Latin America, where migration from countryside to city had wrought a generation of urban workers responsive to leftist politics, Figueres's triumph permitted the ruling order to regain power and retain its hold on national politics if it responded to the demands of a new era. But in Bolivia the feudal aristocracy perished before middle-class revolutionaries of the Nationalist Revolutionary Movement (MNR). During the war MNR officials had occupied important positions in a government that was, in Washington's view, profascist. In the discord that wracked Bolivia in the late 1940s, an era of declining tin prices and agitation among workers, Víctor Paz Estenssoro had effectively purged the volatile Bolivian political arena of his leftist opposition and won labor's support. The Bolivian military, once MNR's ally but now fearful of its political reach, vowed to crush the movement. Unlike the rural dons of Costa Rica, the Bolivian landed aristocracy (believing that a movement of the dedicated without guns posed no real threat) decided to watch the struggle from the sidelines. When MNR organizers called for strikes, the military violently suppressed them, and the party went to the barricades, confronting military units throughout Bolivian cities. In this challenge to the government, MNR lost out, but in the process it had united the tin miners with urban workers. And the ordeal had convinced Paz that the only way to revolution was that long advocated by Juan Lechín and his following of former Trotskyites—defeat and then disband the military.

In 1951, when the MNR made its last attempt to gain power by the ballot, Paz was in exile. But he ran for president at the head of an MNR ticket and the party won a stupendous victory. The army again intervened, installing a rump government, and frantically searched for a civilian political base to sustain it. By now the erosion of Bolivian traditional political life had virtually run its course, and in the cities, where a new political culture had taken its place, MNR leaders began passing out weapons not only to the party faithful but to anyone who would help them gain the power wrongfully denied. Two years before, they had hesitated to arm civilians, fearing a destructive civil war. An unexpected dispute with the United States over the low price Washington was offering for Bolivian tin abetted the rebel cause. Bolivian authorities decided to shut down production, a decision that worsened economic conditions and precipitated more unrest. In April 1952 the party called for the final assault. It seized the armories in the capital and distributed the weapons to the populace. Truckloads of miners descended on La Paz. After three days of intense fighting and six hundred dead, the Bolivian army surrendered.

With its defeat came the collapse of the old order and, more ominously, demands for a revolutionary new order from those who had made the triumph possible. The victors had shifted from Right to Left in their constituency in only six years. Paz Estenssoro and the MNR now had power, but the country's economy was grossly distorted. Tin, the only marketable export, cost more to produce in

Bolivia than anywhere in the world. The country had few manufacturers because it had few consumers of manufactured goods. It had a
landed aristocracy that was largely absentee and whose estates could
be taken without much protest. Its tin owners, if adequately compensated, were eager to rid themselves of inefficient operations. The revolution had assumed political command of an exhausted society, a
wretched economy, and a state with no defense save the masses MNR
had armed. They would not wait for the revolution to fulfill its
promises.

The revolution that had been inspired from above now found itself
pushed from below—from tin miners demanding greater benefits to
Indians (who had historically been denied participation in national
life but who now had the vote. A movement that had begun with
moderate economic plans undertook a social and economic restructuring of the nation. Although their reforms for the tin industry were
unacceptable to the workers, Paz and his MNR chieftains nationalized
the holdings of the tin barons, Patiño, Hochschild, and Aramayo.
More frightening than the urban dislocation was the breakdown of
rural society. Throughout the remainder of 1952 and into the next
year bands of campesinos organized themselves into militias, seizing
estates and expelling their occupants. By the end of 1953 the countryside, which had been largely spared in the revolution, was devastated. The old rural social order, banished from the land, collapsed.

Less than two years in power, with a bankrupt economy, an agricultural system that could not feed the nation, and no money for the
social programs they had promised, the revolutionaries chose the expedient course. Rather than nationalize the entire economy and alienate their middle-class supporters, they chose to accommodate Washington's strictures about running the country. Alert to the pressures
the American government was bringing on the Guatemalan revolution, they offered compensation to the owners—a move that displeased the more radical tin workers but, coupled with a decision not
to nationalize American-owned companies, virtually assured that
Washington would render its polite approval. Within a short time
American officials announced that the United States was doubling its

purchases of Bolivian tin and that Bolivia would begin receiving food exports.

Over the course of the decade Bolivia received $100 million in American aid, more than any Latin American nation.[11] The money flowing from a government dedicated to hemispheric anticommunism provided the Bolivian government with a third of its budget, enabled it to feed its urban population, and made possible the improvement of social services and transportation to its rural people. Indisputably, the price Washington exacted was high: Bolivia had to conform to the economic model the Americans imposed. In 1956, when American aid began trickling off and the MNR confronted yet another economic and political crisis, those who had made the revolution four years before concluded that they had only three choices. They could impose socialism, accept a potentially disastrous inflation, or look again to Washington. They chose the last, and with the approval of American officials and the International Monetary Fund, Bolivia announced a stabilization program.

The Eisenhower administration and the Bolivian revolutionaries did not reconcile their differences out of common purpose or understanding. Bolivia could not afford the social and political costs unleashed by the revolution MNR had begun but feared to complete. The American government chose to subsidize that revolution for fear of something even more destructive. The critical issue was MNR's dismantling of the Bolivian military. Without a loyal army to sustain the new political order, the revolutionary party in power had to persevere until it could create one. That course meant, in turn, U.S. subsidies and U.S. control of a revolution now beholden to Washington.

The Guatemalan Affair

In Central America President Dwight Eisenhower and Secretary of State John Foster Dulles were able to exercise their Cold War policy more forcefully.[12] They were less understanding of the obstacles facing a new generation that had come of age. In 1944, invigorated by a democratic spirit that had swept the isthmus, urban revolutions had

driven from power Jorge Ubico in Guatemala and Maximiliano Her-
nández Martínez in El Salvador. Five years later their Honduran
counterpart, the old dictator Tiburcio Carias Andino, succumbed,
though the quintessential banana republic suffered no disruption of
its social order. Somoza persevered in Nicaragua but not without occasional American disapproval of his meddling in Costa Rican affairs.
Somoza and Pepe Figueres were blood enemies. In 1954 the two
fought a border skirmish when Figueres's enemies, who had been
given sanctuary by Somoza, launched a raid from Nicaraguan soil.
Washington did not especially approve of Figueres and his notions of
state intrusion into the economy, but neither did it want a de-
stabilized isthmus, so the U.S. Air Force dispatched planes to San José
and the OAS intervened to settle the dispute. Somoza backed off from
his personal vendetta, and Figueres emerged from the crisis with
Washington's begrudging support. As he often remarked, Figueres
knew how far he could push the Americans and get away with it.

His kindred spirits in Guatemala did not. Under a formerly exiled
university professor, Juan José Arévalo, they had begun a social transformation in Central America's most rigidly structured social order.
The 1944 overthrow of Ubico, orchestrated largely by reformist students and faculty at the University of San Carlos, heralded profound
changes for the country. Inspired by the wartime rhetoric of commit
ment to a more democratic Latin America and their own disgust at
their nation's debilities, Arévalo's vanguard looked to a national reformation guided by this idealistic generation. Arévalo himself spoke of
"spiritual socialism" with that Latin American intellectual's subordination of material culture and the execration of Guatemala's entrenched oligarchy and its ally, the church. The dream was a new
Guatemala where Indian peasant and urban laborer—theretofore excluded from the political culture—would take their rightful place.

Arévalo showed purpose but had no dependable political support
to sustain his cause. Labor, for example, rapidly increased its economic standing in the new "humane capitalism" but soon fell under
the sway of communists, who began operating schools for future organizers. Like the urban militants of Bolivia and Costa Rica, Guatemalan workers had long suffered from exploitation and indifference.

They had never counted for much in the political and social order. Promised a better day, they became more militant. When Arévalo left office in 1950, Guatemala was a better place for the dispossessed, but "spiritual socialism" had not triumphed. Arévalo had failed to create a cohesive political culture. He did not disband the military, which chafed under his social reformism and twenty times attempted to overthrow him. He managed to hang on, usually by arming the urban faithful, but he left the military intact. Toward the end, ominously, the extremes, Right and Left, moved farther apart. "Spiritual socialism" was neither a reconciling nor a unifying doctrine. But at least Arévalo survived his term.

His virtually handpicked successor, Jacobo Arbenz, was not so fortunate. Assessing the fortunes of a revolution only six years in power, Arbenz decided the only realistic course was invigoration of the government's promise to the Guatemalan peasantry. The Bolivian revolutionaries had made their peace with country peasants by giving them land. In Costa Rica the triumphant rural elite had not given peasants land but provided a benevolent paternalism and acquitted itself with a pervasive myth that in Costa Rica there was no peasantry. By any standard of social decency the Guatemalan country dwellers deserved the agrarian reform that Arbenz announced in June 1952, expropriation with compensation of untilled land above a certain acreage. Landless campesinos could now gain title to lands they had worked as migrants or use of the land in return for a percentage of their crop. In retrospect, the law was mild, but Arbenz did not possess the political stature of the Mexican or Bolivian revolutionaries who had carried out more drastic reforms. More crucially, the Guatemalan revolutionaries were striking directly at the most powerful foreign entity in Central America, United Fruit.

UFCo, which Central Americans derisively called "the Octopus," was not only a huge landowner but also the proprietor of Guatemala's railroad and public utilities.[13] To many the company was Guatemala's last fiefdom, long accustomed to having its way because it had friends in high places, especially in the Eisenhower administration. Under Arbenz's reforms UFCo lost more than two hundred thousand acres, for which the government promised to pay what company officials considered a woefully inadequate compensation. Back in the states UFCo publicists undertook a blistering propaganda campaign to portray "Red Guatemala" as a menace not only to international capitalism but to American security. Largely unseen by American observers—and thus too little appreciated by them—were the disparate but collectively ominous social disturbances caused by roving bands of campesinos. Wanting more than the government was capable of delivering in its agrarian reforms, they had fallen under the sway of militant rural leaders who inspired them to seize not only UFCo lands but the holdings of all foreigners. In time, even sympathetic Guatemalan reformers who lived in the countryside grew fearful of these bands. They had struggled for democracy and national reformation. But the rural disturbances had resurrected old fears that reach deep into Guatemala's history: the unanticipated dangers that sometimes followed political and economic reforms, when formerly oppressed peoples, incapable of being satisfied with moderate, "rational" gestures from their rulers, sense in their collective strength the capability to bring down the prevailing social order and construct their own.

Eisenhower and Dulles required no encouragement to identify the Guatemalans for punishment. Dulles, who had once served in the law firm of Sullivan and Cromwell, which represented UFCo, had already singled out the Guatemalans for their deviation from American guidance in the United Nations. Both Figueres and Arbenz had irritated Washington, but Arbenz was more vulnerable, and, in Dulles's eyes, more culpable. He had not isolated and disarmed the communists but tolerated their rising influence over Guatemalan labor and permitted them to organize the campesinos. In Dulles's mind the communist presence in Guatemala confirmed Soviet penetration of the hemisphere. Other Central American governments, alert to American predilections in the Cold War, joined in the condemnation.

The conspiracy against Arbenz commenced early in the Eisenhower administration. It had already begun within the Guatemalan oligarchy and its supporters in the military in 1952, when Carlos Castillo Armas and Manuel Ydígoras Fuentes vowed war against Arbenz in a gentleman's agreement in San Salvador. But they required American aid and inspiration. Eisenhower was alert to the dangers in an overt assault against the defiant Arbenz, but he remembered his wartime experience and was especially mindful of what could be accomplished by a military intelligence operation. This explains why the Central Intelligence Agency's (CIA) anti-Arbenz plan, appropriately called Operation PBSuccess, was so appealing to an administration dedicated to the dismantling of a leftist government but sensitive to international and especially hemispheric criticism.

One assault against the Guatemalans was carried out through the inter-American system. At the tenth inter-American conference, which met in Caracas in 1954, Dulles led the diplomatic offensive. He introduced a resolution declaring the "domination or control of the political institutions of an American state by the international Communist Movement" a menace to the inter-American system and requiring appropriate response under the Rio treaty. Guatemala, which had not yet signed the pact, denounced this Declaration of Caracas as a pretext for interfering in its internal affairs. The other Latin American republics, though offended by Dulles's preachments, went along when he declared, "I believe there is not a single American state which would practice intervention against another American state."[14] This reassurance, coupled with expectations of U.S. economic aid, got Dulles the authorization he needed. With the declaration in his pocket he headed for Washington, and Operation PBSuccess and the Guatemalan counterrevolution commenced their final drive to extinguish what rightist commentators called "the Red Star over Guatemala."

Anticipating that Castillo Armas would invade, Arbenz frantically tried to shore up his faltering government with political and military measures, but he was frustrated at every turn. Denied arms from the United States since 1948, the Guatemalans looked first to Western European sources. When the Americans blocked them, they appealed to Eastern European governments. News of a shipment from Poland on a Swedish freighter prompted a revival of American charges of Soviet involvement. Within the country, Arbenz's security agents rounded up suspected revolutionaries and subjected them to harsh treatment, including, it was widely reported, torture. On the diplomatic front Guatemala appealed to the U.N. Security Council, proclaiming to the world that the United States, in complicity with United Fruit, was conspiring against a small republic. On the military front, Arbenz withstood Castillo Armas's first attack, destroying two of his three bombers. On both battlefields the initial triumphs quickly deteriorated in frustration, then defeat. In the United Nations, the Americans brought heavy pressure on the British and French, who made a prudent diplomatic retreat. Eisenhower replaced the planes Castillo Armas had lost, and the invaders, beaten on the ground, subjected Guatemala City to a bombardment more psychologically than physically destructive.

Arbenz might have survived if he had been able to rouse an armed populace to the government's defense, but the erosion of his support had gone too far. CIA agents had already gotten assurances from the Guatemalan military that it would not distribute arms to Arbenz's loyal civilian militias. When the air attacks began, Arbenz possessed sufficient airplanes to defend the capital, but the CIA operatives, in a brilliant ploy, broadcast over a rebel station the announcement of the defection of a government pilot. The story was untrue, but Arbenz believed it and grounded his planes. In the final days of late June, threatened by his generals, he tried to shift executive power to a presumably loyal officer. But the American ambassador, John E. Peurifoy, a putative member of the conspiracy from the beginning, foiled his efforts by insisting on a candidate more amenable to Washington.

Its choice, of course, was Castillo Armas. In a national broadcast, Dulles lauded Guatemala's salvation from international communism, and Castillo declared that UFCo's lands would be restored. He demolished the labor unions and disfranchised a generation of Guatemalans who had been incorporated into the political culture in less than a decade. A grateful Washington provided the liberators of Guatemala with a $6 million loan.

The Guatemalan operation ultimately earned the description of "seminal event" in the history of U.S. policy in Latin America, but the implications of this phrase were not readily apparent for many years.

Incorporating Latin America into its postwar global strategy, as it had done to meet the German challenge before the war, the United States had, in an effective and cheap operation, disposed of a nuisance. In the process it had demonstrated not only its priority of security concerns over the principle of nonintervention but, more ominously, the limits of its commitments to the overthrow of governments it considered a threat to those security interests. Had Arbenz dealt with the internal conspiracy against him, he might have survived, for Eisenhower was apparently unwilling to commit American troops to the Guatemalan operation.

The American Colony

There was another limitation to American commitment in the hemisphere. In undermining Arbenz the United States offered no effective rebuttal to the Latin Americans who had reluctantly approved the Declaration of Caracas with the expectation that U.S. economic aid would shortly follow. Marshall had pledged his government to a hemispheric economic conference as early as 1948. When it finally convened in 1954 at Quintandinha, Brazil, Prebisch and the ECLA disciples were prepared with a report on the hemisphere's economic realities. Latin Americans only appeared better off, said Prebisch. In reality, the continent was even more dependent on the industrial north, its share of world trade had declined, and the United States could expect more trouble because of rising expectations and decreasing economic performance. If the challenge were not met, a turbulent future was inevitable. The American emissary, George Humphrey, responded that private not public aid offered the mendicant Latin Americans a more prosperous future.

Others (including the president's brother Milton, who summed up the case for a more aggressive economic program in a special report) warned of a calamitous future for Latin America if social and economic issues were not addressed. The United States was not insensitive to these appeals. Ultimately, in its acceptance of the Inter-American Development Bank and the Alliance for Progress, Washington

adopted a developmental strategy far more ambitious and even revolutionary than any contemplated in the early 1950s. But there were
always limits to what it would or could do for Latin America, just as
there were limits to its tolerance for Latin American governments that
deviated from American prescriptions for economic development.
After Richard Nixon's visit in 1958, when angry crowds in Venezuela
and Peru spewed out their disgust over everything from the Eisenhower administration's coziness with crass dictators to the intrusion
of American multinationals into traditional societies, the American
government supported such programs as the ambitious housing
scheme of the Peruvians to meet the relentless demands of the urban
squatters who had already begun to fester in squalid rings circling
Lima. As the president himself expressed matters, homeownership
deprived the communists of new recruits.[15]

Communism in Cold War Latin America was a perceived rather than
a visible threat to American interests. In the revived anti-Americanism
of the era, the United States mistook the outbursts against its domination as the work of the communists—with less vehemence but essentially the same logic that Nixon used to explain the riots his appearance
provoked. Communist parties throughout Latin America, in fact, went
into decline after World War II. By the mid-1950s, as America's global
anticommunism assumed an uncompromising stridency, most hemispheric governments had broken diplomatic relations with the Soviet
Union (which was still willing to concede to the United States a sphere
of influence throughout the Americas). American liberals who chided
the Eisenhower administration for its inattentiveness to hemispheric
economic concerns and its casual indifference to Latin America's historical antipathy to American intervention correctly identified these
outbursts as potentially troublesome for American policy.[16] With some
persuasiveness, they argued that Castro's revolution was the inevitable product of American economic subjugation. Yet they were often
just as naive in their belief that a more vigorous economic assistance
program would wean a generation of Latin Americans from the
Communist Manifesto of Karl Marx and Friedrich Engels over to *The
Stages of Economic Growth* of Walt Whitman Rostow.

Latin Americans wanted development but *neither* the American *nor* the Soviet model. To the U.S. response that it could not realistically extend aid without stipulations—neither Congress nor the American public would have sustained a program for which the borrower set the terms—they offered a reaffirmation of traditional priorities. As the brilliant Venezuelan man of letters Mariano Picón-Salas expressed it: "Although we Latin Americans are requiring a technology as effective as that of the North American for the improvement of our material conditions, at the same time we wish to preserve our conception of life and culture which, from many points of view, is opposed to that of the United States. The worst thing that could happen to us would be to transform ourselves into second-class Yankees or to have their culture imposed upon us or to suffer an adulteration of native spiritual values, like that which a badly organized North American education has produced in Puerto Rico."[17]

Puerto Rico was an apt choice as an example of Latin American apprehension of Americanization, though few Americans (of that era and today) understood what Picón-Salas was trying to say.[18] The island was an oddity in the American experience in Latin America. In 1917, when it gained what amounted to territorial status, Washington had dispatched a generation of educational zealots to mold an English-speaking culture. By the time the depression set in, the program was in shambles. The New Dealers came along with a Puerto Rican development scheme, which promised much and delivered little, though it did alert a generation of Americans to the severity of what Rexford Guy Tugwell, appointed governor in 1941, called the "stricken land." Just as troubling as the island's depressed social and economic condition, however, was the nationalist agitation of a Puerto Rican elite for independence. In 1937, police, angry over the murder of their chief, fired into a crowd of Nationalist party members in Ponce. During the war anti-Americanism flourished among both the Left and the Right, and in 1945 what to do with (or to) the island remained a conundrum.

Most Puerto Ricans, then and now, recognized that independence would free them from their felt obligation to conform to American culture but would doom them to economic ruin. Moreover, for strategic reasons, the United States would not permit an independent Puerto Rico to pursue a foreign policy that was inimical to American interests. Statehood, at least in 1945, was at first tempting (as it had been to an early generation of Puerto Rican advocates) and then, for both Puerto Ricans and mainland Americans, fraught with uncertainties. *Riqueños*, it was already widely believed, were becoming *Co-colars*, a denigrating term for Puerto Ricans who imported everything they consumed—from clothes and food to philosophy of life—from the mainland. For those Puerto Ricans torn between the cultural identity the independence movement promised and the better life the American connection held out, Luis Muñoz Marín, leader of the Popular Democrats, had a deceptively simple and thus reassuring message. Shortly after the war, when President Truman declared that Puerto Rico had three choices (independence, statehood, or dominion), Muñoz responded by rejecting the first two and, in a modification of the third, called for a "commonwealth of the associated people of Puerto Rico." A commonwealth would enable the island to protect its economy and its cultural distinctiveness.

Muñoz Marín became Puerto Rico's first elected governor in 1948. Two years later, Congress validated the commonwealth in Public Law 600, which it submitted to a plebiscite in an island wracked with uncertainty over what it meant. The Independence party boycotted the voting. The Nationalists called for insurrection. They attacked police stations and even the governor's residence. Muñoz declared a state of emergency and called out the national guard, which took over the University of Puerto Rico, where nationalist sentiment ran strong and its sympathizers regularly gathered. Eventually, the guard suppressed the insurrection, but not before two dozen had perished. In one highly publicized incident on 30 October the guard stormed the home of the fiery old nationalist of the 1930s, Pedro Albizu Campos, who was teargassed into unconsciousness in the assault. The following day two Puerto Rican nationalists tried to assassinate Truman. For years the nationalists kept up their protests, arguing with considerable validity that Muñoz's characterization of Puerto Rico as a "freely associated state" simply masked with deceptive words the reality of a continuing colonial status. Muñoz was less *riqueño*, perhaps, but craftier. He now joined the American delegation in the United Nations in arguing that Puerto Rico no longer belonged on the U.N.'s list of non-self-governing territories because Puerto Ricans had voted to accept Public Law 600.

Already, however, the American colony had begun to assume the economic character that became its blessing and, unintentionally, its burden. In its determination to rid the island of wartime government "socialism," Congress in 1945 authorized the Aid to Industry Program, by which private businesses could lease factories at very low rates, and two years later revolutionized the program with the Industrial Incentives Act, which forgave corporate taxes (and local taxes for a decade). Attracted by Puerto Rico's ready supply of low-cost labor, corporate America moved to the island. Almost immediately the *independistas* condemned the transformation as simply another variety of colonialism—an industrial rather than a plantation colonization but still a self-perpetuating dependence.[19]

In the 1950s Puerto Rican "colonial whining" (a phrase Tugwell often used) diminished noticeably from the spectacular growth rates of the American economic policy, called Operation Bootstrap, which in its most frenzied years led to the establishment of a factory every day. In the decade after 1947 the island's gross national product doubled, and on the eve of Castro's revolution in Cuba, which became in the 1960s the competitive economic model, Puerto Ricans enjoyed the highest per capita income in Latin America. Even as the economy lagged behind that of the mainland, the quality of life for Puerto Ricans rose impressively. Little wonder, then, that Puerto Rico became for the United States the economic model for the Alliance for Progress.

But the island did not become an enduring symbol of economic development and democracy for Latin Americans. The reason is more complicated than the fact that Puerto Rico was yet another example of Washington's efforts to impose a model on them, however benign American intentions. Rather, Puerto Rico stood as an unpleasant reminder of what happens when Anglo and Hispanic are mixed in an experiment in social engineering. If it were to work, Operation Bootstrap required political domination and government involvement in the economy to a degree that would have been thought intolerable on the mainland. In the process the Popular Democratic party held sway, and its leaders, especially Muñoz, ruled as benevolent but stern patriarchs of a factory economy and a government bureaucracy staffed by the faithful. For Americans and many Puerto Ricans, the economic transformation and the paternalism of Muñoz provided opportunities for the sons and daughters of country people who never dreamed of such possibilities in life and thus were able to discard that inherited Hispanic trait of fatalism. Too often, they found in San Juan not success but economic despair in the subculture of poverty. But there was always the prospect that as U.S. citizens they could fulfill the dream on the mainland. Tragically, as Oscar Lewis revealed in *La Vida*, in moving from San Juan to New York they rediscovered the subculture of poverty. Yet the dream persisted.

What Latin Americans found more objectionable than the creation of a "showcase democracy"—in which many Puerto Ricans failed to understand what American-style democracy really meant and thus acquiesced in denial of civil liberties—was the erosion of Puerto Rican culture and with it the Hispanic's need to find reassurance in the social order and in tradition. The *independistas* undeniably distorted the glories of Puerto Rico's cultural heritage, and they were blind to the economic and political benefits of American rule. But in their determination to resist Americanization, whether by legitimate protest or by violence, they expressed the traditional Hispanic *retraimiento*, which literally means *retreat* but also conveys defiance of the alien culture that tries to change one's way of looking at life. To the American tutors of Puerto Rico, the economic and political blessings of Operation Bootstrap had fashioned a new Puerto Rican culture of economic rationality and political benevolence. The United States offered citizenship and economic opportunity. What mattered was the island's future, not its past. Americanization offered material if not spiritual benefits, and it has been a voluntary process, which, Americans believe, absolves the United States from Third World charges of colonialism.

But to Hispanics the voluntary relinquishment of one's cultural tradition can be more frustrating than involuntary servitude to the conqueror. Puerto Ricans have had to pay a cultural price in Americanization. Those who have converted—many with great enthusiasm—not only had to learn English to get ahead but to speak Spanish without an accent, become a *Co-colar*, get a university education not in Puerto Rico but on the mainland, or measure themselves by such slogans as "You Are What You Do" or "Consume." Unlike the earlier wave of European immigrants who arrived between 1880 and 1920—more than 50 percent of whom returned to their homelands—Puerto Ricans could not escape Americanization by returning to the island. They had to reject their past with all its debilities and join the generation of Puerto Rican paranoiacs who are better off but who have lost their cultural identities, who are foreigners in their own land, who are awash in a sea without a cultural anchor.

8   The Cuban Revolution

When Fidel Castro triumphantly entered Havana in January 1959 and ended what most Cubans and many Americans considered an odious dictatorship, progressive elements in the hemisphere cheered his victory. His war against Fulgencio Batista had at last brought down one of the triumvirate of tropical rulers—each identified with the United States presence in the Caribbean—whose long and sometimes ghastly rule ended in the following two decades. The second, Rafael Leonidas Trujillo, Jr., who had wielded power as Caribbean caesar in the nearby Dominican Republic, fell in May 1961, the deserving victim of assassins in his own military. The third, Anastasio Somoza DeBayle, whose father had molded a familial dynasty in the waning days of marine-ruled Nicaragua, fled to the United States during the final days of a civil war that consumed fifty thousand Nicaraguan lives. Unwanted in a nation whose president feared he was conspiring to reverse a revolution most Americans and virtually all Nicaraguans believed offered Nicaragua hope for a democratic future, Somoza sought sanctuary in Paraguay. He died a year later when terrorists ambushed his car.

Before these dictators departed from power, the United States had already distanced itself from them. (In Trujillo's case, the CIA abetted the assassins by providing arms.) In its expressions of support and its offers of economic assistance, the American government welcomed their successors with the twin expectations of furthering hemispheric democracy and charting their economic and social courses. By abandoning the strongmen it had helped to install in power and sustained through long years of misrule, it naively believed that good intentions, economic assistance, and its military credibility would enable the United States to "guide" the revolutions that triumphed. But Castro and later the Sandinistas had their own priorities, their own agendas, their own timetables. Only in the Dominican Republic did the

American political and economic prescription, reinforced by an un-mistakable military presence, hold sway over the new order.

Castro's Revolution—
Challenge to American Power

When Castro launched his revolution against Batista's government with the daring attack on the Moncada barracks in Santiago in July 1953, his rallying cry was the restoration of constitutional government in Cuba, not the removal of American economic and political influ-ence that had shrouded the island from the early years of the century. At his trial, when he delivered the "History Will Absolve Me" speech, he spoke largely for the benefit of Cuba's disgruntled professional and business classes who lived in a country that boasted the fourth highest per capita income in Latin America and had a vigorous intel-lectual and political community but suffered under a crass dictator widely regarded as an American puppet. And he spoke to another generation of Cubans, increasingly discontented and alienated, who believed him when he castigated a presumably modern Cuba where urban dwellers looked visibly prosperous and fun-loving while a countryside of illiterate caneworkers lacked the necessities of life. He reminded Cubans of the ignominy of the foreign presence, largely American, which controlled the nation's utilities and 50 percent of its arable land.

Victorious when the Batista government suddenly collapsed in early 1959, Castro began with pledges to restore Cuban democracy, which heartened those middle-class Cubans who had repudiated Batista. But they quickly realized that they constituted no meaningful opposition to him or his plans for restructuring the Cuban economy. Washington had dispatched a presumably sympathetic ambassador to Havana, Philip Bonsal, who issued no protest when Ernesto "Ché" Guevara, Castro's economic czar, nationalized Cuba's American-owned telephone system. Castro followed with a dramatic visit to the United States, where he was lionized by a still admiring American public and press. Reluctant to appear as a mendicant to wary Cubans who had watched previous leaders make deals with Washington, Castro declared that he wanted not a loan but a new economic understanding with the United States. He met with Vice-President Richard Nixon (President Eisenhower was vacationing in Augusta), who apparently liked Castro but was suspicious of communist influence in the revolution. To allay this and other charges, Castro denounced dictatorship and pledged to his American listeners that his revolution was not communist. As a symbolic gesture of his politics he snubbed the Soviet ambassador during a reception at the Cuban embassy and reminded Americans that his government had not restored the diplomatic relations with the Soviet Union that Batista had broken in 1955. But as he spoke, Cuba's ties with the United States were already unraveling.

Castro severed the American bond because the United States posed the most formidable international opposition to his plan to transform Cuba and refused to treat with him as an equal.[1] He was dedicated to the long held but never realized dream that Cuba can play a pivotal if rarely decisive role in international politics. But the revolution began with a calculated restructuring of the economy. The takeover of Cuba's telephone system was but the first of a series of measures that struck at American property interests in Cuba and, more fundamentally, challenged liberal American beliefs about the social and economic reforms that Cuba merited. In May 1959 the government announced a sweeping agrarian reform law, which applied to American holdings. Ambassador Bonsal upheld Cuba's right to expropriate foreign property if the government compensated the owners. Castro reassured him, then proceeded to move against large American-owned ranches. His rhetoric was alternately strident and conciliatory. Often in the same speech he denounced Washington for trying to control the course of the revolution, then offered soothing words to the same government he had assailed for its history of unjust intervention in Cuban affairs.

During the ensuing months, as seizures continued and irate owners criticized the arbitrariness of revolutionary justice, statements from both governments indicated that disagreements over Cuba's economic policy could be reconciled through continued negotiations. By the end of the revolution's first year, Bonsal was still cautiously optimistic. Early in 1960, when the two governments seemed headed for a fundamental understanding, Castro proposed sending a delegation to the United States to talk about their differences, but he wanted pledges that Cuba's sugar quota, vital to the country's economic interests, would not be reduced. Washington refused.[2]

Afterward, the revolutionary course again shifted to the left. In February, Soviet First Deputy Anastas Mikoyan descended on Havana and signed a commercial treaty with the Cubans. The Soviets were not yet ready to make larger commitments, and Castro waited until May to restore diplomatic relations with Moscow. Even then it was not clear that the revolution was heading inexorably toward the creation of a communist state. What was apparent was Castro's determination to rid Cuban politics of naysayers and to purge the regime of its critics. He molded urban labor and rural campesinos into an alliance. Middle-class Cubans who had not yet abandoned the faith were denounced as enemies of the revolution. In June came the order to foreign refineries to process Soviet crude oil. Under pressure from the Eisenhower administration, they refused, and Castro further infuriated Washington by ordering their seizure. When the companies dispatched key personnel back to the states, Castro brought in foreign technicians to run the plants.

Eisenhower had already suspended Cuba's sugar quota of nine hundred thousand tons, a severe blow to its fragile economy but one that did not deter Castro or mitigate his defiance of Washington. By late summer, as the American presidential campaign between Vice-President Nixon and John F. Kennedy was getting under way, the "Cuban question" had already become a political issue in the United States. By now, American public opinion about Castro had diminished from the early enthusiasm of his first months in power to doubts about where the revolution was heading and widely held skepticism about Castro's democratic professions. This shift in opinion roughly paralleled government policy and explains why Cuba became such a volatile subject in the fall and why Kennedy, in a narrow race for the White House, spoke often about Cuba's "loss."[3]

By then the Eisenhower administration had stepped up its time-table for dealing with Castro as it had dealt with Arbenz in Guatemala six years before, but the plan, which had emanated from Nixon's encounter with Castro in spring 1959, was not one the vice-president could now use as rebuttal to a vigorous young senator determined to exploit the issue of "communism ninety miles from American territory." Fearful of communist penetration of Arbenz's government, the United States had moved quickly to unseat him. Guatemala was a lesson the intelligence bureaucracy often cited as reports of communist intrusion in the Cuban revolution grew more frequent. Washington had rid the hemisphere of a leftist government in Guatemala; for even more compelling reasons it now proposed to dethrone Castro.

The plan was first mentioned by Nixon, but its gestation lay in the CIA, which had Operation PBSuccess (the scenario for the Guatemalan operation) as proof of its expertise in handling such Caribbean irritants. To the generation that had masterminded the Guatemalan affair, the decision to topple Castro was perhaps more problematical and certainly fraught with more difficulties but, to use a favorite bureaucratic word, no less "doable." Castro defied American power and influence in Cuba; his revolution challenged the American prescription for Western Hemispheric development. Arbenz and the Guatemalan revolution had confronted American power, and the United States had rebuffed them, offering no alternative to Latin American liberals of the mid-1950s who were calling for a "Marshall Plan" for the Western Hemisphere.

The American government had learned one lesson from the Guatemalan affair—a revolutionary government that does not have the support of the military can be readily toppled without using American troops. But Castro learned this and more from the events of 1954: if the United States could not accept the Guatemalan revolution, it most certainly would never accept the more radical Cuban variation. But more important to Castro was his conviction that if he raised the stakes of the confrontation between Cuba and the United States to a level at which the United States would *have* to dispatch its soldiers to the island to destroy the revolution, it would not do so. Eisenhower had the benefit of U.S. intelligence operatives in Guatemala who verified the unreliability of the Guatemalan officer corps in the defense of the Arbenz government. Kennedy did not have such a reassurance about Operation Zapata, the outline for the Cuban operation, because Castro quickly stripped the Cuban military of antirevolutionary officers. This, of course, U.S. officials knew, but they came to successive erroneous conclusions about the fighting capability of Cuba's military, the loyalty of a Cuban populace already outspoken in its criticism of the revolution, and what steps Castro would take to remain in power.

Thus was born what has been called the "perfect failure." The plan for unseating Castro had the sanction of the intelligence and military communities and a ready and willing army of former Batistianos, alienated middle-class exiles, and even vengeful former Castroites who had become disillusioned with the revolution and had fled to the United States. In retrospect, the former Castroites had the most persuasive strategy for dealing with Castro. Their spokesman, Manuel Ray, had organized a resistance movement against the *líder máximo* within Cuba, and in fall 1960 still another guerrilla operation had sprung up in the Escambray Mountains. Both sought CIA support but were discounted by agents as too isolated and too weak to cause much damage. Eventually, Castro's counterrevolutionary forces wiped out the Escambray guerrillas and sent Ray into exile.

In the United States, Ray pleaded for a resumption of the anti-Castro guerrilla campaign, but no one in the CIA was much interested. By then, the general plan called for a conventional landing of Cuban exiles in a remote spot along the southern Cuban shore. They would be sustained by American supply ships until they established a beachhead, moved inland (where disaffected Cubans would join them), and created a "legitimate" government that the United States and ultimately the international community would recognize. Ray criticized the plan as hopeless, arguing that the presence of so many former Batista officers among the exiles doomed the credibility of any invasion among even disaffected Cubans. But the CIA, whose agents moved about Miami with cash and advice, was determined to run this operation with the same gusto it had managed Operation PBSuccess. Besides, there was no one in the agency who believed Ray when he said that "Castroism without Castro" was the only way to get support from the large numbers of Cubans who chafed under Castro's rule. Even after the training camps were moved into Guatemalan boondocks, far from prying journalists, CIA trainers brooked little criticism from the Cuban charges and sent the complainers back to Miami. Shortly before the invasion, Kennedy insisted that Ray and his group (who called themselves the Revolutionary Movement of the People) be allowed to participate in the invasion, but the CIA effectively undermined the order by taking its leaders to an isolated farm outside Miami and holding them incommunicado.

Their presence among the invading brigade in April 1961 would probably not have altered the outcome of the battle at the Bay of Pigs, but their plan for toppling Castro, though it called for a prolonged struggle and American support, was in retrospect more realistic than that concocted by the CIA. Kennedy had his doubts about the latter but no acceptable substitute. The bureaucracy that advised him recognized the pitfalls in such an operation, but it is the nature of a government official instructed to plan a military operation to concentrate on goals rather than obstacles. Once Kennedy had acquiesced in the general plan for getting rid of Castro, he inquired as to its feasibility and was dutifully informed that it had a "fair" chance of success, which, he found out later, meant one in four. American military support and, if necessary, the landing of American troops would, of course, have dramatically altered this somber prognostication. But Kennedy was alert to the continuing barrage of invasion rhetoric from Castro's minister to the United Nations and to American credibility in the Third World. He stipulated that no American troops were to take part in the invasion. He was committed to removing the Cuban nemesis but desirous of maintaining the nation's image among Latin Americans historically antagonistic to American intervention.

The success of the operation depended on American actions that the president was loath to take. Those lacking, it rested on variables within Cuba that Castro was able to control. The invaders left Nicaragua, where they had been relocated after publicity had prompted them to vacate Guatemala, believing that American planes would knock out Castro's puny air force, that American supplies would sustain them on the beach, that dissident Cubans would rally to their cause, and more than anything that the American government would not abandon them. In all of these expectations they were mistaken. Castro took command of Cuban defenses, dispatched his planes to the Bay of Pigs to sink one of the supply ships, and ordered the arrest of thousands of Cubans suspected of collaboration with the invaders. In the United Nations the American ambassador, Adlai Stevenson, defended a hopeless cause and stood humiliated. Throughout Latin America Kennedy was condemned for going too far in dealing with the Cubans, a sentiment widely expressed by an American public and press that had become suspicious of Castro, generally supported their government's pressures against him, but in the end were uneasy with the methods employed to overthrow him.[4]

The outcry among Latin Americans was not unexpected; the reaction of the American public to Kennedy's acquiescence in the Cuban invasion and then, when it was imperiled, his inability to make sure it succeeded, damaged his political prestige. Neither, however, was a lasting disability. Castro's revolution and his defiance of American power left other legacies. The Bay of Pigs was a crossroads for both Castro and Kennedy.[5] In its aftermath the prospects for reconciliation dwindled.

"Those Who Make Peaceful Revolution Impossible"

Even before the Bay of Pigs, Castro had carried his challenge to the United States into Latin America. Shortly after returning from his 1959 American trip, he embarked on yet another venture, to participate in a hastily called meeting in Buenos Aires of the Committee of

21, which had been convened to discuss Latin American economic issues. Already the Cuban revolution had increased apprehension about revolutionary outbreaks elsewhere. For the first time the United States encountered the "new Cuba" in a hemispheric forum. Castro himself led the Cuban delegation, sporting the now famous fatigues of his days in the mountains. He was accompanied by fierce-looking bodyguards, but his popularity, especially among younger Argentines, seemed universal. Enthusiastic *porteños* cheered his presence. Even inside the meeting hall, as he sat listening to dreary intonations from the other speakers, he continually distracted the audience with his nervous shifting of his legs and tugs on his moustache. When he rose to speak, few knew what to expect, but after a halting introduction he began what was for him a mild assessment of Latin America's troubles. Hemispheric governments were unstable, he said, because they ruled over backward economies, and they had to change. Latin Americans were not culturally unsuited for democratic governance, as European and American political observers had often said (and Latin Americans themselves too often believed), but they were condemned to political retardation because they were denied the opportunity to develop their economies. He ended with a challenge to the United States to provide the continent with $30 billion in aid for the next decade.

Roy Rubottom, speaking for the American delegation in a noticeably irritated tone, reminded the audience of U.S. support for the Inter-American Development Bank and rejected Castro's proposal. The delegates voted to table the Cuban request. Castro departed and did not participate in later inter-American meetings. When the foreign ministers convened in Santiago, Chile, in September, the Americans pushed for a collective disapproval of Cuba's relations with the Soviet Union. The Latin American response was a restatement of economic priorities, but in early 1960, when the ministers met again in San José, Costa Rica, Cuba's involvement in the domestic politics of Panama, Haiti, and the Dominican Republic prompted the delegates to censure its government. Raúl Roa, Castro's emissary to the meeting, stormed out in protest. When the Committee of 21 met in Bogotá in September, the Eisenhower administration was prepared to support a Social Progress Trust Fund with $500 million to underwrite housing, education, and health projects in the hemisphere. American delegates spoke less of relying on the private sector to underwrite Latin American development needs. It was obvious to the alert Latin Americans that Castro's revolution was largely responsible for this demonstration of American largesse.[6]

In the campaign of 1960 Kennedy spoke forcefully about Cuba, but he also seized on what had been originally a Latin American idea, a bold new development program for the troubled hemisphere, the Alliance for Progress. To a generation of Latin Americans accustomed to hearing shopworn phrases about "hemispheric unity" and "common goals" from American political leaders, Kennedy talked about a hemisphere whose people unjustly suffered authoritarian rule and economic deprivation that only a vast effort could remedy. The task was gargantuan in its dimensions—housing, work, agrarian reform, health, and education for the millions of Latin Americans who had abandoned hope of a better life. It demanded a "peaceful revolution." Without that effort, Latin America confronted violent upheaval.

In some of its proposals, such as the call for a Latin American free trade area and a Central American common market or American financial support to help certain hemispheric nations stabilize the often rapidly fluctuating commodity market, the alliance was not particularly revolutionary. But the thrust of the program was toward social reform and economic development on a scale unprecedented in Latin American history. Agrarian and tax reforms, literacy campaigns, and the extension of health measures to Latin America's poor were not only costly but threatening to the hold of the established social and political order. Kennedy made clear in later statements that such an ambitious program could best be carried out by civilian governments inspired by reformist leaders committed to economic development and social change. Accompanied by his wife, who spoke briefly in Spanish, the president formally inaugurated the Alliance for Progress in a ceremony before the Latin American delegations in March 1961. A month later occurred the fiasco at the Bay of Pigs.

The architects of the program were an impressive group. Though some, such as historian Arthur Schlesinger, Jr., and Richard Goodwin, knew little of Latin America, they were eager students and willing to apply their considerable intellectual talents to overcome the hemisphere's vast but to them not insurmountable obstacles. Others, such as Teodoro Moscoso, Adolf Berle (chairman of the Latin American Task Force), Lincoln Gordon, Robert Alexander, Arthur Whitaker, and Arturo Morales Carrión, were knowledgable about the region and brought a sense of urgency to their mission, as demonstrated by Moscoso's comment, "It is one minute to midnight in Latin America." And Kennedy, unlike his predecessor, did not follow absolutely the dictum of the Mutual Security Act of 1951, which used anticommunist criteria and national interest as the guide for disseminating aid to mendicant Third World countries. The stress on economic development and social reforms appealed to a generation of "action intellectuals" who responded to Kennedy's style of cutting through the bureaucratic maze to "make things happen" with a program that offered Latin Americans a realistic choice to the society Castro's revolution was bringing to Cubans.

In August 1961, when the inter-American economic conference convened at a resort outside Montevideo to discuss hemispheric goals, the Alliance for Progress squad flew down to confront America's ideological adversaries. "Ché" Guevara led the Cuban delegation. Though more ideological than Castro, Guevara nonetheless held out a tentative peace offering to Washington and met formally with the presidents of Argentina and Brazil. But there was little hope of reconciliation, and Guevara renewed the challenge with the affirmation that the Cuban revolution would achieve the goals of the alliance. The Americans were already pressing for the expulsion of Cuba's government from the OAS, and the other Latin American governments, though occasionally grumbling about Washington's harassment of Cuba, recognized American priorities and began cutting diplomatic ties with Havana.[7]

When the Venezuelans shut their embassy doors in November, Castro retaliated with a convoluted address in the Plaza de la Revolución about his "conversion" to Marxism-Leninism. In early 1962, Washington finally succeeded in expelling the Cuban government from the OAS, though its triumph, critics pointed out, resulted from considerable browbeating and bribery. Cynical Latin Americans were already calling alliance funding "Fidel's money." Castro's emissary walked out of the conference with the ringing declaration that Cuba could be kicked out of the OAS but not out of the hemisphere. Shortly, Castro began calling for a united Latin America against U.S. imperialism, which elicited the praise of the Chinese Communists, then international champions of guerrilla war, but irritated the Russians, who were busily promoting peaceful coexistence with Latin America. Castro soon convinced them to pay closer attention by cracking down on dissidents within the country and exhorting Cubans to revolutionary solidarity. Cuba was undertaking the building of a socialist society, he declared, and until it was achieved the revolution must be safeguarded.

Nikita Khrushchev, assailed by Beijing for his betrayal of the revolutionary struggle against imperialism, began looking more closely at this still untamed revolutionary who mocked the United States yet now exhibited the revolutionary prudence to realize that socialism must be constructed within a country before the revolution could be exported. Had the Americans done nothing about Castro, Khrushchev would have understood; had Kennedy followed up the Bay of Pigs with an invasion and gotten rid of Castro, Khrushchev would have understood. In either case the Russians would have done nothing to help the Cubans and have confined themselves to denunciations of American imperialism in the United Nations. But Kennedy had elected a third course and in the process had been indecisive. In his calculation to take advantage of American hesitance, Khrushchev decided that the time of greatest danger was, as Americans are fond of saying, also the time of greatest opportunity.

Thus the Cuban Revolution and the Alliance for Progress, each parading as the inescapable alternative for a distressed hemisphere, became the captives of history and circumstance. Expelled from the hemispheric system, the Cuban government (and Castro personally) embraced the Soviet Union, a union of dissimilar cultures and frankly dissimilar leaders born of Cold War politics and Cuban defiance of all geopolitical logic. When the superpowers squared off in the missile crisis of October 1962, none of the central issues dealt with the alternative Cuban and American proposals for Latin American political and economic change, but the example of the Cuban revolution, despite its obvious economic flaws and dictatorial politics, reminded Washington and especially Latin American governments of American restraints in shifting to the left. In the settlement of the crisis, Kennedy and American policy appeared vindicated by his courageous challenge to the Soviets and the support he received from the Latin American nations. Beneath the glow of victory lay a disconcerting reality: the United States had left the thorn implanted in the American side, a reminder of Cuban defiance.[8]

In the aftermath, Cuba was incorporated into the Soviet sphere, Castro ultimately "tamed," and the revolution consolidated. In a parallel yet connected manner American priorities in the hemisphere altered, and the Alliance for Progress, to use Chilean president Eduardo Frei's words, began to "lose its way." In reality it was already failing, but its diminishing momentum lay not so much in the example of Castro's revolution as alternative but in obstacles, some anticipated and others unforeseen, in the Latin American condition. There were impressive accomplishments in agrarian reform, education, health, housing, industrialization, and employment, but at the end of the 1960s, a U.S. government report gloomily concluded, Latin Americans had actually fallen behind in each of these categories. From 1960 to 1967 a million rural families were resettled, yet ten times that number remained on marginal plots with little hope of a better life. Too often those who had escaped the poverty of the countryside found a similarly depressing environment in the mushrooming slums and squatter settlements that surrounded Latin America's rapidly expanding metropolises. In education the Alliance for Progress sought an enrollment increase of 6 percent annually, an ambitious rate, but the preschool population grew so rapidly that, as in the agrarian resettlement program, programs could not keep pace with demand. Child mortality was reduced but at less than half the goal, and housing fell woefully short of the 15 million units needed. In the 1950s, when Latin America lacked the supportive economic underpinning of the alliance, more newcomers to the job market found employment than in the subsequent decade.[9]

Why had the alliance gone awry? Had Latin American elites, fearful of the disruptiveness of profound changes to the social order and alert to the anticommunist priorities of the United States, placed insurmountable obstacles in its path? Had Washington abandoned its commitment to "peaceful revolutionary change" to achieve peace of mind? Or (as more thoughtful analysts have suggested) when the threat of Castro's revolution receded, did both Latin America *and* the United States decide the social and economic issues of Punta del Este no longer to be so compelling and the cost of achieving them to be so high as to make them unobtainable goals?

For one thing, early in the 1960s the Alliance began to lose the democratic political sustenance required to achieve its social and economic goals. Beginning with the dramatic resignation of President Jânio Quadros of Brazil, who believed his abrupt decision would lead to popular demands for his return, followed by the military ouster of President Arturo Frondizi of neighboring Argentina, who had managed to alienate most of the country's powerful groups, and, in summer 1962, a military coup in Peru, sixteen civilian governments fell to military seizures in the first eight years of the alliance. The official U.S. reaction, at least initially, was hostile. Washington expressed its displeasure at what it considered a return to the political authoritarianism of an earlier day. Kennedy was pointedly critical of the Peruvian military for its violation of the spirit of Punta del Este. Later that summer, as members of the Trujillo family threatened to disrupt a planned election in the Dominican Republic, the president dispatched warships to Santo Domingo to intimidate them.

But there were limits to his antimilitary resolve, and, predictably, Cuba figured heavily in his calculations. In Guatemala, where a military coup forestalled the return to power of Juan José Arévalo (the former president, whose leftist reforms had irritated the United States) Kennedy was discreetly approving. In British Guiana, his concern about the political appeal of Cheddi Jagan, a Marxist, prompted

Kennedy to pressure the British to delay Guianan independence until a more suitable candidate could be identified. In the aftermath of the missile crisis, as Castro's threat lessened, so did Kennedy's hostility to the Peruvian generals who had driven out a civilian leader by ramming a Sherman tank through the gate of the national palace.

Kennedy's death indisputedly deprived Latin Americans of one of the alliance's most spirited defenders. He had championed reform, challenged the established order, praised democracy, and condemned authoritarianism. In the hovels of Latin America's poor his photograph was proudly displayed alongside that of Jesus Christ. In four hemispheric nations he had dedicated alliance projects. But even before his death his priorities in Latin America had subtly but noticeably begun to change. Castro's revolution and the Soviet intrusion had toughened him to the communist challenge, and the Dominican crisis of 1962 had demonstrated his determination to stand against the Trujillo family.

The turning point may have been military coups in Ecuador in July and in Honduras in October 1963.[10] The latter, which brought down the Liberal reformer Ramón Villeda Morales, prompted a rethinking of U.S. policy in the White House and, more fundamentally, the place of the Latin American military in hemispheric strategy. Edwin Martin, Kennedy's assistant secretary of state for Latin American affairs, in a public declaration, ruefully noted the grim prospects for reform under a military regime but acknowledged the difficulty of trying to sustain a civilian leader with economic coercion or even military pressure. Martin believed the most realistic course for the United States would have been to identify its Latin American policies with what scholars were calling the "emerging middle sectors" and to use its influence to achieve a more professional military.[11]

This admission was, at least, a recognition that Latin America was different, but the prevailing wise men in Washington still held fast to the notion that Latin Americans' political, economic, and social priorities were generally those Americans ascribed to them. The complaints that had surfaced about the Alliance for Progress—in Congress and among some of the more grumbling recipient governments—had dealt with costs, procedures, and predictable bureaucratic muddling. Few in Washington or Latin America seriously questioned the Rostowian article of faith that development and democracy went hand in hand, that economic diversification and cooperation offered Latin America an opportunity to break the bonds of an agricultural past, or that civilians were preferable to generals in the running of public affairs.

What was lacking in the American prescription for Latin America was a fundamental awareness not only that Latin America was different but that its politics, its economy, and its social structure fit together differently, worked differently, and expressed different values. If democracy meant the dispersal of power, as Americans believed, then in Latin America, where legislators often represented traditional interests opposed to social and economic reforms, democracy was an obstacle to development. Latin America had to develop its economy, but it needed also to develop a parallel real democracy, which imperiled the ruling social order. Not until 1966 did the American Congress, which had become increasingly disillusioned with the diminishing fortunes of hemispheric democracy, insist that American aid for development projects should be conditioned on participation of local governments and social organizations.[12]

For most Latin American leaders, unaccustomed to sharing decision making with those on the bottom, this was truly a radical notion and precipitated considerable grumbling about American interference, but it revealed that Congress had a vague awareness of the limitations of an aid program that lacked political purpose. Latin America had to identify social and economic goals—in education, agrarian reform, employment, and housing—which it undertook, often with enthusiasm, but it then had to integrate its marginal people into the social order, which the upper and even the middle classes refused to do. They did not do so out of indifference but out of fear— the fear that wretched millions who had "nothing of nothing" would be inspired by a gesture of philanthropy or a fleeting hope for a better life to want more of everything. Americans feared the Cuban revolution—the restructuring of the social and economic order in an

authoritarian state. Latin Americans shared that fear and another—
the prospect conveyed through the alliance of the revolutionary notion that the individual deserved a better life than his parents.

"No More Cubas!"

At Kennedy's death the alliance was not yet in disarray, but Washington's approach toward Latin America had already become more
pragmatic. As the United States increased its financial and diplomatic
pressures, the recipients of its largesse became more defiant. The civilian president of Argentina, Arturo Illia (who had succeeded the
military regime in 1963) had assumed office vowing to cancel foreign
oil contracts, which he believed were illegal. Warned that such a move
would jeopardize American aid and prompt Congress to invoke the
Hickenlooper Amendment (which mandated termination of foreign
aid to any country that did not compensate for seized American property), Illia moved ahead. The Hickenlooper Amendment was not applied, but aid to Argentina fell dramatically, from $135 million in 1963
to $21 million the following year.

President Lyndon B. Johnson had already confronted trouble in
Panama, where a diplomatic squabble over the flying of the U.S. and
Panamanian flags in the Canal Zone had deteriorated into a riot in
January 1964. Only the presence of U.S. troops kept the enraged Panamanians from invading the zone. For several months relations between the two governments were suspended. In the end, and with
his customary flair for the dramatic, Johnson promised the Panamanians that they would eventually get the old canal and held out the
promise of a new sea-level canal—but they had to wait.[13]

This was the pragmatic approach to Latin America. If Latin Americans wanted more control over their economic future, they would
have to pay a political price. The intellectual guru of this policy was
Thomas Mann, who characterized public aid as ineffectual and
favored a businesslike approach to the hemisphere. This idea trans-

lated, his critics charged, into inordinate sympathy for American private investment in Latin America. It was perhaps an exaggeration, but with Johnson's blessing, Mann assumed control over State Department and Agency for International Development (AID) operations in Latin America, replacing Martin and Moscoso. He called in U.S. ambassadors to the hemispheric republics and laid down the new priorities—a preference for economic growth over social reforms, protection of U.S. investments, neutrality toward Latin American governments, whether reformist or rightist, and an unambiguously anticommunist temper to U.S. policy.

Six months earlier, Martin had spoken hesitantly about the resurgence of Latin America's military. Mann's inspirational lecture quickly had its impact. A few weeks later, the Brazilian military, attentive to Washington's demonstration of its displeasure with the populist João Goulart, drove him from office in a coup. Ambassador Lincoln Gordon had learned of the projected overthrow several months earlier from disgruntled São Paulo businessmen, and the CIA had funneled money to U.S. private interests in the country to subsidize anti-Goulart marches in the city. The Johnson administration, which obviously applauded Goulart's fall, recognized the new military government in only twelve days. Once in power, the generals unleashed their wrath on Brazilian reformers, stripping political rights from three former presidents, six governors, fifty-five assemblymen, and prominent labor organizers and intellectuals. Taken aback by their vengefulness, Gordon contemplated resigning in protest, but he was persuaded that the United States could exercise a moderating influence on the Brazilian military.[14] In his most pessimistic forecasts, he could not have foreseen the vigorous economic expansion and political repression that lay ahead for Brazil, which became in the decade after the coup a bloody symbol for those who believed that economic growth flourished in the authoritarian state. Washington demonstrated its appreciation by showering its praetorians with $1.5 billion in aid in the first four years after the military seizure of power.[15]

The Brazilian solution had predictable repercussions elsewhere. In neighboring Bolivia, American dissatisfaction with the presence of Juan Lechín, vice-president in the government of Víctor Paz Estenssoro, grew so intense that Paz turned against his former political ally. In the late 1950s, as the United States pressed its financial stabilization plans on Bolivia, Lechín had shielded the Left. When Paz took him on as vice-president, Lechín became more conciliatory, visiting Washington to affirm his anticommunist convictions. But even a trip to Nationalist China did not convince the Americans that he had abandoned his radical notions and his support of the Bolivian Workers' Central, which Washington and the International Monetary Fund perceived as an obstacle to their Bolivian financial scheme. Alert to American wishes, Paz turned against Lechín and tried to break the grip of the Bolivian Left on the MNR.

When that failed, he turned to the Bolivian military, which the revolution had virtually demolished in its seizure of power in 1952, arguing that the country now confronted the peril of internal subversion. American military advisers streamed into the country to train the counterinsurgency force that three years later triumphed over Ché Guevara's peasant revolution. In a calculated move, Paz cemented his alliance with the military by taking on General René Barrientos as vice-president, but the disintegration of the MNR offered opportunity to the revolution's enemies. Two months after the election, the generals, with Barrientos in the fore, took over. They rejuvenated agrarian reform, declared war on urban labor, and enthusiastically supported foreign investment. And in Argentina, the military, alert to the financial rewards that their Brazilian counterparts had gained, tossed out the middle-class civilian president, Arturo Illia, in June 1966. The generals then installed one of their own in his stead, prorogued the legislative assembly, and banned political parties. Afterward, Washington augmented its aid package to Buenos Aires.

The United States had not abandoned its support of democratic civilian governments in the hemisphere, but Mann had clearly rearranged the hemispheric agenda. In a major speech at Notre Dame in June 1964, he had reaffirmed American support for representative democracy and American commitment to press for elections in countries where the military had seized power. Condemnation of the military for its illegal seizure of power served little useful diplomatic purpose. In any case, the issue of communism was a different matter, for it raised vital questions of hemispheric security and national interest.[16]

The resurgence of the Latin American military paralleled Washington's diminishing concerns with social reform and its escalating anxieties about the communist menace. Ultimately, that menace was traced to a Cuban source. In the aftermath of the missile crisis the United States had successfully mobilized the Latin American countries in an economic blockade of Cuba, but Castro was already proclaiming his anti-imperialist crusades. The Soviet Union had not yet embarked on its policy of forging "normal" relations with some of Latin America's new military regimes, nor had the Russians fully "tamed" the hemisphere's most famous convert to Marxism and transformed him into a pragmatic revolutionary. Guevara left for Africa, returned to Cuba, and departed again—into deepest Bolivia. Castro found a metaphor for his cause in "One, Two, Many Vietnams." Guevara would light the incendiary spark in the Andes of Bolivia.

In retrospect, Washington's reactions to his challenge were exaggerated. Latin American guerrillas and the urban Left often endowed him with heroic qualities and found parallels between the Cuban revolution and their own cause, but just as often they drew on their own experiences for their revolutionary strategy. American officials apparently placed more stock in Castro's boasting than in a realistic appraisal of his ability to foment "Vietnams" everywhere. With the pummeling its military disciples in Latin America were already giving the leftists (and the money and training it was providing them), the United States should have felt more secure about its ability to contain Castro's revolution to Cuba. It did not because its perception of Castro's threat and the reach of the Cuban revolution was actually escalating. Undertaking a military commitment against the global communist menace ten thousand miles away, the United States saw no reason to lessen its anticommunist vigil elsewhere in the hemisphere. It drew the line in the Dominican Republic.

After Trujillo was killed, the American government had identified the policy of the United States with his most popular critic, Juan Bosch.[17] When the Trujillos jeopardized his electoral crusade in 1962, Kennedy dispatched naval vessels to warn them off, and Bosch swept to victory. For seven months, this unpredictable, chain-smoking Dominican poet-revolutionary fascinated a people ground under by indisputably the most gruesome tyrant in the history of the Western Hemisphere. But his American benefactors and the Dominican military grew increasingly, and noticeably, irritated. He did not lead, was weak, and worst of all, they said, allowed the communists to organize. Bosch responded that it was better to have them in the open rather than drive them into the mountains to wage guerrilla war, but this was not the democratic toughness Washington wanted. Neither, apparently, did Bosch's generals. In fall 1963 they drove him into exile.

The generals ran the government for a few months, then installed a triumvirate, headed by Donald Reid Cabral, a civilian. Satisfied that the Dominican military had the Left under control, Washington turned its attention elsewhere in the Caribbean. Reid called for austerity and stability, twin credos that pleased the Johnson administration. They were not especially welcomed by Dominican business and professional elements, who grumbled about his tight-money measures and doubtless welcomed the demonstrations, strikes, and comical plotting that disrupted his tenure. Dominican social conservatives found their hero in Joaquín Balaguer, who had served Trujillo but did so, they believed, under duress, an understandable and to them forgivable predicament. More serious was the challenge of a band of junior officers in the Dominican military who called for the restoration of constitutional government and looked to Bosch as their leader.

These forces pressed on Reid from opposite directions, and the harassed executive turned increasingly to Washington for succor. A new American ambassador, W. Tapley Bennett, arrived to console him and to reiterate Washington's approval of his austerity program. As he became more protective of Reid, the Dominican nationalists, Right and Left, became more shrill in their denunciation. Bennett publicly extolled Reid, but the CIA, in an assessment of the Dominican political situation in early April 1965, gloomily concluded that only 5 percent of the Dominican people supported him. Shortly, Bennett departed for Washington to attend an emergency meeting on the deteriorating Dominican situation. Pro-Bosch organizers in the capital and the military were already organizing to restore constitutional government.

Their revolt, which began on 24 April with the takeover of a radio station and the arrest of a general dispatched to placate Bosch's partisans, appeared initially to offer no serious challenge to Reid. He sent reinforcements to Ozama fortress, and national police readily dispersed crowds that had gathered in the capital's central district. But Reid did not move against the dissident colonels within the military. They renewed their demand for Bosch's return. When Reid refused, they seized the fire station and began taking positions in the city. Unable to rely on his own military for protection, he put in frantic calls to Washington and the American embassy in Santo Domingo.

Washington's principal concerns were the safety of Americans in the capital and, as the situation deteriorated, with communist influence among the pro-Bosch elements. American officials presumed that real power lay with the Dominican generals holed up at San Isidro Air Base outside Santo Domingo, who would, they believed, prevent Bosch's return, even if it meant another military takeover. They had not taken accurate measure of the hesitancy of the generals to maintain Reid, and they underestimated the resolve of the junior officers, who moved decisively by organizing Bosch's civilian partisans. Their leader, Colonel Francisco Caamañó Deñó, personally arrested Reid and proclaimed Bosch's imminent return on Dominican radio.[18]

For the Dominican generals and for Washington, of course, the issue was not constitutional government but the prospect of Bosch returning to power, which they believed would throw the country into civil war. If that happened, the communists would surely take advantage of the chaotic situation to install themselves. Their numbers (as journalists covering these events soon revealed) were grossly exaggerated, as was their influence among the junior officers, who championed Bosch's restoration. Yet in the early calamitous days of the revolt, while Bosch supporters roamed the streets, sending foreigners scurrying into the Hotel Embajador, the grim reports coming into the Operations Center at the State Department made for unsettling reading. The rebels wanted no confrontation with the United States. They vowed to protect American lives and property. When the generals at San Isidro began mobilizing to move against them, they appealed to Washington to mediate. Bennett arrived back in Santo Domingo just as the anti-Bosch military faction unleashed a ferocious attack on rebel positions. Again, the rebels asked for American intercession. Bennett refused. The Embajador and the embassy came under sniper fire, presumably from the rebels. With rifles cracking in the background, Bennett made the frantic call to Washington that precipitated Johnson's decision to intervene. On 28 April five hundred marines from the USS *Boxer* went ashore in Santo Domingo. In a national television address that evening Johnson declared that they had landed to safeguard American lives and to prevent "another Cuba" in the Western Hemisphere.[19]

Within a week reinforcements arrived, taking up position at San Isidro Air Base. Their presence, Johnson argued, was justified by the stream of disturbing reports about communist infiltration in the revolution. Initially, their putative role was to maintain a tenuous neutrality among the armed political factions. In reality, as several prominent Latin American governments charged, their purpose was to provide hemispheric validation of what they called the Johnson Doctrine: unilateral American intervention to prevent a communist takeover. When the American command decided to send the larger San Isidro force into the capital to join with the initial contingent of marines, thus bringing the Americans into conflict with the rebels, all pretense of neutrality evaporated. Johnson was not indifferent to hemispheric criticism, but the outcry provoked his legendary vulgarity. As a hastily assembled Dominican crisis team arrived from Washington, the American government pushed through a resolution in the OAS (which Johnson had said "could not pour piss out of a boot if the instructions were written on the heel") authorizing an inter-American peace force of 9,100 American and 2,000 Latin American (mostly Brazilian) troops to provide for an orderly transition. They remained for almost a year, guaranteeing that Joaquín Balaguer not Juan Bosch would guide what the American government styled a controlled democratic experiment.[20]

The Dominican intervention did not erase the American commitment to Latin American development nor did Latin American criticism shut off the flow of aid, public and private, from the United States. What the dispatch of American and Latin American troops into Santo Domingo symbolized was the chasm between U.S. priorities and Latin America's needs and the American disillusion with the Alliance for Progress dream. Kennedy, in his somber moments, had wondered whether the generation that had been heartened by his call for peaceful revolution in Latin America really knew what economic costs and especially what risks it entailed. Had he lived, this idealist without illusions and political realist, who perceived before his death that something had gone awry in the promise of 1961, would have doubtless responded to the rising conservative business critique of the alliance agenda with sterner demands of Latin American reformers. Yet he would have instinctively sensed the dangers in acquiescing to the resurgent Latin American military. Even Castro, hearing of his death, remarked that Kennedy had understood Latin America's social and economic needs.

In this critical decade, the laudatory social reforms of the alliance—in education, health, agrarian reform, literacy, and the like—collapsed before the demands of private investment and Latin America's increasingly burdensome obligations to use aid to repay debts or to absorb American exports. But they also weakened before unanticipated Latin American priorities. By every economic measure Latin America appeared better off in 1968 than in 1960, but those who benefited were largely those who had been better off in 1960. American planners had believed that commitment to development and democracy would nourish the Latin American middle class, which would in turn sustain the social and economic programs that would serve as a bulwark against communism. They could not foresee that the middle-class beneficiaries of their largesse had a more fearful view of social philanthropy and a more somber appraisal of democracy.[21] In the prognosis of Latin America's future the Anglos were the dreamers and the Hispanics were the realists.

Undeniably, the United States shifted its efforts from social programs to the private sector as the linchpin of economic development. It did so, in part, for security reasons. Thus agricultural development gave way to agricultural pacification. But there was a more fundamental reason. As the decade wore on, the United States was confronted with a dilemma. The model the Alliance for Progress had chosen for its program of economic development was Puerto Rico, hailed as the alternative to the Cuban revolution. Latin Americans did not deny the impressive statistics of the Puerto Rican economy, but they were unwilling to accept its development scheme as one to emulate. Puerto Rico's development architects had taken advantage of the rural labor force on the island and extended incentives to manufacturers and industrialists to relocate there. That was unobjectionable— even to Latin America's elites. But they were hesitant to accept the impact that Operation Bootstrap had on lower-class Puerto Ricans who moved into San Juan. Though the dream eventually vanished before the reality of urban squalor, their expectations had been raised and, more important, the poor of San Juan refused to accept something their parents and grandparents in the countryside had traditionally accommodated—the Hispanic's view of the social order and one's place in it.

Kennedy committed the United States and its economic strength to the Alliance for Progress in the name of America and its political values; he confirmed Latin America's place in United States Cold War strategy. Latin Americans adored him for the first, and they forgave him for the second. His successor continued that aid and reaffirmed with troops Washington's strategic priorities in the hemisphere. Latin Americans disliked him whether he did them good or ill, but neither Kennedy nor Johnson was singularly responsible for the failure of the alliance and the end of the democratic dream in the authoritarian nightmare. Development and democracy coexisted in American developmental theory but not in Latin American reality. In 1960 Latin American dictatorship was in decline and civilian democracies in the ascendancy. In the course of the decade, Latin American militarism and authoritarian governments were reborn, sometimes with U.S. acquiescence and even encouragement and, it must be remembered, with the acquiescence and encouragement of a Latin American middle class that valued its well-being more than it valued the incorporation of Latin America's marginal populations in the social order.

In such circumstances, the lower classes lost out—not in income but in any meaningful social advancement. In a curious and entirely unexpected way, however, they found an opportunity to move up the social ladder—in the military. Americans decried the growing militarization of Latin America in the 1960s as a threat to political democracy but overlooked the impetus that a military career gave to social democracy and, indeed, to the notion that the military can run the state and manage the economy more efficiently than civilians. The American trainers at the School of the Americas in the Canal Zone thought they were tutoring a generation of Latin Americans in the art of counterinsurgency, but they were also conveying to impressionable students (as the U.S. Army had done to the Brazilians in the Italian campaign in World War II) the belief that the soldier can run things if he has to. This was an unintentional but unmistakable legacy of the counterinsurgency program.

America also provided a second route to social advancement for Latin Americans. In a decade in which the United States refused to discard its Cold War globalist strategy in its approach to Latin America, America reinforced the north-south connection. As the United States tried to dispose of Cuban exiles in Cuba at the Bay of Pigs, America began taking in Cubans. In the year that United States forces entered Santo Domingo to end a civil war—an intervention that irreparably damaged the Alliance for Progress—America adopted a sweeping new immigration law that conveyed another message to Latin Americans. That law inspired a wave of immigration that had not yet run its course twenty years later. The major importance of the

1965 law, however, is the alternative it provided for a generation of Latin Americans who wanted to move up the social ladder. They could do so by emigrating to the United States to exploit their skills and to reunite their families. If the United States and Latin America failed to sustain their dream in Latin America, America kept the dream alive.

9   The New Latin America

At the beginning of the 1960s, Latin Americans, it was confidently believed, confronted two choices for their future—the Cuban revolutionary model, which had not yet assumed its Soviet economic or political character, or the agenda offered in the Charter of Punta del Este and the promise of peaceful revolution. Ten years later, Latin America had two unpalatable symbols of what had been wrought: Cuba and Brazil.

For those who had yearned for social justice and a better life in a democratic society neither offered much reassurance of Latin America's political future. Cuba undeniably had achieved much in the decade. In education, public health, and the integration of rural and urban sectors, the revolution went farther than any Latin American country in attaining the objectives of the Alliance for Progress, but as Castro himself confessed, it had not achieved its developmental goals. It was a failure only partially explained by the U.S.-led economic blockade imposed in 1964 or Cuba's isolation in the Western Hemisphere. For democratic Latin Americans, the Cuban model offered little solace. But, then, neither did Brazil, for accompanying its impressive economic growth was a ruthless suppression of liberties carried out with such gruesome effectiveness that it sickened even social conservatives. Brazil at the close of the decade was the domain of generals and technocrats propped up by a coalition of financiers, industrialists, large landowners, and a new middle class. The dissenters (students, labor organizers, intellectuals, the remnants of Goulart's populist forces, and Catholic priests emboldened by liberation theology) were isolated, harassed, imprisoned, and tortured.

Yet there were less noticed variations on these political and economic models. The Peruvian military, which had ousted a civilian government in 1968, offered a curious fusion of social reform and repression—a Peruvian variation of populism in which the generals enthusiastically promoted land reform, nationalized a highly visible foreign company (International Petroleum), throttled the press, and imposed their will on the judiciary. With a logic that befuddled American liberals and conservatives, one of the Peruvian generals explained the zigzag course the junta had chosen: "When one is pursued by a herd of maddened bulls one has three options. One is to kneel, close the eyes, and pray. The second is to fight the bulls, which is as good as the first option. The third is to lead the stampeding herd into terrain that is more advantageous to the pursued. The masses in Latin America are starting to stampede. We the military are the only ones who are capable of leading them—and us—into safe ground."[1]

More palatable was the route taken by Chile, Venezuela, and Colombia, where those in power had resolved to permit their political opponents to campaign more or less freely while promoting economic development and the broadening of the social order. In Colombia, this conciliatory approach (in which Liberals and Conservatives had agreed to alternate in the presidency) had been critical in mitigating the volatile legacies of the civil war. In Venezuela, the Democratic Action party, whose leader, Rómulo Betancourt, had served as Kennedy's prototypical Latin American democrat, had dominated politics through the decade and had carried out reforms that for the time being had placated the Left. In Chile, the Christian Democratic party of Eduardo Frei, with strong U.S. support, had won power in 1964.

With the sustaining influence of the Alliance for Progress, it was said, their example might have spread elsewhere in Latin America, but in 1969 the United States had virtually abandoned the Alliance for Progress. Almost simultaneously, Latin America, disturbed by America's altering priorities, lost its enthusiasm for the OAS. In the Dominican crisis the United States had exploited its dominance of the inter-American system to exact compliance with its interventionist policies. When Johnson left office in 1969, Vietnam was obviously the fulcrum of America's global policy, but for Latin Americans, the turning point in hemispheric solidarity had come four years earlier, when a determined American president had reaffirmed, in what they bitterly called the Johnson Doctrine, Washington's old habits and priorities in dealing with its neighbors. In the humiliation the OAS had remained largely silent. In three conferences of the organization from 1965 to 1967, the distrust of the United States, largely brought on by U.S. intervention in the Dominican Republic, hampered long-standing goals of trying to remold the hemisphere's political structure into a more effective force in the settlement of disputes between member states without invoking the Rio treaty.[2] The determination to prevent another Cuba in the Caribbean may have succeeded, but hemispheric unity suffered for it.

The Rockefeller Mission

When Richard Nixon became president in January 1969, Vietnam, not Latin America, was his concern. The dreary reports about the failures of the Alliance for Progress had confirmed in his mind the direction American policy should take. The United States must maintain its dominating political image and safeguard the interests of the American multinationals with a large stake in Latin America, he argued, yet it must do so without the costs a heavy-handed approach often entailed. This meant supporting "our friends" (the resurgent Latin American militaries) and opposing "our enemies." Latin America had exhausted its efforts to bring about peaceful revolution and in the process had merely inspired the Left to exact ever greater demands on fragile political systems. The generals had reluctantly seized power to preserve the social order. This was a simplistic analysis of the situation, but in considering Latin America, the president and most Americans preferred to think in black-and-white terms. Responding to proposals for greater Latin American access to the American market, which had been raised at the Viña del Mar conference in Chile, Nixon confidently asserted that the Latin Americans wanted not aid but trade, not costly social programs such as the Alliance for Progress but the opportunity for more dynamic free enterprise economies. Such was his developmental strategy for the continent.

Yet in August 1969 Nixon got a report on the condition of the Americas that was disquieting. In the spring he had dispatched his old adversary and former coordinator of inter-American affairs Nelson Rockefeller on a mission southward. Rockefeller had returned bearing grim tidings about the quality of life in the hemisphere. In phrases as compelling and occasionally as eloquent as Kennedy's, Rockefeller spoke of common goals, common bonds, and the need to create a "community of self-reliant, independent nations linked in a mutually beneficial regional system, and seeking to improve the efficiency of their societies and the quality of life of their peoples." This was heady stuff in light of the disappointments of the 1960s, but Rockefeller had not finished. Latin America's dismal condition, he wrote in a remarkably candid passage, was largely a result of American policy. U.S. aid and commercial policies had been carried out in a way that denied the "aspirations and interests of its neighbors," and Washington had often cavalierly displayed a "paternalistic attitude" toward Latin American governments, interfering in their domestic affairs in an "unseemly" manner as if "it knew what was best for them." The United States had spoken of a "new partnership"; now was the time to practice it.[3]

Latin American reformers were initially heartened by such an unusual American self-flagellation but just as quickly disillusioned when they read Rockefeller's recommendations for increased American support for the Latin American militaries and American multinationals.[4] Latin Americans were understandably suspicious of foreign companies because they did not understand the benefits they wrought in the development of democratic societies. Their sufferance of military government was a small but understandable price to pay if their countries were to be shielded from the menaces of guerrilla war and communism. Without order they could not hope to confront the compelling social issues of the day. Devoid of any central social or political purpose in its hemispheric policy, the United States had fallen back on the older (and to Americans more understandable) strategic and economic strictures in dealing with the hemisphere. With these it could not defuse the popular appeal of the still vigorous Latin American Left. In a politically unattainable but challenging recommendation, Rockefeller proposed the creation of a secretariat of Western Hemispheric affairs to direct all U. S. government activities in

Latin America and a hemispheric security council (with its central office outside the United States) to train Latin American military and police in counterrevolutionary tactics. These offices never became a reality, although the U.S. military and even city governments took up the training of Latin American officers and police. Rockefeller's urgency in advocating such measures, coupled with his support for American multinationals, validated in Nixon's mind the approach the United States must take in dealing with Latin America. Some found the report badly flawed by its exaggeration of the threat from the Left—historically more frightening to Americans than Latin Americans—yet Rockefeller had offered the American people a sobering reminder about Latin America's deceptively placid condition.

Nixon spoke loftily about a "new partnership" with Latin America, one in which Latin American recipients of American aid, for example, would not have to "buy American" and could anticipate U.S. support on such diverse matters as debt servicing, technology transfer, and tariff preferences. He coupled these pledges with warnings about Latin American miscreant governments that placed unwarranted barriers against American investment and reminded their leaders of the Overseas Private Investment Corporation, which looked out for American multinationals. Latin American governments that hoped for a marked change in American economic and commercial policy toward the hemisphere were sorely disappointed. Support for development funding to the Inter-American Development and World Bank fell short of Latin American expectations, as did the reduction of tariff barriers. In 1971, when Nixon declared a 10 percent surcharge on imports—aimed primarily at the Japanese—the Latin American imbalance in U.S. trade patterns was further skewed in Washington's favor.[5]

Very shortly, the "new partnership" looked to Latin Americans much like the old relationship of the 1950s. This was not altogether the result of Nixon's failure to adjust to new realities and expectations. Latin America had changed. The Alliance for Progress, arguably, had not achieved the expectations of 1960, but the Latin America Nixon confronted as president was far different from the hemisphere that had so rudely greeted him on his visit of 1958. In Peru, for instance, he had to deal with a military government whose leaders had strong populist instincts and sprinkled pronouncements with socialist rhetoric. Their populism was, apparently, contagious. In Venezuela, the incoming president, Rafael Caldera, allowed the communists to participate in national politics and initiated a dialogue with Castro. The Argentine military, presumably secure since it had tossed out a civilian government in 1966, ran afoul of the working and middle classes with its economic program and narrowly avoided being overturned. And in Bolivia, where Washington's tightening grip had created, it was assumed, a regime subservient to American wishes, yet another general stormed into power and began nationalizing the holdings of Gulf Oil. When he departed after a year, his successor promptly infuriated Washington by nationalizing even more foreign property.

Latin America had yet to take charge of its future (to employ a phrase of the 1980s), but clearly South America in the 1970s began to refashion its international economic ties. The Russians and the Chinese joined the Germans and Japanese in commercial ventures. This was a challenge Nixon could not ignore. He reinforced government support to American multinationals, cut back on public aid to the defiant populist regimes, and lauded the "economic miracle" wrought by the Brazilians. In Peru and Bolivia the American government consciously encouraged rightist military officers. In Bolivia, the military responded by tossing out its reformist colleagues and setting up a pro-American government. Washington acknowledged that deed by reinstituting aid. The changeover was relatively inexpensive and easy.

The Chilean Tragedy

But in Chile the confrontation with revolutionary change produced a bloody climax. In 1970, in a bitterly divisive election that produced no clear winner, the Chilean national assembly had chosen a socialist, Salvador Allende, as president. For more than a decade Allende had capitalized on the alienation of urban workers in a country noted for its middle-class democracy and social tradition. So fearful was the American government of his chances in the 1964 election that it secretly funneled financial support to his adversary, the Christian Democrat candidate, Eduardo Frei. Alert to the heightened international interest in what was happening in Chile, Allende asked for and got support from the Cubans and the Soviets. In the end he proved no match for an opponent who was not only getting American dollars but had the CIA and the American Federation of Labor, using its aggressive Latin American organization, the American Institute for Free Labor Development (AIFLD), working clandestinely on his behalf. In other hemispheric countries where organized labor had become too "political" (that is, too leftist in its orientation) AIFLD performed yeoman service in the anticommunist cause of Washington.[6]

When Frei triumphed, Washington declared him the "last, best hope" of Chilean democracy. He proclaimed a "Revolution in Liberty" and energetically set out to incorporate Christian Democracy's curious mix of traditional and reformist social philosophies into a political culture that was rapidly becoming polarized. In the spirit of the Alliance for Progress, Frei called for agrarian reform and encountered a phalanx of conservative assemblymen. Responding to long-held Chilean resentments against foreign control of the vital copper mining industry, he proposed a gradual nationalization, "Chileanization," which pleased the leftists, but permitted the foreign owners to continue running the companies, which infuriated them. When after three years the economy began to falter with the decline of copper prices and tax revenues, the social programs lost their urgency. Under pressure from the International Monetary Fund and the World Bank, Frei began austerity measures. Bolivia had earlier yielded to American economic prescriptions; so, now, did Chile.

Still, the Chilean economic collapse did not necessarily preordain an Allende victory. In 1970, as in 1964, the American government determined to keep him out of power. The National Security Council, inspired by Henry Kissinger's assessment of the situation ("I don't see why we must sit with our arms folded when a country is slipping toward communism because of the irresponsibility of its own people") allocated $500 million to be distributed among Allende's opponents.[7] Even after he had gotten a plurality of the votes, which virtually assured his selection by the Chilean national assembly, efforts to deny him power did not end. International Telephone and Telegraph (ITT), which had been operating in Chile since the 1920s and had amassed $160 million in assets, was so fretful over a socialist in power that it contrived (apparently with Nixon's blessing) a scheme whereby the Christian Democrats in the assembly would vote for Jorge Alessandri, the former president. He, in turn, pledged to resign, which would mean a new election and another chance to deny Allende the power he had long sought. The plan fell through when the Christian Democrats refused to go along, but ITT immediately followed with Phase II, a plot to cause such economic dislocation that the military would step in, as it had in Bolivia. The CIA, still in the hunt, threw its support to an anti-Allende officer who intended to kidnap General René Schneider, a supporter of Allende's constitutional claim to office. Even Kissinger found the latter too risky, but the Chilean officers went ahead. In the kidnapping attempt Schneider was killed.

In American eyes Allende's triumph was not only a threat to U.S. interests in Chile but a symbolic challenge to its political stature elsewhere in the continent. He was a Marxist, elected to power in a democratic and capitalist society. Chile would be socialized, Allende pledged, but by peaceful means. This meant nationalization of the copper mines and banks and major industry and agrarian reform, as Chileans had anticipated, but it also signaled an independent foreign policy, the end of dependency, and a restructuring of the social order. The last was the most unsettling to middle-class Chileans because it meant, initially, a redistribution of national wealth to Allende's army of marginals and, ultimately, the formation of a new political culture in which the working class would occupy center stage.

Allende's Chile projected a democratic, socialist image before the world.[8] The government raised taxes, froze prices, and increased wages, which had the effect of augmenting the share of national wealth by wage earners from 50 to 60 percent. In the capital unemployment dropped. Rising demand for food and manufactures brought increased productivity in agriculture and industry. When the first local elections were held, in April 1971, the socialist-communist coalition, Popular Unity, won 50 percent of the vote, an impressive showing in Chile's multiparty politics. Allende was hailed as liberator, the "second Fidel," and his program as the protector of the Chilean poor. But in early 1972, as Allende continued with his program of national reconstruction, his political support began to wane, particularly among Chile's middle classes. The economy, which had enjoyed a brief revival, now began to show the stress of his policies. Production had increased, but demand outpaced it, so the government had to satisfy consumers' wishes with increased imports. In the international economy, the price of Chilean copper fell to the level of 1967, and Chile's standing among international lending agencies plummeted with it. Within the country the reformist political consensus that had seemed possible in the beginning now collapsed as middle-class housewives undertook protest marches over rising prices and the falling value of the Chilean *escudo*. Had Allende maintained his links with the Christian Democrats, who had yielded power to him in 1970, he might have been able to weather the economic crisis. Instead, sensing that their political future lay with the old not the new order, the Christian Democrats decided to abandon the Left.[9]

With their departure went whatever middle-class political support Allende had enjoyed. His response was to declare a state of emergency. He banned public meetings, permitted the police to arrest persons without a warrant, and authorized the military to censor the press. In Bolivia or Peru such use of state authority to maintain order would have met with sullen acquiescence, but Chile had a historic tradition of political tolerance, and Allende's toughness inspired the discontented to launch a new wave of protests. In winter 1972 storekeepers, angry over high taxes, closed their doors. A few months later, the truckdrivers struck, citing shortages of spare parts and government-imposed hauling rates. Professional groups and shop owners followed them into the streets in a series of massive demonstrations that shook the government but did not bring Allende down. In the ensuing elections, Popular Unity fared better than in 1970—a sign that Allende was compensating for his declining fortunes among middle-class Chileans by expanding his political base among the urban poor. In the next critical election, in March 1973, the poor turned out in force to renew their commitment. The victory, Allende believed, meant the Chilean people approved the socialist path he had charted for them.

For the Chilean military, however, the electoral reaffirmation of Allende's program meant that the ballot box offered little promise of turning him out. The generals had a forty-year tradition of staying out of politics, but they held solidly anti-Marxist political values and had been suspicious of Allende from the beginning. In the aftermath of the March elections, they watched approvingly as the truckdrivers went out on strike for a second time and, perhaps unexpectedly, found themselves courted by the Christian Democrats, who pressed Allende to appoint more military men to his cabinet. Throughout Latin America, the Christian Democratic party trumpeted civilian domination of the military and condemned military domination of the state. Fearful that Allende would arm urban workers, the assembly authorized the military to search factories and buildings where leftist organizers gathered for weapons. His followers took to the streets in protest, and the politicized urban workers seized factories.

The plotters waited until a prominent general in Allende's cabinet resigned before launching the counterrevolution, on 10 September 1973. Allende died the following day, either by his own hand or by another's. The victors established a military government with General Augusto Pinochet as president, and the Christian Democrats and the rightist National party approved it. In the early days of the coup, soldiers herded thousands into makeshift prisons and executed hundreds of leftists. Then, in a systematic and forceful manner, they began dismantling Chilean socialism and with it the political culture Allende had wrought. They returned the nationalized factories to private ownership, clamped down on the unions, and disbanded the Marxist parties. They broke diplomatic relations with Cuba. They declared the restoration of a capitalist economy and an orderly society. But they did not restore Chilean democracy, nor did they relinquish power.[10]

The collapse of Chilean democracy in 1973 was largely but not solely a domestic tragedy. Allende had become a symbol—the triumph of socialism by constitutional means—that infuriated the Nixon administration and prompted the American government to redefine its anticommunist global strategies. A Marxist government had achieved power in a country with a strong European tradition in its politics. Viewed from this perspective, Allende's Chile was less a harbinger of Marxist takeovers in neighboring Latin American countries than a prototype for the Western European communists to emulate. If they won power by the ballot box, as had Allende, C. L. Sulzberger speculated, the Italian or French communists would be able to split the NATO alliance and destroy the European common market.[11]

In the early months of the Allende government, before Washington's policies had become clear, a consortium of multinational companies, spearheaded by ITT, pressured the administration to block any loans to the Allende government. When Allende nationalized the Chilean copper industry in July 1971, the Agency for International Development cut off the financial spigot. Shortly afterward, the Inter-American Development Bank, which was in the business of making development loans, took Chile off its list of recipients. The World Bank, then under the direction of former Secretary of Defense Robert McNamara, followed the trend in late summer. The Export-Import Bank, which had extended $600 million in credits to Chile since World War II, abruptly announced that it would not certify new credits until the Allende government made pledges that no more foreign property would be nationalized. With the new ITT president, Harold Geneen, enthusiastically supporting a hard-line policy, the Nixon administration in early 1972 declared that future nationalization without proper compensation would result in further curtailment of credit. Later in the year, after random negotiations of the issues of nationalization and credit, Allende got an extension on Chile's debt repayment schedule, but once Washington learned of the military discontent and plotting in early 1973, its position hardened.

Was the Nixon administration directly responsible for Allende's fall? No. Did it bear a responsibility in Allende's overthrow? Undeniably, yes. For more than a decade, the United States had abetted, sustained, financed, and encouraged Allende's opponents. It provided reassurance to the Chilean military. It imposed economic obstacles to Allende's government among international lending agencies. It did not undermine Allende from within, but it encouraged those who did. Allende himself ultimately bore responsibility for the failure of his socialist revolution in trying to reform a society by restructuring it. Even without American disapproval, he courted discontent and, probably, civil conflict, but with American hostility he confronted inevitable disaster. For the United States there was too much at risk—in the symbolic affront of a democratically elected socialist and in Chilean defiance of American direction. President Gerald Ford admitted that the CIA spent $8 million in Chile to facilitate Allende's downfall. What the United States got for its money was stability; what Chile got was the preservation of the social order, at the price of democracy. Therein lay the tragedy of Chile.

The North-South Dialogue

So palpably offensive was the Chilean military's eradication of the Left that within a few years even Kissinger expressed disapproval over the collapse of Chilean democracy and the abuse of human rights by the Pinochet government. By then, of course, new descriptive slogans and causes were reverberating through the inter-American system that indicated the character of the Americas—the end of U.S. hegemony; the New Dialogue and its companion expression, the North-South Dialogue, which inspired the Linowitz report; SELA, the Spanish acronym for the Economic System of Latin America. The last represented the spirited defiance of a Latin America prepared, as yet another slogan confirmed, to "take charge of its future."[12]

SELA included Cuba but excluded the United States. Its principal architects, Carlos Pérez of Venezuela and Luis Echeverría of Mexico, wanted to chart a new course for Latin America in the international economic system. Echeverría's shift to the left represented a symbolic effort to restrain foreign, largely American, economic penetration and appeal to leftist sentiments by advancing Mexico's claim as a Third World leader. Venezuela's defiance of Washington was more complex in its origins. It had been something of showcase of the Alliance for Progress in the early 1960s, but Nixon's indifference to trade issues and congressional measures during the Arab oil embargo (Venezuela was a founding member of the Organization of Petroleum Exporting Countries in 1960) worsened matters. Venezuela had opposed the embargo, but Congress, indifferent to the fact that it was an *Arab* oil embargo, retaliated by withdrawing the General System of Preferences from the Trade Act of 1974. Despite Pérez's protestations of the unfairness of the retaliation, Venezuela stood condemned. Ultimately SELA included twenty-five Latin American governments, a few of them—Honduras, El Salvador, and the Dominican Republic—Cold War allies of the United States. Their purpose was not so much political as economic determination to gain control over commodity prices and to break their dependency with vigorous import-substitution measures, in which governments provided domestic producers with a greater share of the consumer market by the expedient of shielding them from foreign competition.

Concurrently the OAS suffered a noticeable decline and with it a loss of U.S. prestige in the inter-American system. In 1969 the OAS had played a minor role in mediating the hundred-hour war between Honduras and El Salvador (known derisively as the Soccer War). Afterward, the American delegates began to lose their effectiveness in "guiding" the Latin American nations, especially on economic issues. At OAS economic meetings, the Latin American delegates would often repair to another room, decide among themselves on a series of recommendations, then casually inform their American colleagues. A few old Alliance for Progress hands from the early 1960s, disillusioned with such scenarios, began calling for American withdrawal from the organization. When Nixon visited China in early 1972, a number of Latin American governments called for a thaw in Cuban-American relations, beginning with a lifting of the embargo imposed in 1964. They were joined by several outspoken American congressmen, who visited Cuba, interviewed Castro, and returned to Washington with cautious recommendations for a Cuban-American understanding. At the OAS foreign ministers gathering of 1974 in Quito, Ecuador, Washington was apparently ready to acquiesce in lifting the embargo but was joined in abstention by five states—Haiti, Guatemala, Bolivia, Brazil, and Nicaragua—which meant that the measure failed.

Even the smaller states of the Caribbean, most of them newly independent and vulnerable to European and especially U.S. economic and political power, now dared challenge the colossus to the north. Throughout the region there was a pervasive sense that one imperial master had been exchanged for another and they must now, as Michael Manley, the socialist leader of Jamaica expressed it, find some common bond. In the early 1960s they had tried, and failed, to sustain a West Indian federation. Lacking political unity, they had fashioned the Caribbean Free Trade Association and Caribbean Development Bank, followed in 1973 by the Caribbean Community. The United States had not opposed any of these; the Rockefeller Report, in fact, had encouraged such regional arrangements. But the cumulative effect was to fuel Caribbean determination to deal more forcefully with the multinationals that set up operations in the insular Caribbean and to ignore Washington's strictures about consorting with Castro's Cuba. Jamaica established friendly relations with Havana and imported Cuban advisers. In Guyana, where Kennedy had prevented Cheddi Jagan from taking power, President Forbes Burnham proclaimed a "cooperativist republic" and nationalized the holdings of Reynolds Aluminum. Eric Williams in Trinidad/Tobago launched an economic program modeled on the Puerto Rican example, then joined other Caribbean countries in abandoning it.[13]

Cuba, an outcast in the insular Caribbean in the 1960s, won new admirers—not, as Washington believed, for the revolution's economic appeal but for Castro's symbolic role as a Third World leader. To the United States, the Cuban venture into Africa validated the charge that Castro was a Soviet lackey, and his dispatch of troops to Angola virtually killed efforts at any Cuban-American understanding, but to the black Caribbean, which had been swept by a negritude movement early in the decade, his proclamation of a war against imperialism in Africa had powerful appeal.

None of these events, as the Linowitz Report tried to explain, meant that the United States had "lost" Latin America. More concretely, they signaled that Latin America's priorities had moved beyond the Cold War agenda and that Washington must now adjust its policies accordingly. The United States had awakened from the Pan-American dream to a Latin American reality. Policies of the 1960s— when it had dominated hemispheric affairs, established hemispheric priorities, and largely charted the course of hemispheric economies— ill-served U.S. fundamental interests a decade later. Political and economic diversity now characterized Latin America. Several countries, notably Brazil and Mexico, were part of the New Industrial Economic Order. Strategic concerns still dominated American thinking but not Latin America's. Several countries had opened commercial and diplomatic contacts not only with Cuba but also with Eastern European nations, China, and the Soviet Union. The shift represented less a political than an economic realignment of the hemisphere with the global economy.[14]

More than any president since John Kennedy, Jimmy Carter sensed opportunity in Latin America's more assertive posture toward the United States. He spoke movingly and convincingly about renewed American concerns in the hemisphere: vindication of Panama's just demands for a new canal treaty, a fundamental understanding with Castro's Cuba, human rights (an increasingly important issue to Congress), and Central America's distresses along with their implications for American interests. Eschewing the encompassing slogans of previous American leaders who had promised too much and accomplished too little in treating with Latin Americans, Carter (reflecting, perhaps, his engineer's approach to problems) focused on regional and bilateral issues. In the past, he rightly acknowledged, U.S. hemispheric policy had usually floundered because of hard decisions made in specific situations (Castro's revolution, the Dominican crisis, or Guatemala in 1954) requiring a response that inevitably antagonized Latin Americans. In opting for the obverse approach, Carter ultimately found himself condemned for betraying traditional American interests.[15]

The Panama Canal issue befuddled the administration from the beginning. Back in 1973, when the Panamanian economy had begun to slide from the effect of high oil prices, Omar Torrijos, who had seized power in 1968, dramatically announced that the treaties offered by the Johnson administration were unacceptable. He rallied Latin America behind the cause of Panama, and (in a move that embarrassed Washington) invited the U.N. Security Council to Panama. There he virtually forced the American delegate to exercise a U.S. veto to kill a pro-Panamanian resolution. The following year, Kissinger acquiesced in an eight-point agreement to negotiate new canal treaties with the Panamanian minister, Juan Tack. Panama would get a new canal treaty and, by the end of the century, control of the canal. The Canal Zone, a de facto colony in Panamanian eyes, would be terminated. More important, the United States agreed to redefine its security interests on the isthmus.[16]

Perhaps to themselves Americans could admit the justness of Panama's demands, but they deeply believed the canal symbolized American triumph over adversity. Campaigning in 1976, Carter had learned just how attached they were to the waterway, and he responded to their concerns by assuring them that he would not relinquish a vital strategic and commercial lifeline. But retention of U.S. control and Panamanian reconciliation were not compatible, so Carter opted for the latter. He had, frankly, no realistic choice. Among its other recommendations about a new policy with Latin America, the Linowitz commission had urged the negotiation of a new canal treaty with Panama, and shortly before assuming office Carter had learned from seven Latin American leaders that failure to settle this long-standing issue would align the hemisphere against him. A few weeks after his inauguration, he named Ellsworth Bunker (old but skillful in dealing with Latin Americans) and Sol Linowitz to head his negotiating team. They adopted the Kissinger-Tack formula and by August had produced two agreements (a canal treaty and a neutrality treaty).

Torrijos and Carter signed the treaties in a dignified ceremony in September. In both countries a furious debate ensued. Torrijos had to use his considerable popularity to persuade Panamanians to accept treaties that fell short of Panamanian aspirations. Carter had to convince a coterie of hard-line senators that the neutrality treaty permitted U.S. military action to preserve canal security and then had to reassure the harassed Torrijos that the reservation did not mean "intervention" in Panamanian internal affairs. The narrow victory in the Senate was, Carter believed, the triumph of moral principle and political determination, and he *had* preserved vital American interests. But the cost was diminution of his political prestige. Panama had no constituency in the United States, but the canal did. For both governments, predictably, the symbolic importance of the canal (for Panamanians, a continual reminder of the American economic and military presence; for Americans, a monument to American engineering and determination) overshadowed the more somber analyses about the pressing need for a new treaty. In the election of 1980 came the inevitable reminders that Carter had "given away our canal." His policy toward Panama was a textbook lesson of an American leader doing what all Latin America and many Americans said was right and suffering for his deed.

Panama brought Carter plaudits but no victories elsewhere in Latin America. Neither did his abrupt call for a dialogue with Castro work to his benefit. In the 1976 campaign he had voiced caution about altering Cuban policy, citing Cuba's disturbing role in the Angolan civil war, but as president he declared that the United States should have "normal relations" with all countries. The two governments signed a fishing agreement and opened "Interests Sections" in Havana and Washington. Carter lifted restrictions on travel to Cuba. And in a media coup, Barbara Walters interviewed Castro, who promised to release a few American prisoners and hinted that full diplomatic relations might be possible in Carter's second term. But within the year

Carter had grown suspicious of Castro's meddling in Angola, a concern that escalated in 1978 when Castro dispatched troops into Ethiopia. By the third year of his presidency, as tales of a Soviet brigade in Cuba swept through Washington cocktail parties, the vaunted Cuban-American reconciliation of 1977 had deteriorated into mutually recriminating exchanges.

Elsewhere, especially in the Southern Cone, Carter's determination to fuse morality, reason, and power (which can be mixed but rarely blended) in American policy toward the hemisphere brought not compliance but, increasingly, defiance. In 1976, a military junta in Argentina, declaring that inflation and political disorder threatened the nation, had overthrown the government of Isabel Perón. Determined to break the Left, the military launched a war against terrorism that ultimately reached gruesome severity. Fifteen thousand, it was estimated, "disappeared" in the Argentina of the junta. They were swept away in the middle of the night, tortured, killed, and interred without markers. Their families never learned of their whereabouts. Even if discovered, the torso of one victim was sometimes buried with the head of a second and the limbs of a third. Some of the more outspoken, such as the journalist Jacobo Timerman, survived incarceration and went into exile. Timerman wrote a despairing account of his suffering in *Prisoner without a Name, Cell without a Number*. Despite the odious character of Argentina's war against terrorism and the accumulating evidence of the junta's violation of human rights, the Carter team divided over policy. Cyrus Vance, the secretary of state, argued for sanctions; Zbigniew Brzezinski, the president's national security adviser, who had already spoken of ending Washington's hegemonic pretensions in the hemisphere, viewed a vigorous human rights policy as injurious to American relations not only with Argentina but with Chile and Brazil.[17]

The president sided with Vance, a decision that accurately reflected the hostile mood in Congress toward Latin America's authoritarian regimes. Carter singled out the Argentine junta for its human rights violations and reduced its foreign aid allotment by 50 percent.[18] Argentina denounced the American move, but Congress wanted to go even farther by cutting off all military assistance to the generals in

Buenos Aires. For a few months the president resisted the pressure, then finally acquiesced, citing Argentina's gross violations of human rights. Other financial pressures against the junta in the Inter-American Development and Export-Import banks followed. But the severity of the Argentine government's internal policies lessened only slightly under these sanctions. In retaliation, the junta singled out American multinationals, subjecting them to such intense pressures that they inundated Washington with complaints. Carter softened his Argentine policy. The junta promised the restoration of civilian rule in 1979—a promise it did not keep—and gave Timerman respite from his ordeal in an Argentine torture chamber. A trickle of American aid reentered the country. After the Soviet invasion of Afghanistan in 1979, which brought a grain embargo from Washington, Carter tried to persuade the Argentines not to increase their grain exports to the Soviet Union. As compensation, the Argentines wanted a relaxation of administration pressures, but Pat Derian, assistant secretary of state for human rights, threatened to resign. In the end, the Argentines sold more grain to the Russians, the military sanctions remained in effect, and Derian stayed at her post.

In Brazil, which Brzezinski called one of the "new influentials" in the Third World, Carter encountered further obstacles to his policy of forceful benevolence. In size, population, and economy, Brazil (together with Mexico) symbolized the New Industrial Economic Order that had come of age in the 1970s. Thus it was of greater importance to Carter than either Argentina or Chile. Yet, as Carter had declared in the 1976 presidential campaign, however crucial Brazil was to Washington's strategic and economic calculations, the repressiveness of the Brazilian military government warranted American disapproval. Afterward, the Human Rights Office of the Department of State cited Brazil for serious violations of political rights, the first step toward shutting off military aid. Before that occurred, however, the Brazilian government peremptorily canceled its military assistance pact with the United States (which had been in force since 1952) and declared that it would not accept U.S. aid. Carter's protestations over a West German offer to supply the Brazilians with nuclear technology (Brazil had not signed the treaty banning nuclear weapons from Latin

America)—which Washington followed up with pressures on Bonn to cancel the arrangement—so infuriated the Brazilians that it took three years for Carter to mollify them. As had the Argentines, the Brazilians refused to cut back on their grain exports to the Soviet Union.

In retrospect, Latin American hostility overshadowed Carter's occasional but significant small victories. He kept up fairly consistent pressure on Latin America's most egregious violators of human rights. Without such pressure, they doubtless would not have lessened the severity of their rule. The process of Latin American democratization that Ronald Reagan later lauded (and took credit for) owed its provenance not to Reagan primarily but to the human rights activism of Carter in Latin America. Carter also criticized his predecessors for neglecting Mexico and used his influence to assure that Mexican laborers in America, even those without proper documentation, were not deprived of their human rights. Yet when he drew attention to the increasing numbers of illegal entries of Mexicans into the United States, Mexico joined the chorus of Latin American critics of his policies.

Latin American governments came to regard Carter as yet another American leader who promised much and delivered too little. He spoke about human rights. They talked of internal security problems and the unavoidablity of "dirty wars" against terrorism. He talked of a north-south dialogue. They responded with renewed pleas for access to markets, technology, and financial assistance from the modern industrial nations. There was a noticeable gap between his rhetoric about what he wanted to do for Latin America and his performance. In all fairness, Carter administration officials concerned with Latin America often fought hard for a policy but lost out to more persuasive advocates of a contradictory policy. And, as Abraham Lowenthal has astutely observed, a surprisingly powerful array of private enterprises and organizations—international banks, labor unions, oil companies—can often frustrate American policy in Latin America, and *their* priorities sometimes get more attention from Congress. Latin American aspirations and needs required more than a new administration whose leader called for a new policy. What Latin America wanted in the 1970s was the benefits of a modern economic order without the strains it often places on the social order. This ideal was beyond the ability of Carter or any American leader to bring about.[19]

Carter's failure lay not in flawed priorities or the lack of will to achieve them but rather in his unwillingness to recognize that no nation can easily blend morality and power into an effective foreign policy and in his inability to harness those diverse public and private American interests and enterprises with a stake in the hemisphere to carry out his goals. No American leader, however well-intentioned, can readily succeed with policies that are crafted to shape events but instead are shaped by those events.

Carter saw Latin America as he wanted it to be, not as it is. He expressed the aspirations of America, not the definable hemispheric goals of the United States. When democracy resurfaced in the Latin America of the 1980s, Americans gave Ronald Reagan much of the credit. But Latin Americans knew better, and Carter joined John F. Kennedy as the most admired modern U.S. presidents in Latin America.

10 Central America and the Hemispheric Agenda

In an era when American hegemony in Latin America declined, Washington's hemispheric strategists took their stand in Central America.

Until the Nicaraguan and Salvadoran upheavals of 1979 sent the isthmian economy downward, Central America had been one of the post–World War II economic successes in Latin America. Even under the strain of a rapidly growing population (from 8 to more than 20 million from 1950 to 1979), its national economies had expanded vigorously. In 1960, before the Alliance for Progress got under way, its often combative governments had fashioned the Central American Common Market. Despite squabblings between competitive states and the inability of isthmian producers to shield themselves against the intrusion of American companies, the isthmian economy grew and the middle class expanded.[1]

As the expectations of a generation of Central Americans for a better life heightened, those who ruled failed to produce a more democratic political or social order. And in the countryside the demands for land of an expanding agro-export economy sometimes took a heavy toll on traditional peasant cultures. Cattle grazing and cotton growing—twin programs encouraged by U.S. agricultural development policies—took food lands out of production. In the process the expanding state economy drove campesinos from their meager holdings.[2] A generation of Salvadoran rural people, pushed off the land to make room for bigger and more powerful growers, migrated into relatively sparsely settled Honduras. The growing hostility to their presence ultimately drove many back into El Salvador and precipitated the confrontation between the two governments in the 1969 Soccer War.

237

The war ended after one hundred hours, but the severity of the agrarian situation worsened. It was especially grim in Guatemala, where a "dirty war" had gone on in the countryside off and on since 1954. Peasants sometimes organized, as in Honduras, and compelled a usually indifferent government to respond to their needs, but in Honduras and elsewhere they were generally too weak or too frightened to fight. They went elsewhere—into more isolated regions or into the crowded national capitals, where their presence and their demands created new problems.

As the decade ended, the "inevitable revolution" Robert Kennedy had warned about came not in Guatemala (where the soothsayers had predicted) but in Nicaragua and El Salvador.

The Central American Crisis

In his first two years Carter had articulated a benign policy for Latin America and tried to apply it to Central America. Despite cynicism about the gap between American professions and actions, especially in human rights diplomacy, he had made converts—even among American conservatives—and his sustained commitments to this cause *had* made a difference. Human rights violations declined noticeably in those nations whose governments denounced American interference in their internal affairs and repudiated their military assistance pacts with Washington.

But the revolution in Nicaragua against Somoza posed more difficult choices. In 1970 the Somozas had appeared as secure as ever, but in 1972 Somoza perpetuated his familial rule in a fraudulently unconstitutional manner. When Managua was devastated by an earthquake in the same year, he committed the government to rebuilding the capital on land he had acquired at a pittance and resold at enormously inflated prices. By the mid-1970s, the corruption of the regime had reached such proportions that it sickened all Nicaraguans. He began moving in on businesses formerly reserved for other Nicaraguan families. The mix of greed and ambition transformed those who had quietly tolerated his excesses into an increasingly vocal protest group. The acknowledged leader of the moderate opposition was Pedro Joaquín Chamorro, editor of *La Prensa*, who put together a coalition of labor organizations and anti-Somoza politicians in the Democratic Union of Liberation.

Chamorro and the union denounced Somoza's misrule, but they fought mostly with words. The Sandinista Liberation Front (FSLN), which in 1974 had perhaps no more than a hundred soldiers, began to challenge the urban opposition for attention. In late 1974 the FSLN kidnapped a dozen prominent Nicaraguans and held them for a million-dollar ransom, release of fourteen of their comrades, and safe-conduct passes to Cuba. Somoza was so outraged by the incident that he began a brutal campaign the following year to eradicate the guerrillas. With American aid, he initiated a counterinsurgency in the northern mountains, where the guard drove campesinos from their homes into resettlement areas (a policy, ironically, which the Sandinistas themselves have occasionally followed in the war against their enemies, the Contras). The outrages brought down on Somoza the condemnation of the church and eventually of the American government. Somoza's credibility in Washington rapidly diminished. The assassination of Chamorro in January 1978 brought on a general strike in Managua and prompted demands from the moderates for Somoza's resignation. For a few months, the Sandinistas appeared to be losing control of the direction of the revolution, but in August, Edén Pastora led a dramatic capture of the national assembly. He demanded a ransom and safe passage for his men to the sanctuary of Omar Torrijos's Panama. Crowds of Nicaraguans along the route to the airport cheered him. The incident convinced Carter that Somoza might not be able to survive.[3]

Despite his distaste for this man whose father had abetted the marines in the Sandino war a half-century before, Carter astutely perceived the limited choices he confronted in Nicaragua. Perhaps unwittingly, his human rights policies had inspired the Nicaraguan opposition, which grew stronger with every week, into believing that the United States, which, as Nicaraguans argued, had put the

Somozas into power, would now remove them. Not only in Nicaragua but elsewhere, especially in Costa Rica, Venezuela, and Panama, the disgust with Somoza reached frenzied levels. Somoza had to go, but for Carter the troublesome matter was his successor. Somoza confronted a popular opposition, it was clear, and if he tried to stay in power, Nicaragua would plunge into civil war. If anything, the United States had to intrude to prevent that, but, more important, it had to find some alternative to the core of Marxists in the FSLN who, if Somoza fell, would doubtless install an anti-American government.

Fifty years before, the solution would have been simple—dispatch the marines and hold an election. But Carter had already made it clear that he would not ask Somoza to resign or, if Somoza refused to quit, forcibly remove him. Given this self-imposed limitation on the use of American power—which Latin Americans should have applauded—he moved quickly to introduce the OAS mechanism into the disturbed Nicaraguan political scene. When the OAS pressed the dictator to hold a plebiscite, Somoza, sensing he might be able to manipulate Washington into giving him enough time to crush the Sandinistas, toughened. Carter showed his displeasure a month later by shutting off aid to the Somoza regime, but by then the dictator had strengthened the guard. It would, he believed, defend the family to the death.[4]

Somoza had rejuvenated the guardians of the dynasty, but his armed enemies had also consolidated. Once split into three factions—each with a different strategy for the war against him—they consolidated into a liberating army. In May and June, a steady flow of supplies from Cuba came through Panama and Costa Rica to sustain them in their final assault. Only toward the end, as Somoza subjected the cities of Nicaragua to a vengeful, destructive bombardment that roused the urban populace against him, did the moderate opposition have an opportunity to put itself in a position to succeed him. In the last week of the civil war, American pressure on Somoza to step down, carried out through the OAS, escalated, but the moderates saw in this no discernible advantage. The Sandinistas realized the American effort would effectively deny them the power they had won by armed struggle and successfully opposed it. Mexico, Panama, Venezuela, and Costa Rica supported them. Shortly afterward, Somoza left the country.

Thus in less than a year Nicaragua's plunge into social and political chaos had reached a point where American pressure, once decisive in the history of the republic, was no longer a determining influence. Rejecting intervention, Carter had tried persuasive and, increasingly, forceful diplomacy in Nicaragua. Throughout he had blended moral concern and reason. But in retrospect his policy had not determined the course of Nicaraguan history in the final year of the Somoza dynasty. Rather, the calamitous events of that year had established a fearful and destructive pattern that made Nicaragua a victim of its tormented history and the United States ultimately a bystander to the exorcism of the demon the Sandinistas believe it had wrongfully imposed on them fifty years before.

In the beginning neither the Sandinistas nor the Carter administration consciously sought a confrontation. With Marxists in the core of their movement, they were presumably committed to a reconstruction of Nicaraguan society, yet they began with a practical course—a mixed economy, nonalignment, and political pluralism. With the first they hoped to absorb the small but influential business and professional class; with the second they professed to keep Nicaragua out of the Cold War; and with the last they offered a stunted political culture the opportunity to create "real democracy" in which elections dominated by narrow political elites are less determining than the participation of popular organizations, labor unions, and campesinos. The *comandantes* and the FSLN would mold Nicaragua along socialist lines but would not exclude the private sector from the new Nicaragua, where all labored for the common good. They made the anticipated overtures to the Cubans, who sent teachers and medical personnel to assist in the literacy and health campaigns. Castro advised them not to make Cuba's mistakes by cutting themselves off from the United States. Their approach impressed neighboring Costa Rica and Panama, two countries whose support had been vital to the Sandinista victory, and apparently persuaded Carter that the United States, by using desperately needed foreign aid as a lever, would be able to bolster the Nicaraguan middle class and contain the revolution.

But events now pressed on American policy in Central America. Three months after the Sandinista victory, as the president was putting together a significant aid package for Nicaragua, the military government in El Salvador (which had received Washington's moral disapprobation for its human rights violations) fell to a reformist military cadre that brought civilians into the government and spoke of ending the grip of the military-elite alliance that had been fashioned in the early 1930s. Hard-liners, mostly in the Defense Department, saw the isthmian condition increasingly in a strategic context, and within the foreign policy bureaucracy they harassed those who called for American support for Salvadoran reform with grim scenarios about falling dominoes and threats to America's national interests "in our backyard." As it had done in Nicaragua before Somoza's fall, the American government expressed its commitments to reform, but it was apprehensive about the means, particularly the inclusion of popular organizations in the political process, to obtain them. So Carter hesitated, giving the Salvadoran ruling elite the opportunity to fashion its solution to the leftist challenge—paramilitary vigilantes and death squads, which began a systematic, increasingly grisly campaign to dispose of those who defied the social order.

In the months after the October coup, the lasting hope of Washington was the continued participation of the Christian Democrats in the succession of juntas. On this middle-class, reformist political movement the United States had staked its commitment in Chile in the 1960s. In El Salvador, however, it had abruptly allied itself with a Christian Democracy that had already begun to splinter over a fundamental party principle—civilian dominance of the military. Through 1980, as successive months brought new horror stories from El Salvador—the most repulsive were the assassination of Archbishop Oscar Romero and Mario Zamora, a Christian Democratic leader. These were accompanied by announcements of an agrarian reform program, which began in the spring with Phase I, the dividing of estates larger than 1,250 acres. Even here, the elite was able to retain its hold by parceling out the land to relatives or unleashing the death squads on peasants who dared to claim it. By the end of the year, when three American nuns and a Catholic lay worker were raped and murdered near the international airport, the policy of reform and repression had wrought little reform and many deaths. And in this year the Christian Democratic party and its leftist allies dissolved their momentary political alliance, and then the Christian Democrats—rent by internal disputes, challenged by a rightist coalition, its leaders harassed and murdered—fled to the Left and Right on the political spectrum.

One of them sensed opportunity. José Napoleón Duarte, wrongfully denied power in 1972, made his pact with the generals. They would permit him to rule if he did not tell them how to fight their war.

The Strategic Option

Surprisingly, Americans retained a fleeting belief in a middle course in Central America, but in 1980 their growing estrangement from the world and its troubles (symbolized in the 444-day ordeal of American hostages in Tehran) took its toll. By summer, when the national political conventions took place, they were ready for the reassurance of the more militant voice of Ronald Reagan. Carter had taken limited but visible steps to deal with the deteriorating isthmian situation—he had furthered the cause of democracy in Guatemala and Honduras—but he had not resolved the crisis in El Salvador nor had he brought the Sandinistas to heel with promises of American aid. The Mariel boatlift, when 125,000 Cubans whom Castro allowed to emigrate, piled on boats hastily dispatched from Miami and sailed for Florida while the American government warned over its radios that they lacked permission to enter the United States, served as a metaphor for American debility in the Caribbean. What had begun as apparent triumph several months before (when Cuban exiles had visited the island with their enthusiastic tales of life in Miami) and continued with Cubans flooding into Latin American embassies demanding asylum, Americans disconsolately argued, had ended with Castro unloading the residue of his mental hospitals and prisons on a United States too embarrassed to refuse them. Most of the Marielitos were soon absorbed into the vigorous Cuban-American community, but Castro exploited the episode.

What Reagan proposed was not so much a different strategy to confront the Central American crisis but different tactics to attain American objectives.[5] For inspiration he drew on Truman's resolve in the 1947 Greek crisis, genesis of the containment doctrine, and Theodore Roosevelt's display of American power to show how the United States responded when Latin Americans, as TR often said, "got in the revolutionary frame of mind." Carter had offered the American people a realistic but complex and therefore disturbing assessment of the hemisphere's problems. Reagan substituted tough talk and new priorities. The United States had slipped in Central America because it had lost its commitment to confront the "evil empire" of the Soviet Union. Détente had been a chimera. It had not diminished Soviet meddling in the Third World, as Americans (though not Russians) had anticipated. The Sandinista victory, the "giveaway of our canal," the Soviet invasion of Afghanistan and its military commitments to Ethiopia, the Salt II treaty, guerrilla war in El Salvador—the list went on but the story of American weakness was depressingly familiar.

A band of Reagan ideologues had best expressed this presumably unarticulated public disenchantment in a thought-piece entitled the Santa Fe doctrine. Coupled with renegade Democrat Jeane Kirkpatrick's damnation of Carter's tolerance of the excesses of U.S. enemies (in the cause of revolutionary change) and his relentless pressure on our friends (in the cause of human rights), the Santa Fe doctrine made an emotionally persuasive case for drawing the line. Central America offered the most sensible place to take a stand. The Soviets—even the Cubans—dared not confront U.S. power there, nor would they pay the economic price for sustaining "another Cuba," whatever the psychological or political self-satisfaction it might offer. Containment, which had begun in Europe after World War II, now shifted to Central America, where American power and the will to use it would bring victory.[6]

With Carter gone, the hard-liners were now in the ascendancy in the bureaucracy. Their ideologue was Secretary of State Alexander Haig. The guerrilla war in El Salvador, he averred, was yet another episode in the East-West struggle. Defeat of the insurrection in that country would be symbolically equivalent to "rolling back the communist tide" elsewhere. More concretely, momentum was on Washington's side. In late 1980 the Salvadoran guerrillas had persuaded the Sandinistas to help them, and early in the following year they had unleashed their urban commandos to bring down the fragile coalition government. The attack proved a disaster: the resurgent Salvadoran military used the occasion to brutalize and cower its urban opposition. Though Carter had grown more skeptical of Sandinista professions and had labored to prevent the triumph of the Salvadoran Left by political means, he had not, either in his rhetoric or his actions, drawn those clear divisions that Americans apparently wanted to see. Untroubled by political ambivalence, in Latin America or at home, Reagan did. In the early years of the new administration, the only meaningful debate within the administration lay between those who wanted to contain the Sandinista revolution to Nicaragua and those who wanted to overthrow it.

El Salvador provided a means to reconcile these twin groups. Until the Contra revolution in Nicaragua in 1982, the latter were apparently content with an enhanced American military presence in Honduras and support for the Salvadoran military's struggle against the guerrillas in the countryside. The traditionalists who were uneasy with the militarization of the isthmus ultimately found philosophical satisfaction in Reagan's support for Duarte in El Salvador, a commitment that would produce in 1982 a coalition government of rightists and Christian Democrats and, following a "demonstration election" in 1984, a victory for America's "last, best hope" in El Salvador.

Reagan's approach to Central America had stated objectives and, presumably, sufficient American political and military commitment to achieve those objectives, but from the beginning he encountered unanticipated problems. Some could be attributed to his failure to create a bipartisan consensus for his Central American policy, others to the hesitance of Congress to fund an increasingly costly and dangerous enterprise that would ultimately necessitate the use of American troops. Determined to fashion a coalition, Reagan delivered a bracing speech in April 1983 in which he applauded "democratic" El Salvador and castigated "Marxist" Nicaragua. The wallowing moderates in Congress stood forewarned about the perils of remaining on the sidelines in a battle in which the issues seemed so clear.

But, then, that was the problem—even if the issues had been clear, the way to resolve them was not. Americans listened to the president, liked what they heard, liked the way he said it, and certainly liked him, but were disturbed and frustrated by Central America and its complexities. Not only was the public uncertain about the issues in Central America, but an embarrassing number of Americans could not have identified the Central American countries or correctly located them without a map. ("Where is Nicaragua?" was not only a query; it became the title of a book.) Geographical and cultural ignorance had proved no impediment to earlier generations of Americans confronted with an isthmian crisis. With determination, power, and economic and political leverage, the United States could resolve the modern predicament of Central America.

The insular Caribbean, too, found itself snared by the American strategic option. There were renewed efforts to isolate Cuba, which had made some diplomatic headway in the region in the 1970s and unsubtle reminders to Suriname and especially Grenada, which had opted for alternative development strategies that increasingly displeased Washington. Unlike most other powers with historic interests in the region, which (save for the Conservative government of Margaret Thatcher in Great Britain) extended their aid largely without political conditions, the U. S. government always extracted a political price for its benevolence. Strategic considerations, the Caribbean recipients soon learned, determined American priorities for development assistance. In the first year of the Reagan watch, Secretary of State Alexander Haig met with Canadian, Mexican, and Venezuelan representatives in the Bahamas and laid out what appeared at first to be the basis of a mini–Marshall Plan for the Caribbean. They were initially heartened by Haig's economic agenda and the subsequent announcement of the Caribbean Basin Initiative (CBI) but within the year were embarrassed by its overtly political implications.

To get the money, the Caribbean countries had to distance themselves from Cuba, Nicaragua, and Grenada, which were excluded. Though the aid package (with its initial outlay of $350 million) was a sorely needed boost for devastated economies, only a few—notably the pro-American government of Edward Seaga in Jamaica—alertly sensed American priorities and rhapsodized about the benefits of the free market. It took extensive lobbying from the administration and concessions to American textile and shoe manufacturers before Congress finally approved the CBI. In the end, the biggest beneficiaries were American exporters and not the neediest Caribbean recipients.[7]

The cause of the strategic option improved somewhat—as did public awareness of Central America—after the October 1983 "liberation of Grenada" from a band of tropical Marxists (who had taken out their leader and shot him), the Kissinger Commission Report (which undergirded the administration's isthmian policy), Duarte's victory in El Salvador, and Reagan's landslide victory over Walter Mondale in 1984. Congressional Democrats still warned of the dangers of another Vietnam but narrowly supported aid to the Nicaraguan "freedom fighters," the Contras, whose struggle had begun to weaken the already precarious Nicaraguan economy.[8] American aid became the life line to the Duarte government and, ultimately, to the Salvadoran military. But the American public remained skeptical, and virtually every major religious denomination was divided over American policy. Outspoken critics of American policy in many churches dispatched support groups to Nicaragua.

Nor was Reagan able to create a hemispheric support group for his Central American policy. Fearful of U.S. military intervention in Central America, the larger countries pressed Washington to disengage from the isthmian morass by reversing its policy of militarization. When that failed, four regional governments—Panama, Venezuela, Colombia, and Mexico—initiated discussions on the island of Contadora (off Panama) in 1982. Reagan at first ignored their efforts, but

Contadora's widespread public appeal compelled him to offer lukewarm support. When the Contadora group pleaded for a cessation of American military buildup in the region, the administration responded with a large military exercise in Honduras. Contadora eventually produced a draft proposal in 1984, which at least offered a beginning for a negotiated settlement in Central America, but American pressure on El Salvador, Honduras, and Costa Rica—each beholden to U.S. economic assistance— killed its chances.

Regarding Central America the American people expressed convictions, American business charted markets, American leaders identified "legitimate" strategic interests, and each called for analyses to achieve consensus. The National Bipartisan Commission on Central America (known as the Kissinger Commission) tried to fashion one. Reagan wanted confirmation of Soviet and Cuban involvement in Central America. With some qualification, the commission provided it but observed that the isthmus's profound social and economic inequities were equally persuasive explanations for the political convulsions that had wrought the Sandinista triumph in Nicaragua and guerrilla war in El Salvador. The United States must confront the Marxist challenge in the first, its report concluded, and should address the second.

Too few Americans paid attention to Kissinger's solemn observation in delivering the commission's report in early 1985. In Central America, he said, there is an argument for "doing nothing" and for "doing a great deal more," but worse than "doing nothing" would be "doing too little." Perhaps unintentionally, he provided the president, the Congress, and the American people—few of whom wanted to "do nothing" or "a great deal more," especially if it might mean dispatching American troops to fight in a counterinsurgency campaign—with the rationale for choosing the worst option. Sometime later, when neither increased military commitment nor economic aid had resolved the isthmian crisis, a sardonic Kissinger suggested that the United States bomb Nicaragua with the Kissinger Commission Report. He had failed to perceive that the United States had chosen a hard-line policy in Central America, but America, with its expressed doubts about the moral and human costs of the strategic option, had elected another course.

In any event, critics of U.S. Central American policy have observed, the "real battle" in Latin America is not the struggle for political power in Central America. The isthmian conflict is a symptom of deeper ailments far more menacing to the peace of the region—Latin America's crushing debt burden, its continuing dependence on the northern industrial nations for technology and capital, its vulnerability to price fluctuations for its produce, and, less apparent but no less threatening, environmental deterioration and the perceived troublesome condition of its social order. For the most part, these problems can be addressed but not resolved by the American government, however well-intentioned or determined.

After years of U.S. aid, Central America was no closer to resolution of its inner conflict. Frustrated by eight years of war, the isthmian presidents convened in Guatemala in 1987 and there signed the first of several accords, more inspirational than precise in their wording, calling for peace. For his noteworthy efforts in this process, Costa Rican president Oscar Arias was awarded the Nobel Prize for Peace. What he had secured was mitigation of conflict and a dialogue among peoples at war with themselves. His was a struggle, as Hispanics know, that is without resolution but must be fought. Arias ventured to Washington to explain why Central Americans found *their* pact— even with its faith in dialogue between warring political factions and the uncertainty of its future—preferable to *our* plan to resolve their conflict. He eloquently conveyed how Central Americans had suffered since 1979, but he could not explain to an American audience why Central Americans view the uncertainties of political turbulence as a less frightening prospect than the collapse of the social order.

Earlier, when his policy had expressed determination and a sense of purpose, Reagan had reminded Americans of the cumulative record of social and economic injustice in Central America, noted that larger amounts of U.S. aid went toward economic than military support, and (as had the U.S. government a half-century earlier) called for fair and impartial elections. What he did not explain (because no

American admits such irrationality into his thinking) was the Central American's seemingly unshakable conviction that social conflict could not be resolved—mitigated, perhaps, but not resolved.

The Economic Agenda

In the 1980s Latin American democracy, in part inspired by Carter's human rights policy, changed the form if not the content of hemispheric political culture. For this political sea change from the dismal 1970s, Reagan took undeserved credit. The heroes of the democratic restoration were those Latin Americans who decried the lingering power and influence of dictatorships or military governments. In 1980, when authoritarian politics was the rule, few observers would have anticipated that by 1987 it would be the exception. Even in Central America, the determination of strife-ridden countries and their peoples to prevent the erosion of democratic processes stood as symbolic defiance of those who believed they held real power because they held the guns. And in Panama, strategically vital to the United States, a generation of thugs and thieves who followed Torrijos confronted in summer 1987 a people divided by economic and social cleavages but united in their disgust for military rule.

As the decade wore on, however, there were recurring questions about the survival of democracy amid economic decline. After World War II, Latin America's economic analysts spoke of "structural problems"—uneven growth, the failure to develop domestic markets, dependence on foreign investment, and bloated state bureaucracies. Latin American governments carried these economic debilities into the modern era, even as their economies registered impressive gains. Some took corrective measures, but in general Latin America entered the 1980s with inadequate economic systems. As in the 1930s, the outside world and its economic pressures plunged the hemisphere into another cycle of debilitating economic downturns. Escalating oil prices severely damaged the oil-poor countries. In a perverse way, because of rapid expansion of the public sector, financed largely by foreign loans, the oil producers, particularly Mexico, found themselves awash in credit and when the oil glut hit just as quickly adrift in a sea of debt.[9]

By 1988 Latin Americans owed international banks almost $400 billion. Production, real income, and wages had fallen sharply since 1980. The gains of the previous decade dissolved in red ink. With them went much of the promise of economic modernization. In 1982, when the economic crisis struck Mexico, the United States arranged an emergency bailout, but the price for Mexico and especially for its people was high. Mexico had to impose an austerity that caused real wages to decline by almost 50 percent. Elsewhere, the demands of the International Monetary Fund (which largely reflects American international economic policy) proved so severe that *El Fondo* became as despised a symbol of American power as, for example, United Fruit Company had been a generation earlier in Central America. Latin America could not pay its debts or even the interest. From 1981 to 1986, debt interest remittances swallowed $130 billion of Latin America's productivity (relatively twice the size of Germany's reparations obligations to Britain and France after World War I). Capital departed Latin America to finance the escalating budget deficit in the United States. The impact in the hemisphere was withering investment and declining consumption.[10]

Out of economic self-interest if not altruism, the United States responded to Latin America's debt crisis but in a way that Latin Americans increasingly found inadequate. Washington's understandable preoccupation with strategic concerns in Central America diverted its attention from the depths of the economic crisis. And following emergency assistance to Mexico (and Brazil) in 1982, the United States disappointed Latin America's indebted with its reluctance to push World Bank loans for hemispheric development or to press the private international banks to reschedule the Latin American debt in accordance with its priorities. In 1985 the American government put forward the

Baker plan, which called for $29 billion in loans over a three-year period, but in return Latin American governments had to adopt market-oriented practices, lower trade barriers, and encourage foreign investment. Given their statist economic philosophies, naturally, most—Mexico proved a notable exception—found these too demanding.

Castro, predictably, entered this debate by suggesting that Latin Americans seriously consider debt repudiation, as several did in the calamitous 1930s, or at least become more aggressive on the issue. For the most part, they have not been receptive to such a severe measure as repudiation, but a signal of Latin America's distress was Peruvian president Alan Garcia's declaration that his government would adjust its debt repayment to Peruvian income from exports and the Brazilian moratorium on its debt interest payments. And they have become more defiant of Washington's self-appointed economic leadership in the hemisphere. Meeting in Acapulco in late 1987, eight Latin American presidents called for the reincorporation of Cuba into the inter-American system. This meant, presumably, not only the reentry of Cuba into the OAS but its membership in the Inter-American Development Bank and the Latin American Association for Development and Integration, the successor of the Latin American Free Trade Association. Cuba's profound economic differences apparently posed no severe deterrent to these eight countries—the largest, save for Panama and Uruguay, in Latin America—in their recommendation. The proposal was yet another sign of Washington's diminishing political influence in Latin America.

Despite the demands of seemingly insurmountable external forces, Latin American governments in the 1980s became increasingly more sophisticated in assessing their economic condition. Their statist economies have inherited defects but must be lived with until something better comes along that will provide growth but without its manifest social injustices. For the Left, of course, the only realistic future lies in planned economies, preferably without the rigidity of the Cuban model but with its emphasis on equity. The Cubans have chosen equity over growth. Most Latin American governments would like the benefits of both; what depresses them is the realization that they are not yet ready to take charge of their economic futures. But they are at least more conscious of past errors in their economic strategies. Under past industrialization schemes, for example, they inadequately managed the operations of transnationals within their borders. Foreign companies produced goods they needed—farm equipment and electric motors—but were permitted to flood local markets with excessively priced and often inappropriate consumer goods that satisfied only the narrow middle-class market. Protected industries did not have to compete in an international market and thus could turn out shoddy goods for the captive domestic market and received energy at often ridiculously low prices. Where foreign technology was available, usually only the transnational concerns had the capacity to exploit it. Smaller industries, which have proved important in the development of more advanced industrial societies, have in the past received too little attention in Latin American economies.

When their economies recover, will Latin Americans follow a similar pattern? Will they turn inward (as some are prophesying) and adopt even more stringent protectionist measures out of pessimism that the international lending agencies and banks have wearied of Third World debt and that the more advanced industrial nations are themselves leaning toward protectionism? Or will they revive some of the heretofore feeble efforts to promote regional economic integration and increased intra–Latin American trade so as to demonstrate a collective strength in dealing with the north? In the United States and to a lesser extent in Western Europe, international bankers may persuasively argue that Latin America has no other recourse but to look north for assistance and, presumably, the advice that goes with it about how to run their economic affairs. But the exchange is between debtor and debtor, and Latin American borrowers realize that the Americans may have the development schemes, but the Japanese have the money. The prospect of Latin America's economic future is a variation on old themes but with a sobering reminder that Latin Americans must "stop expecting the solutions to our problems to come from outside."[11]

The Social Agenda

More disturbing was the harmful effect hemispheric debt had on fragile democracies. The downward economic spiral of the decade had increasingly severe social costs and, it was feared, ultimately would have political costs as well. The rural dispossessed and unemployed of a generation ago have become the urban dispossessed and unemployed of the modern age. The malnourished rural child of 1958 is the underemployed father of 1988, whose children cling to life in one of the endless hillside shanties of every Latin American metropolis. Campesino families that once lived precariously on the land now live on the margin of existence in the city. The "revolution of rising expectations," a popular slogan of the 1960s, has given way to more ominous comments about the inability of Latin America to pay much more without disturbing social and political repercussions.

Most Latin Americans have moved up a notch or two on the economic ladder, but they have shifted sideways in the social order. In a material sense, they appear better off in the cities, but often the quality of the social services they receive has diminished. Education has expanded at every level and is as accessible for ordinary urban Latin Americans as for Americans, but its quality has lessened. Health care, too, has improved, but the emphasis has been on curative rather than preventive medicine and large urban hospitals rather than small neighborhood or rural clinics. The redistributionist impact of the tax structure has been limited by oversized and inefficient state bureaucracies, subsidies, military expenditures, and a widespread sentiment among middle- and upper-class Latin Americans that the vast majority of the poor are properly compensated by relatively inexpensive education and medical services and ridiculously cheap public transportation. In reality, of course, Latin America's poor wind up paying relatively more than their more affluent countrymen through indirect or value-added taxes, which can be double what sales taxes are in the United States. Particularly frustrating about the cumulative effect of Latin America's social structure is that inequity of income distribution is worse in those countries that have shown the most remarkable economic growth since World War II, Mexico and Brazil.

Within every country an internal migration—inspired by a dream—was begun. The Mexican sociologist Pablo González Casanova, writing in the mid-1960s, described it as the belief that the modern economic miracle in his country, which had begun two decades before, would make the son of a country peasant an urban worker and make *his* son a professional.[12] Mexico intended an industrial future and so desperately needed its rural labor force that in 1947 the Mexican government pressed the American government to stop the flow of Mexicans illegally entering the United States. Mexican farm youths did move to the city, did get jobs in factories, but did not go on to become professionals. By the time González made his analysis, the ability of Mexican industry to absorb this labor force had leveled off, compelling the government to accommodate the excess in the public sector. When government could no longer provide employment, this vast army of migrants joined Mexico's marginal population. They have settled in the rabbit-warren *colonias* of the poor in Mexico City, alien creatures one generation away from a village back in Oaxaca. They know better than to expect very much, but they expect more than their rural parents did. They learn to make do; some form community organizations, creating "Little Oaxaca" in the midst of misery.

In time, here and elsewhere in the exploding metropolises of the continent, they will become more secure. The man will get on-again, off-again employment for two or three months a year, perhaps more if he is lucky. He may acquire a sidewalk "business" selling fruit or tacos or cheap plastic combs and may even move up to a sidewalk magazine distributorship. Then he will probably abandon his woman, and she will set up her fruit stand and supplement her meager income by dispatching the children her runaway husband has bequeathed to her into the street to sell Chiclets to the perpetually stalled drivers on city streets. These rural dispossessed in search of the dream are the lucky ones. But they have become the culturally anonymous of Mexico's burgeoning urban population, people who once had a sense of place, who were part of a community and were ripped from it to make way for modern Mexico. They and the millions of marginals who have flocked into every Latin American capital in the past generation form by their numbers and their presence an unsettling portent of Latin America's future. They constitute a vast, still captive labor force that economic planners can mobilize against organized workers and then discard. Political parties of every persuasion vie for their votes but fear their absorption into the political culture in any meaningful way. For the present they have become attached to but not absorbed by the prevailing social order. They are needed yet feared, and they cannot be ignored. They have transformed Latin America into a Third World continent, and the uncertainty of what they want or what they will do befuddles and frightens those who are charting the hemispheric agenda.

The United States confronts with modern Latin America a migration of peoples, largely from the Caribbean Basin and Mexico, of unparalleled magnitude and consequence for the future of the Western Hemisphere and, in a more immediate sense, of increasing importance to American policy. In the past, economic and political concerns have occupied a central place in Washington's strategic calculations in Latin America, but the 1980s migration within the hemisphere—once a secondary issue in the history of the Americas—has assumed a critical and a more determining place in its international politics. In part, this modern migration derives its strength from older patterns, not only in the New but in the Old World, of movement into sparsely settled regions or to satisfy the labor demands of modern industrial economies to the north. For more than a century, laborers have migrated north from Mexico, in peace and wartime, to meet the needs of a dynamic U.S. economy, especially in the Southwest. And American companies have moved assembly plants southward into Mexico, Central America, and the Caribbean to take advantage of a labor supply that does not migrate northward. An international American economy has spawned an international labor force. Dependency theorists argue, sometimes persuasively, that it has not only fostered economic dependency but retarded Latin American democracy.

Economic downturns, especially those afflicting Latin America in the 1980s, have fueled new migrations, often of desperate people who have lost all hope save the fleeting prospect that they will find "on the other side" a temporary job to sustain them. They are the dispossessed of the Third World. Occasionally their plight generates powerful social concerns and prompts the response of governments or the international community or private voluntary organizations. In Central America, civil war and economic debility have pushed them from their country huts into the cities, into neighboring countries, into refugee camps of the United Nations, or, ultimately, into the United States—to New Orleans, Houston, Washington, Los Angeles. The confrontation of Cuba and the United States, sustained for more than twenty-five years by the cynical international posturing of the two governments, has made a generation of Cuban migrants pawns of Washington.

Latin America's population, almost 400 million today, will approach 600 million in 2000. The growth will be especially dramatic in Brazil, Central America, and Mexico. It is a demographic reality that cannot be addressed with such socialist homilies as "Latin America is rich in resources but has poor people." These are people who cannot readily be fitted into rational economic schemes because they are on the move. They may be Cubans or Haitians or Dominicans or Central Americans or Mexicans, and those who assess their plight may endlessly debate the "push-pull" forces or the political uncertainties that explain their movement northward.[13] Their expectations are greater than their parents', and the customary political or economic responses to their condition may no longer suffice to confront the challenge they pose to the Western Hemisphere and its future.

Hemispheric governments have reacted to this migration largely with unilateral measures, occasionally with benevolent intentions. In 1980 the United States expanded political refugee status beyond those fleeing communist systems to accommodate peoples with well-founded grounds of political persecution from noncommunist countries as well. For the most part, however, American immigration policy has become increasingly restrictive, reflecting the declining needs of the American economy for immigrant labor and the growing public resentment over the vast numbers of "illegals" who have crossed the two-thousand-mile U.S.-Mexican border into *El Norte*. In 1986, after a decade of debate, a coalition of liberals and conservatives produced a major revision of America's immigration law, making "illegal immigration" truly illegal by establishing fines for American employers who hire anyone without proper documentation to work in this country. In what was properly described as a generous offer, the same law offered "legalization" and ultimately citizenship to those "illegals" who were in the country before 1 January 1982. Southwestern agribusiness, which fought such changes for years on the grounds that it could not depend on a domestic labor force, supported the new law only after Congress stipulated that migrant agricultural workers would come under less restrictive measures.

In the beginning, at least, this ten-year debate over immigration reform reflected largely economic concerns and the increasing social costs of the undocumented. (In the debates over the Caribbean Basin Initiative, for example, supporters of immigration reform argued that Caribbean development would stem illegal entry into the United States by offering employment in the sending country.) Americans became increasingly fearful about the changing social character of the country, particularly in south Florida and southern California, and irritated over the rising costs of social services provided for these people. There was an apprehension that the newcomers were "Latinizing" America and a sometimes unarticulated fear of a vanishing Americanness. The "illegals," they believed, were forming a subculture of the dispossessed, people doomed to live in the shadows who lived in America but could never be Americanized. In "Latinized" America the older binding ties of a common public language (English), commonly held political values, and common social priorities were unraveling. Such fears were ordinarily manifestations of regional or local resentments—the furious debate over bilingualism in the schools—but inevitably they led to somber assessments about "what kind of nation do we want to be." Not surprisingly, many

Americans with strong feelings of social justice supported immigration reform because they believed the "illegals" were being exploited.

This debate revealed the differing ways in which the United States and America confront the needs of the American economy for a labor force that stretches beyond our borders. The U.S. economy employs Latin Americans—principally Mexicans, Central Americans, and Caribbean peoples—in U.S. multinationals in their countries and as undocumented or documented workers in the United States. For those who employ them, the understandably critical issues are the cost and reliability of their labor. America looked beyond such calculations to the social status of Latin American workers. It has not only addressed their social condition in this country but has become alert to such issues as child labor and unsafe working conditions in U.S. multinationals in Latin America. Put another way, the United States and America express qualitatively differing measures about the Latin American in the workplace of the Americas.

One values his labor; the other, his person.

Epilogue:
The United States, America,
and the Americas

More than two centuries ago American revolutionaries spoke to a "candid world" about "self-evident truths" and "inalienable rights" and with British liberals and French ideologues inspired a generation of Spanish Americans to reject monarchical rule, as had Anglo-Americans. Then America stood as the metaphor for the aspirations of a hemisphere and its European peoples, the United States as the symbol for what political man could achieve. America held no conviction that government could be perfected, only that man could be liberated, that he could define his place in life rather than occupy the place history and tradition bequeathed to him. Americans believed that this was a struggle most likely achieved in a United States secure within its borders and in a Western Hemisphere unshackled by the economic and political "systems"—then a menacing term—of the Old World. That the national security of the United States took precedence over the aspirations of America was—at least for Americans—an indisputable truth.

Rarely were the goals that sustained the quest for national security called into question, only the means used to bring them to reality. And sometimes, as occurred in 1987, when revelations of a bungled operation aimed at diverting funds from sales of arms to Iranians to the Nicaraguan Contras aroused congressional ire, the architects of policy invoked national honor and patriotism in their defense of expediency and illegality. There were the predictable confessions of errors in judgment about the means but no admission that the goal of the policy (to undermine the Nicaraguan government) may have been wrong and no realization that a democratic country that persists in its undemocratic behavior in hemispheric affairs with a single-minded determination to isolate its enemies (who themselves may be undemocratic) is unwittingly isolating itself from a hemisphere it professes to lead. In the end, Congress and the public tried to identify in the Iran-Contra affair villains and heroes but wound up mostly with characters who turned out to be heroic villains—persons of unquestionable, even naive, loyalty to a cause, who took impish delight in breaking the rules.[1] After the self-absolution of yet another inquiry and a stern reminder that the president does not make foreign policy toward Nicaragua or any other country without the Senate's approval (and certainly not in defiance of its wishes), the senators adjourned for the holidays.

Virtually unnoticed was the Senate's overwhelming reaffirmation of the Monroe Doctrine. With the exception of a reference to the Deity, its profession of faith was not much different from that of Mary Baker Eddy, founder of Christian Science, a century ago: "I believe in God, the Constitution, and the Monroe Doctrine." In a sense, the Senate's return to the fundamental principle of the nation's Latin American policy was predictable. It was not the first occasion on which the doctrine, ordinarily employed to justify a more aggressive and usually successful policy, was resurrected to provide comfort for one that had apparently failed. In the early 1920s, as one generation of Americans was trying to retrench from the Caribbean empire wrought by its predecessors, Secretary of State Charles Evans Hughes reaffirmed the doctrine as a reminder of the country's nobler purpose in the hemisphere. The European menace to Latin America had diminished with Germany's defeat, American power stood unchallenged in the Western Hemisphere, and American export capital and multinationals had penetrated into remote South America. There was no questioning the retention of the doctrine in the lexicon of foreign policy principles or its value as a basis for action in the future.

In the past American leaders—some more than others—have generally been able to forge at least a momentary political consensus to justify policy in the hemisphere, generally by pointing to national self-interest or long-standing American concerns. But they have too often fashioned public support for American policy by appealing to the irrational and emotional instincts of the general public. Such appeals can often generate tremendous support for a questionable policy, but ultimately they exact a price when the task requires more than the public anticipates, when the public loses its early enthusiasm for a venture, or when troops have to be dispatched to woebegone places that the U.S. military does not want to send them. From the turn of the twentieth century, when Alfred T. Mahan precisely categorized U.S. foreign policy—"In Europe, abstention; in Asia, cooperation; in the Western Hemisphere, domination"—only the last survives, and its strength has dissipated considerably. What has weakened the centrality of the United States in the international life of the Western Hemisphere is the lessening of American will to maintain commitments and interests undertaken early in the twentieth century and the parallel strengthening of the determination and the ability of Latin American countries to resist.

In the late nineteenth century, as the British Empire required ever greater military commitments to sustain, British leaders were nonetheless able to persuade even industrial workers that whatever prosperity they enjoyed depended on the economic well-being of empire. But years before two world wars ultimately brought down that empire, those British statesmen who had fashioned it quietly worried that it could not last, that one day the costs of defending it would exact too high a price. By a less dramatic but no less consequential process, the United States confronts a similar prospect in Latin America. Theodore Roosevelt looked south and contemptuously spoke of "warring little republics" in the "revolutionary frame of mind" and vowed to mitigate if not resolve their conflicts. With a similar arrogance but without Roosevelt's astuteness, Ronald Reagan similarly characterized those who raised the revolutionary banner against American power. In Sandinista Nicaragua, he confronted a government seething with an inherited anti-Americanism, whose leaders acquired a sense of national purpose largely through their defiance of the United States.

Clearly, if the United States or any of the hemispheric governments continue to inject such irrationality into the inter-American political arena in the future, the idea of Western Hemispheric unity will never become reality. If American leaders persist with arguments that international law and the inter-American tradition of reconciliation of disputes are secondary to American national interests, they are—unintentionally but unmistakably—declaring that the United States, as self-ascribed leader of the Western Hemisphere, is above the law. As much as the republican model it projected to the new Latin American nations, the United States symbolized the primacy of law and institutions in its governance. The nation's security and, certainly, its survival may occasionally justify a momentary departure from this tradition, but the hemispheric security of the United States depends on hemispheric unity and a reaffirmation of fundamentals. It calls for restating not only the Monroe Doctrine but George Washington's dictum about observing "good faith" toward all nations.

In the past—and, it can be argued, in our time—the primacy of U.S. security interests in Latin America over America's plea for a hemisphere of common purpose made sense. U.S. presidents from Jefferson to Reagan (their arguments reinforced by military strategists) have persuasively made the case for protecting the weak southern flank of the United States. In Jefferson's day the menace lay in the continuing European imperial presence; in Polk's, in the determination of European powers to create a balance of power in North America that would threaten U.S. security and impede America's mission to spread the blessings of republican liberty; in Theodore Roosevelt's and Wilson's, in German ambitions in the Caribbean and Mexico and the perceived threat to the Panama Canal; in Franklin Roosevelt's, in the fascist intrusion into a vulnerable Latin America; and since World War II, in the appearance of defiant or hostile anti-American governments whose ideological, economic, political, and military links to Eastern Europe, the Third World, and the Soviet Union have undermined the hemispheric security the American people sensed they had achieved at the end of two world wars.[2]

America, too, has sought security in the Western Hemisphere, and it has done so by following a riskier but ultimately more reliable course: a sustained belief that the New World held out the promise of a better life and would bring forth a new man, that republican government would ultimately bring forth more democratic societies, that individual opportunity and endeavor would deliver more material blessings than statist economies. This is a demonstrably fanciful and unarguably naive quest. But America, without a government to articulate its goals or a military to sustain them, has in many ways achieved a security still denied to the United States in the Americas.

America has found that security by exercising restraint on the more vigorous and forceful intrusions of the United States into Latin America. Where the United States spoke of manifest destiny in the nineteenth century, America professed mission. Early in the twentieth century, when the United States reinforced its security concerns with troops dispatched into unruly tropical places, America pledged democratic tutelage and material blessing. Granted, not much was achieved, but the crass dictatorships that often followed had their origins in the example of the honest but undeniable military rule of the United States, not in the ethnocentric benevolence of America. Since then, the United States has alternated between forceful measures and economic development programs, occasionally blending them to achieve its purpose in Latin America. Whatever the assessment of their worth (and they are generally defensible even if not always admirable in their purpose) they have not wrought the security this country is seeking.

But America has sought elsewhere for its security, not among governments but among their peoples, not in the reach of its economy or its military but in its belief in freedom and community. In the course of two centuries, the United States sought to supplant Great Britain, then confronted Germany and the Soviet Union in the Western Hemisphere. But in its cultural strength in the hemisphere, America more closely resembles France, a nation largely bereft of its imperial role and lacking a dynamic economy or a reassuring political system but which continues to wield tremendous influence in a hostile world. Unlike the United States, which too often defines its Latin American friends as those who support U.S. policies or those who oppose our adversaries, America recognizes that true friendship should not demand that a Latin American, however much abused, should denounce his country to demonstrate his convictions. For America with its faith in a better world—more than the United States with its forceful presence—holds out the promise that even Cuba, the most authoritarian society in the Western Hemisphere, may one day rejoin the Americas. With the passage of the 1986 immigration law, which now makes the employment of "illegals" truly illegal, U.S. multinationals may shift even more of their operations into Latin America—perhaps including Cuba, which no longer offers a market for U.S. products but which could provide a labor force. Conceivably, U.S. leaders might one day accept such an arrangement between politically hostile governments. But America will not until Cuba reaffirms its commitment to the hemispheric credos of liberty and freedom.

There are signs—fleeting and too often obscured by distressing events—that the peoples of the Western Hemisphere have a sense of common aspiration if not a common culture and political ideology. They may not be able to articulate it but they feel it. Their leaders may speak in trite phrases about Bolívar or Monroe, about the "destiny of the Western Hemisphere" or the "cosmic race" or "hands across the border," but these slogans do not forge hemispheric unity. Governments have faltered in their efforts to inspire unity through the myriad structure of the inter-American system or through contrived programs to promote inter-American cultural awareness.

Their peoples are not failing in this quest. In often unnoticed and too little appreciated ways they are redefining the hemispheric purpose. A more democratic Latin America may yet be a dream, but the social order of Latin America—in every country, whatever its political structure—is shuddering from below. Identified by those who rule as that centuries-old latent violence of the masses, which state and society have always managed to suppress, it is a force less destructive but more threatening to government, whether of the Right or the Left. It is an awareness, even among ordinary people unaccustomed to questioning tradition and authority, of the possibility of a different future for oneself and especially one's children. The Left decries it as the intrusion of "imperial television" and its portrayal of material bless-ing; the middle class derides it as the unwarranted demand for social services from those who will not pay for them; and the traditional order sees in it an unspeakable menace to church and family. (An average of four hundred Latin American Catholics convert every hour to evangelical Christianity.) Economic development schemes from the top may not be creating more equitable societies, but "penny cap-italism" is flourishing. The long-admired American experience of un-shackling the individual so that society may benefit from his creativity and human capital or of encouraging small business and en-trepreneurship is an idea taking hold among even the lowliest street vendors in Latin America. This is the "informal revolution" that is sweeping the continent, and the Right and the Left fear it, for the urgency of its message can only signal that their peoples have re-tained a faith in themselves, and they have that faith because America has sustained it.

America and the United States are the same, but the smugness with which Americans assert that may conceal some inner doubts of its truth. In any event, Americans and a great many Latin Americans certainly want to believe it, and that means positive acts can be under-taken to bring about the spiritual union. U.S. policy toward Latin America, however strategically fashioned and soundly executed, can-not circumvent America's priorities and aspirations for the Western Hemisphere. Until the United States joins the Western Hemisphere in spirit as well as in geographical identity, it will remain in but not of the Americas. Three steps are necessary.

The first requires ridding ourselves of the ingrained belief that most Latin Americans are chaotic in thought and incompetent in deed. We may respond that we certainly do not believe that—which is probably true—but we act as if we believe it, and, tragically, too many Latin Americans have come to believe it. The ill effects of this legacy of contempt have left the peoples of the hemisphere countless silly no-tions about one another, which have accumulated in a great un-truth—that because the United States can identity Latin America's problems, it can fix them. Americans may be good pathologists of the Latin American condition, but the United States cannot provide the cure until it is willing to join with the other nations of the hemisphere (as equals) in combating the diseases that afflict the Americas—the perilous condition of human rights, the precarious state of the hemispheric environment, and the most insidious threat, the hemispheric drug trade. If the United States—on the specious argument that it alone is blameless for these hemispheric debilities—insists on undertaking these gargantuan battles alone, it will one day wind up alone.

A related issue concerns the debate over the "Latinization" of the United States. Running throughout has been a fear, implicit if not always visible, that Hispanics in the United States are creating a Spanish-speaking "Quebec" with all its divisive connotations. As the Hispanic head count rises with each census, the concerns resurface. In the process Americans forget a vital distinction between French and Hispanic cultures: France is a cultural island, and the French convey the notion of separateness wherever they are; but Hispanics hold to the belief that society is a unity of diverse races and ethnic peoples. The person should not have to relinquish his cultural identity to take his rightful place in the larger society. The "inner world" of the family may sometimes conflict with the "outer world" of the community and nation, but what is necessary for social unity is not so much resolution of these conflicts as dialogue. To Anglo-Americans, Hispanics retain a clannish loyalty to their *familia* and exhibit more interest in endless discussion of community issues than in resolving problems, but their commitment to the nation is no less strong than that of any other American ethnic group. Hispanics have died alongside other Americans in the wars of the United States. But like those fellow Americans, they have fought and died not so much for the United States as for America.

The second is a latent issue that causes no visible, immediate harm but must be addressed. Americans are continually reminded that Mexico deserves a "special place" in our hemispheric agenda for strategic and economic reasons. This is undeniable, but Mexico merits this distinction for another, largely forgotten reason. No country save Great Britain has a greater claim to a share of America's cultural identity than Mexico, and it should be recognized. One-third of the United States was carved from one-half of Mexico in the Mexican War.

True, the American victory assured North America a more secure and ultimately more democratic future. But Mexico's legacy to the American Southwest, largely measured by the value of the labor force it dispatched northward, has been cultural as well, and the cultural ingredient the 12 million Americans of Mexican heritage have given to America has not received its deserved place in American estimation. The rectification of this injustice does not require a reversal of the Mexican War or even an apology. Mexico and the Mexicans do not want them. But it does demand that we deal with Mexico and Mexicans with the respect due a two-thousand-year old culture—for what Mexico is, not just where it is, and for a people who know who they are, not just for their labor.

But the most crucial issue that confronts the United States lies in Puerto Rico. The island must be given its freedom or be made a state. Since the former act—for strategic reasons—is presently unacceptable, statehood is the proper course. There are at least a hundred reasons why mainlanders (Puerto Ricans are already U.S. citizens) are reluctant to incorporate the island as a state. The most obvious are that it would be the poorest state and it would be our only Spanish-speaking state. If we preserve what is in fact a colony, however, the agitation on the island over the status question will never subside, and we may ultimately confront in Puerto Rico the explosive defiance the French and British encountered in their empires. Further, statehood for Puerto Rico reinforces our strategic and cultural presence in the Caribbean. The act would satisfy the need of the United States for a place in the Caribbean that we would never give up (and, frankly, a location for the Southern Command of the U.S. Army when it leaves Panama), and (because the states are equal under the U.S. Constitution) it would demonstrate to Latin Americans that the United States is willing to accept a Spanish-speaking culture as equal.

It would mean that the United States and America are the same in thought and deed.

Notes

Introduction

1. Arthur P. Whitaker, *The Western Hemisphere Idea: Its Rise and Decline* (Ithaca, N. Y., 1954), 1.
2. Luis Quintanilla, *Pan Americanismo*, quoted in ibid., 4.
3. From 1821 until 1823 Mexico and much of Central America was a monarchy under Iturbide.
4. Bolívar's teacher, Simón Rodríguez, described Europe as a "bright veil covering the most horrible picture of misery and vice" (quoted in Leopoldo Zea, *América como consciencia* [Mexico City, 1953], 130.)
5. John Bassett Moore, *The Principles of American Diplomacy* (New York, 1918), 400.
6. On these themes see Marano Baptista Gumucio, *Latinoamericanos y norteamericanos: Cinco siglos de dos culturas* (La Paz, Bolivia, 1986), esp. 35–44; and Samuel Shapiro, ed., *Cultural Factors in Inter-American Relations* (Notre Dame, 1968), esp. 39–68.
7. By *Latin America* Rangel means *Spanish America:* "Europeans, Asians, or Africans . . . tend to overlook . . . the profound humiliation this North American success constitutes for the other America, still unable to provide itself, or the outside world, with an acceptable rationale for its own failure" (Carlos Rangel, *The Latin Americans: Their Love-Hate Relationship with the United States* [1976; Eng. ed. New York, 1976], 23). Lawrence Harrison emphasizes the cultural impact in explaining Latin American economic development in *Underdevelopment Is a State of Mind: The Latin American Case* (Cambridge, Mass., 1985).

Prelude: The Western Design

1. On the buccaneers see Alexander Esquemelin, *History of the Bucaniers* (London, 1678); and Clarence H. Haring, *The Buccaneers of the West Indies in the XVIIth Century* (1910; rpt. Hamden, Conn., 1966).

2. Thomas Gage, *The English-American, His Travail by Sea and Land: or, A New Survey of the West-Indias* (1648).
3. Quoted in Timothy Severin, *The Golden Antilles* (New York, 1970), 195.
4. For other accounts of the Western Design see Roland Hussey, "Spanish Reaction to Foreign Aggression in the Caribbean to about 1680," *Hispanic American Historical Review* 9 (August 1929): 286–302; Frank Strong, "Causes of Cromwell's West India Expedition," *American Historical Review* 4 (1889): 228–45.

1. Transatlantic Empires

1. Harry Bernstein, *Origins of Inter-American Interest, 1700–1812* (New York, 1956), 66–67.
2. Much of this chapter relies on Peggy Liss, *Atlantic Empires: The Network of Trade and Revolution, 1713–1826* (Baltimore, 1983).
3. Stanley Stein and Barbara Stein, *The Colonial Heritage of Latin America: Essays on Economic Dependence in Perspective* (New York, 1970), 1–53.
4. The standard account is C. H. Haring, *The Spanish Empire in America* (New York, 1947).
5. Liss, *Atlantic Empires*, 1–25, persuasively argues that the Peace of Utrecht ended the wars of religion and initiated the eighteenth-century transatlantic struggle for commercial supremacy, which placed new demands on colonies within competing empires.
6. Richard Pares, *War and Trade in the West Indies, 1739–1763* (Oxford, 1936), portrays these conflicts as wars for trade. See also Trevor Reese, "Georgia in Anglo-Spanish Diplomacy, 1736–1739," *William and Mary Quarterly* 3d ser., 15 (April 1958): 168–90.
7. Liss, *Atlantic Empires*, 48–49, contends that the Bourbon reforms did not exclude the landed order or the church from social prominence, did not initiate a revolution in agriculture and technology, and did not extend meaningful power to the Spanish assembly, the Cortes. The British had accomplished all these changes by 1763.
8. For its detail if not its questionable interpretation of American innocence in the corrupting world of European politics no work on Revolutionary diplomacy in English has surpassed Samuel F. Bemis's *The Diplomacy of the American Revolution* (1937; 3 ed.Bloomington, 1957).

9. For European perspectives on the Franco-Spanish connection after 1760 see Francis Renault, *Le pacte de famille et l'Amérique: La politique coloniale Franco-Espagnole de 1760 à 1792* (Paris, 1922).

10. The standard Spanish account is Juan F. Yela Utrilla, *España ante la independencia de los Estados Unidos*, 2 vols. (Lérida, 1922). Vol. 2 contains documents from the Spanish archives relating to American independence.

11. John Caughey, *Bernardo de Gálvez in Louisiana, 1776–1783* (Gretna, La., 1934).

12. Liss, *Atlantic Empires*, 127–46.

13. For this account of the Spanish-American frontier I have used J. Leitch Wright, Jr., *Anglo-Spanish Rivalry in North America* (Athens, Ga., 1971); and *Britain and the American Frontier, 1783–1815* (Athens, Ga., 1975).

14. J. Leitch Wright, Jr., "The Creek-American Treaty of 1790: Alexander McGillivray and the Diplomacy of the American Southwest," *Georgia Historical Quarterly* 51 (1967): 379–400.

15. Arthur Whitaker, *The Spanish-American Frontier, 1783–1795: The Westward Movement and the Spanish Retreat in the Mississippi Valley* (Lincoln, Neb., 1927), 13.

16. Arthur Whitaker, *The Mississippi Question, 1795–1803: A Study in Trade, Politics, and Diplomacy* (Washington, D.C., 1934), 155–58.

17. Quoted in Alexander DeConde, *This Affair of Louisiana* (New York, 1976), 100.

18. Quoted in Winthrop D. Jordan, *White over Black: American Attitudes toward the Negro, 1550–1812* (Chapel Hill, 1968), 381.

2. America and the Revolutions of the Americas

1. *Archivo de General Miranda, 1750–1810*, 15 vols. (Caracas, 1929), 15:207.

2. Quoted in Thomas Ott, *The Haitian Revolution, 1789–1804* (Knoxville, 1973), 194; see also E. Cordoba Bello, "La revolución haitiana y la independencia hispano-americana," *Revista Historia* (Caracas), 1 (April 1961): 27–48.

3. Whitaker, *The Western Hemisphere Idea: Its Rise and Decline* (Ithaca, N.Y., 1954), 28–29.

4. Salvador de Madariaga, *The Fall of the Spanish American Empire* (New York, 1947), 376–77.

5. Harry Bernstein, "Las primeras relaciones intelectuales entre New England y el mundo hispánico (1700–1815)," *Revista Hispánica Moderna*, 5 (1938):8.

6. Secretary of state to U.S. minister to France, 2 November 1810, in William R. Manning, ed., *Diplomatic Correspondence of the United States Concerning Latin American Independence*, 3 vols. (New York, 1925), 1:8; Secretary of state to William Pinkney, 22 January 1811, ibid., 10–11. Isaac J. Cox virtually exhausts the topic in *The West Florida Controversy, 1798–1813* (Baltimore, 1918), but see also Clifford Egan, "The United States, France, and West Florida, 1803–1807," *Florida Historical Quarterly*, 47 (1969): 227–53.

7. Peggy Liss, *Atlantic Empires: The Network of Trade and Revolution, 1713–1826* (Baltimore, 1983), 229, contends that the American and Latin American revolutions represented similar "outgrowths of internal expansion and changing attitudes, international struggles, shifting international economic arrangements, and new outlooks on colonies by the metropolis and the other way around."

8. Arthur P. Whitaker, *The United States and the Independence of Latin America, 1800–1830* (1941; rpt. New York, 1964), 94–99.

9. Not surprisingly, the Monroe Doctrine has a dual history in the United States and Latin America. Donald Dozer, ed., *The Monroe Doctrine, Its Modern Significance* (New York, 1975), gives a sampling from both perspectives. The doctrine's "biographer," Dexter Perkins, wrote a three-volume history covering 1823 to 1907 and followed that with a one-volume summation covering the twentieth century in *A History of the Monroe Doctrine*, rev. ed. (Boston, 1963). In this account I have relied heavily on Whitaker, *Western Hemisphere Idea*.

10. Quoted in Whitaker, *United States and the Independence of Latin America*, 126.

11. John Quincy Adams, *Memoirs of John Quincy Adams*, ed. Charles Francis Adams, 12 vols. (Philadelphia, 1874–77), 5:176.

12. Speech, 20 January 1816, *Annals of Congress*, 14th Cong., 1st sess., 727.

13. Adams to George Erving, 28 November 1818, in Worthington C. Ford, ed. *The Writings of John Quincy Adams*, 7 vols. (New York, 1913–17), 6:487–88.

14. The standard treatment of the Transcontinental Treaty is Philip C. Brooks, *Diplomacy and the Borderlands: The Adams-Onís Treaty of 1819* (Berkeley, 1939), which emphasizes frontier pressures. C. C. Griffin, *The*

United States and the Disruption of the Spanish Empire, 1810–1822 (New York, 1937), stresses American commercial acquisitiveness amid Spanish decline.

15. Whitaker, *United States and the Independence of Latin America*, 211.
16. Quoted in ibid., 336.
17. Ernest R. May, *The Making of the Monroe Doctrine* (Cambridge, Mass., 1975), stresses the domestic political implications of a unilateral statement. For William A. Williams, "The Age of Mercantilism: An Interpretation of the American Political Economy, 1763–1828," *William and Mary Quarterly* 3d ser, 15 (1958): 419–37, the doctrine was the culminating statement of American mercantilism.
18. Quoted in Harold Bierck, ed., *Selected Writings of Bolívar*, comp. Vicente Lecuna, trans. Lewis Bertrand, 2 vols. (New York, 1951), 2:458–59. See also José Vasconcelos, *Bolivarismo y Monroismo* (Santiago, 1937).
19. Glen Dealy, *The Public Man: An Interpretation of Latin America and Other Catholic Countries* (Amherst, Mass., 1977), explains this divergence. In the United States, capitalism and its cultural credos (the Protestant ethic, the fusing of private and public morality, the acquisition of wealth as a symbol of status, and so on) set the guidelines for the political culture. Latin Americans drew their political lessons from Saint Thomas Aquinas and Nicoló Machiavelli, both of whom distinguished between private and public morality. The "public man" acquired influence and stature not by following the law (i.e., the constitutional restrictions on his office) but by acquiring a following. To accomplish that he had to rule authoritatively and convincingly. Otherwise, his following would desert him for someone who exhibited the manly traits of the leader. In such a setting the "issues" or the "facts" are ignored or left unresolved if they inhibit the mandatory expression of influence and power. For Latin Americans this is the "rational" way to look at public life and the obligations of the leader.

3. The Model Republic and Its Image

1. Joseph B. Lockey, "Diplomatic Futility," *Hispanic American Historical Review* 10 (August 1930): 265.
2. Quoted in William Manning, ed., *Diplomatic Correspondence of the United*

States: Inter-American Affairs, 12 vols. (Washington, D.C., 1932–39), 5:503–4. For a Colombian view of this incident see vol. 1 of Germán Cavelier, *La política internacional de Colombia*, 2d ed., 4 vols. (Bogotá, 1959).

3. Hunter to Secretary of State John Forsyth, 10 February 1837, in Department of State, Despatches, Brazil, National Archives (microfilm).

4. *El Tiempo*, 19 February 1829, in Despatches, Argentina, National Archives (microfilm).

5. Forbes to secretary of state, 25 May 1829, in ibid.

6. Francis Baylies to secretary of state, 26 September 1832, in Manning, ed., *Diplomatic Correspondence*, 1:165.

7. David Pletcher, *The Diplomacy of Annexation: Texas, Oregon, and the Mexican War* (Columbia, Mo., 1973), is unsurpassed for its balance and objectivity in chronicling American expansionism in the 1830s and 1840s.

8. James Hook to Lord Palmerston, 30 April 1841, in E. D. Adams, ed., *British Diplomatic Correspondence Concerning the Republic of Texas* (Austin, 1918), 38.

9. Buchanan to Slidell, 10 November 1845, in Manning, ed., *Diplomatic Correspondence*, 8:173.

10. In this section I have relied heavily on Frederick Merk, *Manifest Destiny and Mission in American History: A Reinterpretation* (New York, 1963); and *The Monroe Doctrine and American Expansionism, 1843–1849* (New York, 1966); Carlos Bosch García, *Historia de las relaciones entre México y los Estados Unidos, 1819–1848* (Mexico City, 1961); and Gene Brack, *Mexico Views Manifest Destiny, 1821–1846* (Albuquerque, 1975).

11. *New York Herald*, 11 April 1848, quoted in Robert Johannsen, *To the Halls of the Montezumas: The Mexican War in the American Imagination* (New York, 1985), 303.

12. Thomas Hietala explores this theme in *Manifest Design: Anxious Aggrandizement in Late Jacksonian America* (Ithaca, N.Y., 1985), 255–57.

13. On racial ingredients of expansionist philosophy and politics see Reginald Horsman, *Race and Manifest Destiny: The Origins of American Racial Anglo-Saxonism* (Cambridge, Mass., 1981), 217.

14. Gustave A. Nuermberger, "The Continental Treaties of 1856: An American Union Exclusive of the United States," *Hispanic American Historical Review*, 20 (February, 1940):32–55; John P. Harrison, "Science and Politics: Origins and Objectives of Mid-Nineteenth Century Government Expeditions to Latin America," *Hispanic American Historical Review* 35 (May 1955):

175–202, shows how the United States blended scientific interest and manifest destiny in its policies.

15. Basil Rauch, *American Interest in Cuba, 1848–1855* (New York, 1948), covers the U.S. urgency in dealing with Cuba but should be supplemented with the monumental work of Herminio Portell-Vilá, *Narciso López y su época*, 3 vols. (Havana, 1930–58), who argues that López favored independence and was not a pawn of the southern "slavocracy."

16. C. Stanley Urban, "The Africanization of Cuba Scare, 1853–1855," *Hispanic American Historical Review* 37 (February 1957): 29–45; and Lester D. Langley, *The Cuban Policy of the United States: A Brief History* (New York, 1968), chap. 2.

17. Robert E. May, *The Southern Dream of Caribbean Empire, 1854–1861* (Baton Rouge, 1973), demonstrates how southerners believed the pursuit of a tropical empire would restore the South to its preeminence in the Union.

18. "British Aggression in Central America," *U.S. Magazine and Democratic Review* n.s., 1 (January 1851): 14.

19. Squier to secretary of state, 12 September 1849, in John Clayton Papers, Library of Congress. The standard biography of Chatfield is Mario Rodríguez, *A Palmerstonian Diplomat in Central America: Frederick Chatfield, Esq.* (Tucson, Ariz., 1964).

20. For a summary of this era in Central America see Lester D. Langley, *Struggle for the American Mediterranean: United States–European Rivalry in the Gulf-Caribbean, 1776–1904* (Athens, Ga., 1976), 81–106, but special aspects are covered in David Folkman, *The Nicaraguan Route* (Salt Lake City, 1972); A. Z. Carr, *The World and William Walker* (New York, 1963), a psychological biography; William O. Scroggs, *Filibusters and Financiers* (New York, 1916); Charles Brown, *Agents of Manifest Destiny* (Chapel Hill, 1980), which ignores the considerable Central American literature; and William Walker, *The War in Nicaragua* (Mobile, Ala., 1860). On the Central American side see Comisión de Investigación Histórico de la Campaña de 1856–57, *Documentos relativos a la guerra contra los filibusteros* (San José, C.R., 1956); Lorenzo Montúfar, *Walker en Centro-América*, 2 vols., (Guatemala, 1887); and Enrique Guier, *William Walker* (San José, C.R., 1971).

21. Gregorio Delgado, "Walker, Nicaragua, y Cuba," *Revista del Archivo y Biblioteca Nacional*, 33 (November–December 1954, January–June 1955): 383–93.

22. Quoted in Comisión de Investigación Histórico, *Documentos relativos a la guerra contra los filibusteros*, 64.

4. The Destiny of the Americas

1. Quoted in Germán Arciniegas, *Latin America: A Cultural History* (New York, 1966), 379.

2. Agustín Cué Canovas, *Juárez, los Estados Unidos y Europa: El Tratado McLane-Ocampo* (Mexico City, 1959), 159–60; Ralph Roeder, *Juárez and His Mexico*, 2 vols. (New York, 1947), 1:224–25.

3. William S. Robertson, "The Tripartite Treaty of London," *Hispanic American Historical Review* 20 (May 1940): 178, 188–89; Christine Schefer, *Los orígenes de la intervención francesa en Mexico, 1858–1862*, trans. Xavier Ortiz (Mexico City, 1939), 169–70; Genaro Estrada, *Don Juan Prim y su labor diplomático en Mexico* (Mexico City, 1928), 107–8.

4. For this account I have relied heavily on Alfred Hanna and Kathyrn Hanna, *Napoleon III and Mexico: American Triumph over Monarchy* (Chapel Hill, 1971).

5. Thomas Schoonover, *Dollars over Dominion: The Triumph of Liberalism in Mexican–United States Relations, 1861–67* (Baton Rouge, 1978), finds the Mexican-American bond of this era in the sharing of laissez-faire economic views between Republicans and Mexican liberals.

6. *Vida de Abrán Lincoln: Décimo sexto presidente de los Estados Unidos* (New York, 1866). For a persuasive summary of the impact of the Civil War see the chapter "Latin America" by Harry Bernstein in Harold Hyman, ed., *Heard Round the World: The Impact Abroad of the Civil War* (New York, 1969).

7. On this and related themes see E. Bradford Burns, *Progress and Poverty* (Berkeley, 1979), which should be measured against Bill Albert, *South America and the World Economy from Independence to 1830* (London, 1983), who argues that dependency did foster some material progress.

8. Leopoldo Zea, *Positivismo y la circunstancia mexicana* (Mexico City, 1985), 187–88. For more on American economic penetration into Mexico in the late nineteenth century see David Pletcher, *Rails, Mines, and Progress: Some American Promoters in Mexico, 1867–1911* (Ithaca, N.Y., 1958), 307, who observes that Americans failed to see the "raw materials of a great social revolution" when the Indian and lower classes were uprooted by

the expanding capitalist state. They did not get their fair share of the new prosperity. Those who triumphed in the revolution, however, disowned neither the power of the state nor profoundly altered the social structure. *Los de abajo* got land but not liberty.

9. Walter LaFeber, *The New Empire: An Interpretation of American Expansion, 1860–1898* (Ithaca, N.Y., 1963), 1–61.

10. Sumner Welles, *Naboth's Vineyard: The Dominican Republic 1844–1924*, 2 vols. (Washington, D.C., 1928), 1:140–41, 238–39, 324–25; C. C. Tansill, *The United States and Santo Domingo, 1789–1893* (Baltimore, 1938), 432–33; J. J. Montllor, "Oposición dominicana a la anexión a los Estados Unidos," *Boletín del Archivo Nacional* (Dominican Republic) 4 (December 1941): 395–407.

11. Ramiro Guerra y Sánchez, *Guerra de los diez años, 1868–1878*, 2 vols., (Havana, 1950), 1:166. For a general discussion see Lester D. Langley, *The Cuban Policy of the United States: A Brief History* (New York, 1968), chap. 3.

12. David Pletcher, *The Awkward Years: American Foreign Relations under Garfield and Arthur* (Columbia, Mo., 1962), 7–8, 23–24, 31–33; Robert Burr, *By Reason or by Force: Chile and the Balancing of Power in South America, 1830–1905* (Berkeley, 1974), 260–63. William Sater, *Chile and the War of the Pacific* (Lincoln, Neb., 1986), is definitive.

13. D. C. M. Platt, *Latin America and British Trade, 1860–1914* (London, 1972), 78–86. Joseph Smith, *Illusions of Conflict: Anglo-American Diplomacy, 1865–1896* (Pittsburgh, 1979), argues that the British intended to remain economic but not political competitors to the United States in Latin America.

14. For a scathing Latin American assessment, see Alonso Aguilar, *Pan-Americanism: From Monroe to the Present, A View from the Other Side* (New York, 1968), 36–42.

15. H. Ramírez Necochea, *Balmaceda y la contra-revolución de 1891*, 2d ed. (Santiago, 1969), portrays the martyred president as a nationalist who wanted to use the nitrate resources to develop the Chilean economy.

16. This section relies largely on Lester D. Langley, *The United States and the Caribbean in the Twentieth Century* (Athens, Ga., 1985), 3–14, modified by the brilliant analysis of Louis A. Pérez, Jr., on the destructive purpose of the Cuban revolution in *Cuba between Empires, 1878–1902* (Pittsburgh, 1983).

17. Latin America's elites, writes Carlos Rangel in *The Latin Americans: Their Love-Hate Relationship with the United States* (1976; Eng. ed. New York,

1976), retained an admiration for the United States in the 1890s. Even the Nicaraguan poet Rubén Darío, who later wrote scathingly of American power, inscribed a paean, "Saluting the Eagle":

E Pluribus Unum! Glory, victory, work!
Give us the secrets of the hard-working North
And may our sons, forsaking the Latin heritage
Learn tenacity, vigor, strength of soul from the Yankees.

18. David Healy, *The United States in Cuba, 1898–1902* (Madison, 1963), 44–56; J. J. LeRiverend Brusone, "Historia económica," in Ramiro Guerra y Sánchez, *Historia de la nación cubana*, 10 vols. (Havana, 1952), 9:287–300.

5. New World Policeman

1. I have pursued this theme in greater detail in *The Banana Wars: United States Intervention in the Caribbean, 1898–1934* (Lexington, Ky., 1983). Louis Pérez, Jr., assesses the historiography of U.S. intervention in "Intervention, Hegemony, and Dependency: The United States in the Circum-Caribbean, 1878–1980," *Pacific Historical Review* 51 (May, 1982): 165–94.
2. Langley, *Banana Wars*, 227–33.
3. Roosevelt to Trevelyan, 9 September 1906, Roosevelt Papers (microfilm), reel 413; Allan Millett, *The Politics of Intervention: The Military Occupation of Cuba, 1906–1909* (Columbus, Ohio, 1968), 90–91.
4. Langley, *Banana Wars*, 20–33.
5. Arthur P. Whitaker, *The Western Hemisphere Idea: Its Rise and Decline* (Ithaca, N.Y., 1954), 86–87. The Latin American position, wrote Alonso Aguilar, was "legally and politically unobjectionable," but The Hague adopted the Porter doctrine, which forbade the use of force to collect debts if the debtor nation agreed to the decision of the arbitrator (*Pan Americanism; From Monroe to the Present, A View from the Other Side* [New York, 1968], 52).
6. Dana G. Munro, *Intervention and Dollar Diplomacy in the Caribbean, 1900–1921* (Princeton, 1964), 146–74; Pedro Joaquín Chamorro, *Orígenes de la intervención americana en Nicaragua* (Managua, 1951), 13; Scott Nearing and Joseph Freeman, *Dollar Diplomacy: A Study in American Imperialism* (New York, 1925), 151–68.

7. Langley, *Banana Wars*, 77–165; Berto Ulloa, *La revolución intervenida: Relaciones diplomáticas entre México y los Estados Unidos, 1910–1914* (Mexico City, 1971), 136–56.

8. Whitaker, *Western Hemisphere Idea*, 114–18. Mark Gilderhus elaborates on Wilson's hemispheric "vision" in *Pan American Visions: Woodrow Wilson in the Western Hemisphere, 1913–1921* (Tucson, Ariz., 1986).

9. Joseph Tulchin, *Latin America and World War I* (New York, 1971), 10.

10. American propaganda efforts against Germany in Latin America were successful; see James Mock, "The Creel Committee in Latin America," *Hispanic American Historical Review* 22 (May 1942): 262–79. Emily Rosenberg explores the Mexican-Argentine "bloc" against the United States in "World War I and 'Continental Solidarity' ", *Americas*, 31 (January 1975): 313–34.

11. A. Conil Paz, *La neutralidad argentina y la Primera Guerra Mundial* (Buenos Aires, 1976).

12. Robert Freeman Smith ably catalogs the U.S. confrontation with Mexican revolutionary nationalism in *The United States and Revolutionary Nationalism in Mexico, 1916–1932* (Chicago, 1972).

13. Quoted in Robert Seidel, *Progressive Pan Americanism: Development and United States Policy toward South America, 1906–1931* (Ithaca, N.Y., 1973), 592.

14. C. H. Haring, *South America Looks at the United States* (New York, 1929), assesses anti-Americanism in the 1920s.

15. Jean Franco, *The Modern Culture of Latin America: Society and the Artist* (New York, 1967), 71–72.

16. On the banana business and isthmian politics see Thomas Karnes, *Tropical Enterprise: The Standard Fruit and Steamship Co. in Latin America* (Baton Rouge, 1978), 70–88. Dana G. Munro, *The United States and the Caribbean Republics, 1921–1933* (Princeton, 1974), remains the standard work.

17. Samuel G. Inman, *Inter-American Conferences, 1826–1954* (Washington, D.C., 1965), 86–104.

18. Langley, *Banana Wars*, 181–223. On Sandino see the classic biography by Neill Macaulay, *The Sandino Affair* (1967; rpt. Durham, N.C., 1986); and Gustavo Alemán Bolaños, *Sandino: El libertador* (Mexico City, 1952).

19. Robert Ferrell, "Repudiation of a Repudiation," *Journal of American History* 51 (March 1965): 669–73.

6. Good Neighbors

1. Quoted in Donald Dozer, *Are We Good Neighbors? Three Decades of Inter-American Relations, 1930–1960* (Gainesville, Fla., 1959), 4.

2. Doubtless Roosevelt bore responsibility for acquiescing in the Caribbean despotism. "Somoza may be an s.o.b., but at least he's *our* s.o.b.," a remark often attributed to Roosevelt, served as metaphor for the new political reality. Donald Schewe, nine years at the FDR Library in Hyde Park, searched in vain for this quotation in the Roosevelt papers. See Robert Pastor, *Condemned to Repetition: The United States and Nicaragua* (Princeton, 1987), 3.

3. Dick Steward, *Trade and Hemisphere: The Good Neighbor Policy and Reciprocal Trade* (Columbia, Mo., 1975), 1–12, 100–122.

4. Quoted in Glen Barclay, *Struggle for a Continent: A Diplomatic History of South America, 1919–1945* (New York, 1972), 51–52.

5. The final settlement required another three years to achieve. Though not impartial, it did bring peace to the Chaco. See Leslie Rout, *Politics of the Chaco Peace Conference, 1935–39* (Austin, 1970).

6. Tulio Halperin Donghi, *Historia contemporánea de América Latina* (Madrid, 1969), 356–75.

7. R. A. Humphreys, *Latin America and the Second World War*, 2 vols. (London, 1981), 1:4–38.

8. David Haglund, *Latin America and the Transformation of U.S. Strategic Thought, 1936–1940* (Albuquerque, 1984), 85–95.

9. Holger Herwig, *The Politics of Frustration: The United States in German Naval Planning, 1889–1941* (Boston, 1976), 187.

10. Quoted in Haglund, *Latin America*, 105.

11. Quoted in ibid., 108.

12. Steward, *Trade and Hemisphere*, 273–75; David Green, *The Containment of Latin America: A History of the Myths and Realities of the Good Neighbor Policy* (Chicago, 1971), 60–74.

13. John A. Logan, *No Transfer: An American Security Principle* (New Haven, 1961), 309–45.

14. Gerald Haines, "Under the Eagle's Wings: The Franklin Roosevelt Administration Forges an American Hemisphere," *Diplomatic History* 1 (Fall 1977): 373–88; J. Manuel Espinosa, *Inter-American Beginnings of U.S. Cultural Diplomacy, 1936–1948* (Washington, D.C., 1976).

15. E. Cárdenas de la Peña, *Gesta en el Golfo: La segunda guerra mundial y México* (Mexico City, 1966).

16. In the process, Frank McCann argues, the "alliance" and its debilitating connotation of dependence laid the basis for anti-Americanism in Brazil ("Brazil, the United States, and World War II," *Diplomatic History* 3 [Summer 1979]: 57–76). For a discussion of the military relationship see his *The Brazilian-American Alliance 1937–1945* (Princeton, 1974).

17. Michael Grow, *The Good Neighbor Policy and Authoritarianism in Paraguay* (Lawrence, Kan., 1981), 59–113.

18. Michael Francis, *The Limits of Hegemony: United States Relations with Argentina and Chile in World War II* (Notre Dame, 1977); and Randall Woods, *The Roosevelt Foreign Policy Establishment and the Good Neighbor: The United States and Argentina, 1941–1945* (Lawrence, Kan., 1979).

19. Quoted in Humphreys, *Latin America and the Second World War*, 2:177.

20. Randall Woods, "Conflict or Community? The United States and Argentina's Admission to the United Nations," *Pacific Historical Review* 46 (August 1977): 361–86, argues that the United States was persuaded to support Argentina's claim out of commitment to the principle of sovereignty and nonintervention.

21. Demetrio Boersner, *Relaciones internacionales de América Latina* (San José, C.R., 1982), 249, observes: "The Second World War had a stimulating impact on economic and social development in Latin America and contributed to future standard changes or the impetus to achieve such changes." Frederick W. Marks III, in *Wind Over Sand: The Diplomacy of Franklin Roosevelt* (Athens, Ga., 1988), 217, cites Senator Hugh Butler's scathing indictment of the Good Neighbor "purchase" of Latin America's wartime loyalty without getting a good return from them. What is overlooked here is the Latin American admiration of the leader who senses the importance of dialogue and style and who recognizes that disputes between nations cannot be resolved but must be mitigated. Further, in its aspirations the Good Neighbor conveyed a higher purpose.

22. Fredrick Pike, "Latin America and United States Stereotypes in the 1920s and 1930s," *Americas* 42 (October 1985): 131–62. There was, indisputably, a murkiness to Frank's views, but Latin American intellectuals once influenced by Rodó and Ugarte found him a refreshing North American intellectual spirit.

7. The Cold War in the Americas

1. Quoted in Samuel Baily, *The United States and the Development of South America, 1945–1975* (New York, 1976), 44.
2. On the Argentine affair see David Green, *The Containment of Latin America* (New York, 1971), 25–54.
3. Quoted in Baily, *The United States and the Development of South America*, 60.
4. Quoted in Roger Trask, "The Impact of Cold War Relations on United States–Latin American Relations, 1945–1949," *Diplomatic History* 1 (Summer 1977): 281.
5. Quoted in ibid., 278.
6. Raúl Prebisch, "El desarrollo económico de la América Latina y sus principales problemas," *Revista de Economía Argentina* 48 (1949): 211–21, 254–66.
7. Y (Louis Halle), "On a Certain Impatience with Latin America," *Foreign Affairs* 27 (July 1950): 568.
8. Quoted in Thomas Bohlin, "United States–Latin American Relations and the Cold War, 1949–1953" (Ph.D. dissertation, University of Notre Dame, 1973), 67. Shortly before leaving the State Department in 1950, Kennan wrote a lengthy analysis of U.S. policy toward Latin America. He urged an end to "moralizing" about the region and gloomily observed: "It seems to me unlikely that there could be any other region of the earth in which nature and human behavior could have combined to produce a more unhappy and hopeless background for the conduct of human life" (Department of State, *Foreign Relations of the United States, 1950* [Washington, D.C., 1861–], 2:600).
9. Ibid., 319; F. Parkinson, *Latin America, the Cold War, and the World Powers* (Beverly Hills, 1973), 26–30.
10. For a penetrating analysis of this critical year in Costa Rica see John P. Bell, *Crisis in Costa Rica: The 1948 Revolution* (Austin, 1971).
11. For a statistical analysis of American aid see J. W. Wilkie, *The Bolivian Revolution and U.S. Aid since 1952* (Los Angeles, 1969).
12. Much of this section relies on Richard Immerman, *The CIA in Guatemala* (Austin, 1982).
13. The sordid role of UFCo in the overthrow of Arbenz is candidly retold in Thomas McCann, *An American Company: The Tragedy of United Fruit* (New

York, 1976), 42–62. See also Guillermo Toriello, *La batalla de Guatemala* (Mexico City, 1955), 161–91.

14. Quoted in Cole Blasier, *The Hovering Giant: U.S. Responses to Revolutionary Change in Latin America, 1910–1955,* rev. ed. (Pittsburgh, 1985), 168.

15. Thomas Zoumaras, "Containing Castro: Promoting Homeownership in Peru, 1956–1961," *Diplomatic History* 10 (Spring 1986): 161–82.

16. As R. Harrison Wagner observed, those who decried the inadequacies of Eisenhower's policies toward Latin America in the 1950s exaggerated the impact of peacetime economic assistance by drawing on the unusual wartime experience as an example of what was possible *(United States Policy toward Latin America: A Study in Domestic and International Politics* [Stanford, 1970], 161).

17. *El Tiempo* (Bogotá), 15 February 1948, quoted in Donald Dozer, *Are We Good Neighbors? Three Decades of Inter-American Relations, 1930–1960* (Gainesville, Fla. 1959), 305.

18. For this section I have relied heavily on Raymond Carr, *Puerto Rico: A Colonial Experiment* (New York, 1948).

19. Juan Angel Silen, *Historia de la nación puertoriqueña* (Rio Piedras, P.R., 1973), 326–28; Gordon Lewis, *Puerto Rico: Freedom and Power in the Caribbean,* paperback ed. (New York, 1968), 113–33.

8. The Cuban Revolution

1. On Castro's "conversion" to Marxism see Richard Welch, Jr., *Response to Revolution: The United States and the Cuban Revolution, 1959–1961* (Chapel Hill, 1985), 9–14. For an assessment of the intellectual origins of the Cuban revolution see Sheldon Liss, *Roots of Revolution: Radical Thought in Cuba* (Lincoln, Neb., 1987).

2. Philip Bonsal, "Cuba, Castro, and the United States," *Foreign Affairs* 45 (January 1967): 260–76; and his book *Cuba, Castro, and the United States* (Pittsburgh, 1971), 108–9.

3. Michael Francis, "The U.S. Press and Castro: A Study in Declining Relations," *Journalism Quarterly* 44 (Summer 1967): 257–66.

4. Arthur Schlesinger, Jr., *A Thousand Days: John F. Kennedy in the White House* (Boston, 1965), 226–56; Karl Meyer and Tad Szulc, *The Cuban Inva-*

sion: The Chronicle of a Disaster (New York, 1962); and Haynes Johnson et al., *The Bay of Pigs: The Leaders' Story of Brigade 2506* (New York, 1964).

5. The official Cuban account can be found in *Playa Girón, derrota del imperialismo* (Havana, 1961).

6. Jerome Levinson and Juan de Onis, *The Alliance That Lost Its Way: A Critical Report on the Alliance for Progress* (Chicago, 1970), 46–49.

7. E. V. Corominas, *Cuba en Punta del Este* (Buenos Aires, 1962).

8. Robert Divine, ed., *The Cuban Missile Crisis* (Chicago, 1971), 7–57, offers a summary and follows with selections that debate the issues. Herbert Dinerstein, *The Making of the Missile Crisis, October 1962* (Baltimore, 1976), concludes that neither the United States nor the USSR wanted a confrontation.

9. U.S. Congress, House of Representatives, Committee on Foreign Affairs, Subcommittee on Inter-American Affairs, *New Directions for the 1970s: Toward a Strategy of Inter-American Development: Hearings* (Washington, D.C., 1969), 699, 715.

10 Edwin Lieuwen, *Generals vs. Presidents: Neo-Militarism in Latin America* (New York, 1964), 63–68.

11. Levinson and de Onis, *Alliance That Lost Its Way*, 86–87.

12. Robert A. Packenham, *Liberal America and the Third World: Political Development Ideas in Foreign Aid and Social Service* (Princeton, 1973), 100.

13. Lester D. Langley, "U.S.-Panamanian Relations since 1941," *Journal of Inter-American Studies and World Affairs* 12 (July 1970): 339–66; Victor F. Goytía, *La tragedia del Canal* (Panama City, 1966), 5.

14. *New York Times*, 3, 4 April 1964; Levinson and de Onis, *Alliance That Lost Its Way*, 90–91.

15. Without U.S. acquiescence, the Brazilian military would not have undertaken the repressive policies that followed the coup nor would they have systematically "denaturalized" Brazilian cultural identity (Jan Knippers Black, *United States Penetration of Brazil* [Philadelphia, 1977], 260). Considering American influence on the Latin American militaries in the 1960s, Lyle McCalister concluded: "Militarism in Latin America is an indigenous phenomenon. It is a response to tensions in societies which have not yet achieved true national identities or established basic norms of political legitimacy. While it would be foolish to deny that North American policy and personnel have some impact on the thinking of the Latin American

military, the influence is peripheral." (quoted in Samuel Shapiro, ed., *Cultural Factors in Inter-American Relations* [Notre Dame, 1968], 101–2).

16. The speech is reprinted in Martin Needler, *The U.S. and the Latin American Revolution* (Boston, 1972), 145–53.

17. John Bartlow Martin, *Overtaken by Events: The Dominican Crisis from the Fall of Trujillo to the Civil War* (New York, 1966), 547–90, 637–45.

18. Abraham Lowenthal, *The Dominican Intervention* (Cambridge, Mass., 1972), 42–61; Tad Szulc, *Dominican Diary* (New York, 1965), 65–77.

19. Lyndon Johnson, "The Dominican Republic: A Target of Tyranny," *Vital Speeches* 31 (15 May 1965): 450–52.

20. Theodore Draper, *The Dominican Revolt: A Case Study in American Policy* (New York, 1968), 183–200. For Bosch's view that the intervention reaffirmed American imperialism in a different guise see his book *Pentagonism: A Substitution for Imperialism* (New York, 1968), 20–22, 106–7, 108–22.

21. The most optimistic statement on the role of the middle class in Latin America's future is John Johnson, *Political Change in Latin America: The Emergence of the Middle Sectors* (Stanford, 1958).

9. The New Latin America

1. *New York Times*, 26 January 1970.

2. John C. Dreier, "New Wine in Old Bottles: The Changing Inter-American System," *International Organization* 22 (1968): 477–93. In the last years of the decade—in spite of the disapproval of Washington—Latin American governments expanded their economic and political ties with communist governments. See Herbert Goldhamer, *The Foreign Powers in Latin America* (Princeton, 1972), 23.

3. Quoted in Samuel Baily, *The United States and the Development of South America, 1945–1975* (New York, 1976), 118.

4. Nelson Rockefeller, *The Rockefeller Report on the Americas* (Chicago, 1969), esp. chap. 1.

5. Latin America had responded with unsettling threats of possible nationalization of U.S. properties. See Eric Baklanoff, "The Expropriation of

United States Investments in Latin America," SECOLAS *Annals* 8 (1977): 48–60.

6. Leonard Gross, *The Last Best Hope: Eduardo Frei and Chilean Democracy* (New York, 1967).

7. These and other revelations of U.S. complicity are contained in U.S. Congress, Senate, Committee on Foreign Relations, *Hearings on the International Telephone and Telegraph Co. in Chile, 1970–1971*, 2 vols. Washington, D.C., 1973).

8. Richard Feinberg, *The Triumph of Allende: Chile's Legal Revolution* (New York, 1972), is largely sympathetic.

9. U.S. Congress, House of Representatives, Committee on Foreign Affairs, *Hearings: The U.S. and Chile during the Allende Years, 1970–1973* (Washington, D.C., 1975), offers assessments from varying positions.

10. Chilean socialism and Allende's downfall have generated much scholarly heat, occasionally some light. Among others, see Allende's own account, *La conspiración contra Chile* (Buenos Aires, 1973); James Petras and Morris Morley, *The United States and Chile* (New York, 1975), who blame foreign companies; and Federico Gil et al., *Chile, 1970–1973: Lecciones de una experiencia* (Madrid, 1977), who believe the United States influenced the conspirators but did not determine Allende's fall.

11. *New York Times*, 13 January 1971.

12. For the implications of Latin America's economic defiance see R. H. Swansborough, *The Embattled Colossus: Economic Nationalism and the United States Investors in Latin America* (Gainesville, Fla., 1976); and Shoshona Tancer, *Economic Nationalism in Latin America: The Quest for Economic Independence* (New York, 1976).

13. Gérard Pierre-Charles, *El Caribe contemporánea* (Mexico City, 1981), 292–332.

14. Commission on United States–Latin American Relations (the Linowitz Commission), *The Americas in a Changing World* (New York, 1975), esp. 11–61.

15. On Carter's policies see Gaddis Smith, *Morality, Reason, and Power: American Diplomacy during the Carter Years* (New York, 1986), 109–32; and Demetrio Boersner, *Relaciones internacionales de América Latina* (San José, C. R., 1986), 334–39.

16. Much of this section is based on Walter LaFeber, *The Panama Canal: The Crisis in Historical Perspective* (New York, 1978), 160–227.

17. Arthur Schlesinger, Jr., "Human Rights and the American Tradition," *Foreign Affairs* 57 (1979): 503–26.
18. U.S. Congress, House of Representatives, Committee on Foreign Affairs, *Report: Human Rights in the International Community and in United States Foreign Policy, 1945–1976* (Washington, D.C., 1977), is a compilation.
19. Abraham Lowenthal, "Latin America: A Not-so-Special Relationship," in *Foreign Policy on Latin America, 1970–1980* (Boulder, Colo., 1983), 128–38.

10. Central America and the Hemispheric Agenda

1. Henry Kissinger et al., *Report of the National Bipartisan Commission on Central America* and *Supplement* (Washington, D.C. 1984), are required reading. The modern isthmian condition is explored in Lester D. Langley, *Central America: The Real Stakes* (New York, 1985); Walter LaFeber, *Inevitable Revolutions: The United States in Central America* (New York, 1983); Morris Blachman et al., *Confronting Revolution: Security through Diplomacy in Central America* (New York, 1986); and Daniel Camacho and Manuel Rojas B., eds., *La crisis centroamericana* (San José, C.R., 1984).
2. By promoting cattle grazing and cotton growing, which take food-growing land out of production, in its development programs, American policy contributes to rural discontent. See Robert Williams, *Export Agriculture and the Crisis in Central America* (Chapel Hill, 1986).
3. For a detailed analysis, written from the perspective of one who helped to shape Carter's Latin American policy, see Robert Pastor, *Condemned to Repetition: The United States and Nicaragua* (Princeton, 1987).
4. Richard Millett, *Guardians of the Dynasty* (New York, 1977), critically assesses the role of the national guard in Nicaragua.
5. José Miguel Insulza, "La crisis en centroamérica y el caribe y la seguridad de los Estados Unidos," in Jaime Bastida et al., *Centroamérica: Crisis y política internacional* (Mexico City, 1984), 193–226.
6. For the impressions on the Latin American Left of the "Reagan doctrine," see Luis Maira, ed., *La política de Reagan y la crisis centroamericana* (San José, C.R., 1982).
7. Anthony Payne, *The International Crisis in the Caribbean* (Baltimore, 1984), 62.
8. Nicaragua's economic problems were not altogether caused by the Contra

war. See Carlos Vila, *The Sandinista Revolution: National Liberation and Social Transformation in Central America* (New York, 1986).

9. Marcela Serrato, "Las dificultades financieras de México y la política petrolera hacia el exterior," in Olga Pellecer, ed., *La política exterior de México: Desafíos de los ochenta* (Mexico City, 1983), 287–303.

10. On the debt crisis see Rosemary Thorpe and Laurence Whitehead, eds., *Latin American Debt and the Adjustment Crisis* (Pittsburgh, 1987).

11. Víctor Urquidi, "The World Crisis and the Outlook for Latin America," in Miguel Wionczck, ed., *Politics and Economics of External Debt Crisis: The Latin American Experience* (Boulder, Colo., 1985), 51. The view that Latin America must develop "within" to bring about a more equitable, autonomous, democratic society is the theme of Gonzalo Martner, ed., *América Latina hacia el 2000* (Caracas, 1986).

12. Pablo González Casanova, *La democracia en Mexico* (Mexico City, 1965), a work that has gone through sixteen printings.

13. For the often unappreciated impact of immigration on development see Robert Pastor, ed., *Migration and Development in the Caribbean The Unexplored Connection* (Boulder, Colo., 1985). For the implications of this population growth see Gonzalo Martner, comp., *América Latina hacia el 2000* (Caracas, 1986), 245–67.

Epilogue: The United States, America, and the Americas

1. Theodore Draper, "An Autopsy" [of Irangate], *New York Review of Books* 34 (17 December 1987): 67–77.

2. Cole Blasier reaffirms three rules of U.S. policy in Latin America: (l) no Soviet military bases in Latin America; (2) no unilateral U.S. military intervention against any hemispheric government; and (3) no use of U.S. military or economic influence to determine the political outcome of any election in Latin America (*The Giant's Rival: The USSR and Latin America* [Pittsburgh, 1985], 158).

Bibliographical Essay

This essay assesses general works relating to United States relations with Latin America and the ideas and forces that have shaped the inter-American experience. For articles and books dealing with specific events or U.S. policy toward individual countries, the reader should consult the notes.

The most comprehensive bibliography of United States–Latin American relations is David Trask, Michael C. Meyer, and Roger Trask, *A Bibliography of United States–Latin American Relations since 1810* (Lincoln, Neb., 1968), with a *Supplement* (Lincoln, Neb., 1979). For those interested in related items that may have been excluded from these volumes, the *Handbook of Latin American Studies* (Cambridge, Mass., Gainesville, Fla., and Austin, Texas, 1936–) provides a virtually exhaustive bibliography in all fields of Latin American studies. Six of the forty chapters in *Guide to American Foreign Relations since 1700* (Santa Barbara, Calif., 1983), edited by Richard Dean Burns, pertain to Latin America.

General works on United States–Latin American relations, in English and Spanish, are often too laboriously structured to convey an overarching theme, so attentive to immediate issues that they fail to explain fully the lasting features of the inter-American relationship and how and why they have developed, or too determined to justify or condemn U.S. policy toward Latin America.

In the first category, the most notable work is Graham Stuart and James L. Tigner, *Latin America and the United States*, 6th ed. (Englewood Cliffs, N.J., 1975), which is immensely detailed but lacks thematic unity. For those looking for a more concise summary, J. Lloyd Mecham, *A Survey of United States–Latin American Relations* (Boston, 1965), focuses largely on U.S. strategic concerns; and Federico Gil, *Latin American–United States Relations* (New York, 1971), identifies the cycles of U.S. interest. Wilfrid Hardy Callcott, *The Western Hemisphere: Its Influence on United States Policies to the End of World War II* (Austin, 1968); and J. Lloyd Mecham, *The United States and Inter-American Security, 1889–1960* (Austin, 1961), maintain that U.S. policy has been consistent. Excellent parallel texts from the Latin American view are G. Pope Atkins, *Latin*

America in the International Political System (New York, 1977); Harold Davis et al., *Latin American Diplomatic History: An Introduction* (Baton Rouge, 1977); and Harold Davis and Larman Wilson, eds., *Latin American Foreign Policies: An Analysis* (Baltimore, 1975). Demetrio Boersner, *Relaciones internacionales de América Latina* (San José, C.R., 1986), is socialist in tone but often displays balance in its assessments.

In the second category, the most useful works are by political scientists: Abraham Lowenthal, *Partners in Conflict: The United States and Latin America* (Baltimore, 1987), which makes the case for Latin America's "transformation" since 1961; Harold Molineau, *U.S. Policy toward Latin America: From Regionalism to Globalism* (Boulder, Colo., 1986), which makes an eloquent argument for a policy of nonintervention; and Michael Kryzanek, *U.S.–Latin American Relations* (New York, 1985), which examines the internal forces, official and private, that act on hemispheric policy. Cole Blasier, *The Hovering Giant: United States Responses to Revolutionary Change in Latin America* (Pittsburgh, 1985), which focuses on Mexico, Bolivia, Cuba, Guatemala, Grenada, and Central America, is a model study. Richard Newfarmer, ed., *From Gunboats to Diplomacy: New U.S. Policies for Latin America* (Baltimore, 1984), is especially good on specific countries and alertly incorporates essays on current economic questions and the often unmeasured impact of immigration.

In the third category, the essential starting point is Samuel Flagg Bemis, *The Latin American Policy of the United States: An Historical Interpretation* (New York, 1943), a classic account that is unsurpassed for its sustained defense of U.S. policy and has yet to be satisfactorily answered. Even critics regard it as essential reading. Gordon Connell-Smith, *The United States and Latin America: An Historical Analysis of Inter-American Relations* (New York, 1974), is a mild critique. Juan José Arévalo, *The Shark and the Sardines* (New York, 1961), may be the most widely read polemic on U.S. policy in the Western Hemisphere. Other writers have followed parallel themes in Spanish: Genaro Carnero Checo, *El Aguila Rampante: El imperialismo Yanqui sobre América Latina* (Mexico, 1956); Ramón Oliveres, *El Imperialismo Yanqui en América: La dominación política y económica del Continente* (Buenos Aires, 1952); and Pablo Franco, *La influencia de los Estados Unidos* (Montevideo, 1967), which emphasize economic themes. Alonso Aguilar, *Pan Americanism from Monroe to the Present: A View from the Other Side* (New York, 1969), argues that the United States has historically exploited Latin America. Jules Benjamin, "The Framework of U.S. Relations

with Latin America in the Twentieth Century: An Interpretive Essay,"
Diplomatic History 11 (Spring 1987): 91–112, is essential reading.

In both Latin America and the United States a few writers have attempted
exploratory and interpretive essays on comparative cultures of the Americas
or coped with the unanswerable question: Do the Americas have a common
history? A convenient summary of the latter is contained in Lewis Hanke,
ed., *Do The Americas Have a Common History?: A Critique of the Bolton Theory*
(New York, 1964). Of those who have explored "culture" (defined in its
broadest sense) to find some explanation for the political and economic differences between the United States and Latin America, the most suggestive
are Glen Dealy, *The Public Man: An Interpretation of Latin American and Other
Catholic Countries* (Amherst, Mass., 1977); E. Lawrence Harrison, *Underdevelopment Is a State of Mind: The Latin American Case* (Cambridge, Mass., 1985),
which lays the blame for Latin America's economic debilities on its cultural
priorities and relies heavily on Carlos Rangel, *The Latin Americans: Their Love-
Hate Relationship with the United States* (New York, 1977). Jacques Maritain,
Reflections on America (New York, 1958); Luis Alberto Sánchez, *Existe América
Latina?* (Mexico City, 1945); and Mariano Baptista Gumucio, *Latinoamericanos y
Norteamericanos: Cinco siglos de dos culturas* (La Paz, Bolivia, n.d.) are generally
favorable to the United States. Eduardo Galeano attempts in a trilogy, *Memory
of Fire* (New York, 1986–88), to make a statement through historical vignettes
on the experience of Latin America over five centuries. Samuel Shapiro, ed.,
Cultural Factors in Inter-American Relations (Notre Dame, 1968), explores in
twenty-four essays the varied imprint of culture on the hemispheric relationship. Germán Arciniegas, *Latin America: A Cultural History* (New York,
1967), esp. the Introduction and pp. 487–522, deftly integrates cultural and
literary themes. Akira Iriye, "Culture and Power: International Relations as
Inter-Cultural Relations," *Diplomatic History* 3 (Spring 1979): 115–28, suggests
that diplomatic relations between nations often derive their character from
the interactions between differing cultures.

Lamentably, modern students are less persuaded by the power of ideas in
the hemispheric experience than earlier scholars, thus political, economic,
and strategic themes have dominated the literature on United States–Latin
American relations for the past quarter-century. Arthur P. Whitaker, *The Western Hemisphere Idea: Its Rise and Decline* (Ithaca, N.Y., 1954), explores the impact
of an idea on generations of American and Latin American leaders from

Jefferson to Franklin Roosevelt. Albert K. Weinberg, *Manifest Destiny: A Study of Nationalist Expansion in American History* (Baltimore, 1935), retains its authoritativeness, as does Frederick Merk, *Manifest Destiny and Mission in American History: A Reinterpretation* (New York, 1963). In two works Harry Bernstein assesses inter-American intellectual links: *Origins of Inter-American Interest, 1700–1812* (Philadelphia, 1945); and *Making an Inter-American Mind* (Gainesville, Fla., 1961). The first explores how tentative commercial ties inspired individuals in differing cultures to learn more about one another. Three volumes that are distinguished for their measure of culture on international politics are Whitaker, *The United States and South America: The Northern Republics* (Cambridge, Mass., 1948); *The United States and the Southern Cone: Argentina, Chile, and Uruguay* (Cambridge, Mass., 1976); and especially Fredrick Pike, *The United States and the Andean Republics: Peru, Bolivia, and Ecuador* (Cambridge, Mass., 1977).

From the European rivalries in the Americas in the early eighteenth century there evolved a hemisphere of competing empires and nations with an obverse, private character that evolved from the traders and entrepreneurs of that era to the array of business, religious, social, educational, and charitable institutions of our times. Their collective imprint on policy is often difficult to measure, but it is central to an understanding of the inter-American experience. Peggy Liss, *Atlantic Empires: The Network of Trade and Revolution, 1713–1826* (Baltimore, 1983), effectively demonstrates that theories of empire or economic models often fail to explain the realities of transatlantic rivalries in the eighteenth century. No one did more to explore the private and personal actors in the United States–Latin American experience from 1783 to 1830 (when the hemispheric relationship took on its fundamental character) than Arthur P. Whitaker. In *The Spanish American Frontier, 1783–1795* (Cambridge, Mass., 1927); *The Mississippi Question, 1795–1803: A Study in Trade, Politics, and Diplomacy* (Washington, D.C., 1934); and especially *The United States and the Independence of Latin America, 1800–1830* (Baltimore, 1941), Whitaker traced two parallel stories, one of rivalrous governments and nations, the other, more consequential, of conflicts and agreements between their peoples that often influenced political decisions. As befitted a student of Frederick Jackson Turner, he began with the eighteenth-century frontier in his inquiry into the United States–Latin American experience. For the era of manifest destiny, David Pletcher, *The Diplomacy of Annexation: Texas, Oregon, and the Mexican War* (Columbia, Mo., 1973), bears the mark of careful research, balanced judgments, and authoritativeness. For the late nineteenth century, Walter LaFeber, *The New Empire: An Interpretation of American Expansion, 1860–1898* (Ithaca, N.Y., 1963), often finds in Latin American policy evidence to sustain his economic determinist theme. Often critiqued, the work has yet to be effectively rebutted. Lester D. Langley, *Struggle for the American Mediterranean: United States–European Rivalry in the Gulf-Caribbean, 1776–1904* (Athens, Ga., 1976), is a convenient summary.

Yet another topic of current inquiry into the state of the Americas is Latin American economic development and dependency. The succinct study by Stanley Stein and Barbara Stein, *The Colonial Heritage of Latin America: Essays on Economic Dependence in Perspective* (New York, 1970), offers a depressing assessment of Latin America in the twentieth century as the lamentable outcome of a colonial economy that has not achieved modernity. From there the reader can move to the more turgid (and more detailed) analyses in C. F. S. Cardoso and Hector Pérez Brignoli, *Historia económica de América Latina*, 2 vols. (Barcelona, 1979); F. H. Cardoso and E. Faletto, *Dependency and Development in Latin America* (London, 1979); André Gunder Frank, *Capitalism and Underdevelopment in Latin America: Historical Studies of Chile and Brazil* (New York, 1967); Celso Furtado, *Economic Development of Latin America: Historical Background and Contemporary Problems* (Cambridge, Eng., 1977); William Glade, *The Latin American Economies: A Study of Their Institutional Evolution* (New York, 1969); Albert O. Hirschman, *The Strategy of Economic Development* (New Haven, 1959); the works of D. C. M. Platt, especially *Trade, Finance, and Politics in British Foreign Policy, 1815–1914* (Oxford, 1968), and *Latin America and British Trade, 1806–1914* (London, 1972); and Raúl Prebisch, *The Economic Development of Latin America* (New York, 1950).

A useful summary, with appropriate case studies and an excellent bibliography, is Christopher Abel and Colin Lewis, eds., *Latin America, Economic Imperialism and the State: The Political Economy of the External Connection from Independence to the Present* (London, 1985). On the impact of the debt crisis see Jonathan Hartlyn and Samuel Morley, eds., *Latin American Political Economy: Financial Crisis and Political Change* (Boulder, Colo., 1986). Thomas McCann, *An American Company: The Tragedy of United Fruit* (New York, 1976), provides a casebook example, written by a longtime publicist for the company, of a multinational enterprise in Central America and the Caribbean. Two important special studies on American investors and companies in Latin America are Robert Swansbrough, *The Embattled Colossus: Economic Nationalism and the*

United States Investors in Latin America (Gainesville, Fla., 1976); and Paul Sigmund, *Multinationals in Latin America: The Politics of Nationalization* (Madison, 1980).

In assessing the Monroe Doctrine and Pan-Americanism most scholars have focused largely on political, economic, and security issues. A handy collection of essays is Donald M. Dozer, ed., *The Monroe Doctrine: Its Modern Significance* (New York, 1965), which contains representative American and Latin American views. Isidro Fabela, in *Intervención* (Mexico City, 1959), covering the legal ramifications of the subject from 1865 to 1954, reinforces the anti-U.S. Mexican view and thus should be judged alongside Ann Van Wynen and A. J. Thomas, Jr., *Intervention: The Law and Its Import in the Americas* (Dallas, 1956). John A. Logan, *No Transfer: An American Security Principle* (New Haven, 1961), traces the history of a corollary of the doctrine. Dexter Perkins, *A History of the Monroe Doctrine*, rev. ed. (Boston, 1963), sums up his three-volume account from 1823 to 1907 and concludes with an assessment of the doctrine in the twentieth century. Two opposing interpretations of the inter-American system are Gordon Connell-Smith, *The Inter-American System* (New York, 1966), who is critical; and J. Lloyd Mecham, *The United States and Inter-American Security, 1889–1960* (Austin, 1961), who is generally favorable to U.S. policies.

For a general survey of U.S. policy toward the circum-Caribbean, see Lester D. Langley, *The United States and the Caribbean in the Twentieth Century*, 4th ed. (Athens, Ga., 1989). The early twentieth-century interventions are detailed in Lester D. Langley, *The Banana Wars: United States Intervention in the Caribbean, 1898–1934* (Lexington, Ky., 1983), which details the military's involvement; and especially the two-volume account of Dana Gardner Munro, *Intervention and Dollar Diplomacy in the Caribbean, 1900–1921* (Princeton, 1964), and *The United States and the Caribbean Republics, 1921–1933* (Princeton, 1973). For the Good Neighbor era and after, I have relied on Donald Dozer, *Are We Good Neighbors? Three Decades of Inter-American Relations* (Gainesville, Fla., 1961), which incorporates considerable Latin American disenchantment with postwar U.S. policy to show how the wartime unity deteriorated. Irwin Gellman, *Good Neighbor Diplomacy: United States Policy in Latin America, 1933–45* (Baltimore, 1979), provides a balance to the hostile account in David Green, *The Containment of Latin America: A History of the Myths and Realities of the Good Neighbor Policy* (Chicago, 1971). Bryce Wood gives a meticulous analysis in *The Making of the Good Neighbor Policy* (New York, 1961) and in *The Dismantling of the Good Neighbor Policy* (Austin, 1985), which focuses on Argentina, Bolivia, and Chile to explain the collapse of the policy.

In an indictment of U.S. policy, Samuel Baily, *The United States and the Development of South America, 1945–1975* (New York, 1975), demonstrates how American planners foiled hemispheric aspirations for economic integration. Stephen Rabe, *Eisenhower and Latin America* (Chapel Hill, 1988), shows the president's activist role in shaping hemispheric policy. For the Alliance for Progress, Jerome Levinson and Juan de Onis, *The Alliance That Lost Its Way* (Chicago, 1970), retains its freshness and sense of immediacy. Two important collections of essays are Richard Gray, ed., *Latin America and the United States in the 1970s* (Itasca, Ill., 1971); and Kevin Middlebrook and Carlos Rico, eds., *The United States and Latin America in the 1980s* (Pittsburgh, 1986), which ranges over political, economic, social, and security issues in its essays. Margaret Daly Hayes, *Latin America and the U.S. National Interest: A Basis for U.S. Foreign Policy* (Boulder, Colo., 1984), should be read alongside Lars Schoultz, *National Security and United States Policy toward Latin America* (Princeton, 1987). Tom Farer, *The Grand Strategy of the United States in Latin America* (New Brunswick, N.J., 1988); and Lars Schoultz, *Human Rights and United States Policy toward Latin America* (Princeton, 1981), are indicative of the often unbridgeable chasm between those who debate the conflicting goals of the "United States" and "America" in the Americas.

For those who see U.S. policy in Central America as metaphorical explanation for the essential character of U.S.–Latin American relations, a good beginning (among the seven hundred or so books on Central America published since 1979), is Walter LaFeber, *Inevitable Revolutions: The United States in Central America*, rev. ed. (New York, 1984). A less damning indictment of U.S. policy, with more sensitivity to the legacy of isthmian culture and history, is Lester D. Langley, *Central America: The Real Stakes* (New York, 1985). The reader who is pursuing the "new hemisphere" should look to the publications and activities of the myriad private social, educational, environmental, health, business, and especially religious organizations that have a deepening reach among hemispheric peoples. I have pursued a parallel theme in *MexAmerica: Two Countries, One Future* (New York, 1988).

Index